TIME

TURNING POINT OF THE CIVIL WAR

Reunited *Veterans of Gettysburg, Confederates on the right, shake hands in 1913, on the 50th anniversary of the battle, at the "Angle" where Pickett's Charge failed on July 3, 1863*

TIME

MANAGING EDITOR Richard Stengel
ART DIRECTOR D.W. Pine
DIRECTOR OF PHOTOGRAPHY Kira Pollack

Gettysburg
Turning Point of the Civil War

EDITOR, WRITER Kelly Knauer
DESIGNER Ellen Fanning
PICTURE EDITOR Deirdre Read
MAPS Jackson Dykman
RESEARCH Tresa McBee
COPY EDITOR Bruce Christopher Carr

TIME HOME ENTERTAINMENT

PUBLISHER Jim Childs
VICE PRESIDENT, BRAND AND DIGITAL STRATEGY Steven Sandonato
EXECUTIVE DIRECTOR, MARKETING SERVICES Carol Pittard
EXECUTIVE DIRECTOR, RETAIL AND SPECIAL SALES Tom Mifsud
EXECUTIVE PUBLISHING DIRECTOR Joy Butts
DIRECTOR, BOOKAZINE DEVELOPMENT AND MARKETING Laura Adam
FINANCE DIRECTOR Glenn Buonocore
ASSOCIATE PUBLISHING DIRECTOR Megan Pearlman
ASSISTANT GENERAL COUNSEL Helen Wan
ASSISTANT DIRECTOR, SPECIAL SALES Ilene Schreider
DESIGN AND PREPRESS MANAGER Anne-Michelle Gallero
BRAND MANAGER Michela Wilde
ASSOCIATE PRODUCTION MANAGER Kimberly Marshall
ASSOCIATE BRAND MANAGER Isata Yansaneh
ASSOCIATE PREPRESS MANAGER Alex Voznesenskiy

EDITORIAL DIRECTOR Stephen Koepp

SPECIAL THANKS
Katherine Barnet, Jeremy Biloon, Stephanie Braga, Susan Chodakiewicz, Rose
Cirrincione, Brian Fellows, Jacqueline Fitzgerald, Christine Font, Jenna Goldberg,
Hillary Hirsch, David Kahn, Amy Mangus, Amy Migliaccio, Nina Mistry,
Dave Rozzelle, Ricardo Santiago, Adriana Tierno, Vanessa Wu, TIME Imaging

Copyright © 2013 Time Home Entertainment Inc.
Printed in the U.S.A.

Published by TIME Books, an imprint of Time Home Entertainment Inc.
135 West 50th Street, New York, NY 10020

Portions of the Lee's invasion story and the 7/1, 7/2 and 7/3 battle chapters have
been adapted from the Time-Life Books volume *Gettysburg, The Confederate High
Tide* (1985), Champ Clark, writer. Profiles and all other unbylined stories are by
Kelly Knauer. Sidebar matter is by Tresa McBee.

ISBN 10: 1-61893-053-2
ISBN 13: 978-1-61893-053-8
Library of Congress Control Number: 2012954684

We welcome your comments and suggestions about TIME Books.
Please write to us at:
TIME Books
Attention: Book Editors
P.O. Box 11016
Des Moines, IA 50336-1016

To order any of our hardcover Collector's Edition books,
please call us at 1-800-327-6388.
Hours: Monday through Friday, 7 a.m.–8 p.m., or Saturday,

Marble men *This monument to the 1st Pennsylvania Light Artillery
company, commanded by Captain R. Bruce Ricketts, is located on
Cemetery Hill at the Gettysburg National Military Park*

RICKETTS' BATTERY
1st PENNA. LIGHT ARTILLERY   PENNA. RESERVE CORPS

Contents

Ready for posterity's gaze
*Members of the 139th Pennsylvania
Volunteer Infantry Regiment pose for
the camera circa 1863. Two memorials
on the battlefield commemorate their
service on the left flank of the Army of
the Potomac on July 3*

Why Gettysburg Matters

By James M. McPherson

WHEN CONGRESS CREATED GETtysburg National Military Park in 1895, the Gettysburg Electric Railway Co. owned part of the land on which the battle had been fought. The company was building a trolley line to carry tourists to Devil's Den and Little Round Top. When the owners refused to sell their property to the park, the government began proceedings to seize it under the power of eminent domain. The case went all the way to the Supreme Court, which ruled unanimously in 1896 that Gettysburg was vested with such importance to the fate of the nation that the government had a right to "take possession of the field of battle, in the name and for the benefit of all the citizens of the country … Such a use seems …so closely connected with the welfare of the republic itself as to be within the powers granted Congress by the Constitution for the purpose of protecting and preserving the whole country."

The court in effect followed the lead of President Abraham Lincoln, who had spoken 33 years earlier at the dedication of the cemetery at Gettysburg that would receive the bodies of most of the 5,000 Union soldiers who were killed or mortally wounded in the battle. Lincoln's Gettysburg Address was a prose poem of 272 words that evoked the meaning of their sacrifice. The war that he described as a "testing" of whether the nation founded in 1776 would "long endure" or "perish from the earth" still raged over a front of 1,000 miles on that November day in 1863 when Lincoln rose to speak. He looked out over the graves of those who "gave their lives that the nation might live." He told the crowd of 10,000 people that it was the task of the living to take up the "unfinished work … for which they gave the last full

measure of devotion." That unfinished work included the abolition of slavery. Having issued the Emancipation Proclamation almost a year earlier, and eager to pass a constitutional amendment outlawing slavery in the U.S., Lincoln was determined that "this nation, under God, shall have a new birth of freedom."

With these words, the President called forth the historic consequences of the Civil War, of which the Battle of Gettysburg was a crucial linchpin. The war's outcome ensured the survival of the U.S. as one nation, indivisible, and freed from the incubus of slavery that had made a mockery of that nation's professions of liberty. Lincoln's Gettysburg Address has become a classic because no one before or since has so eloquently and succinctly defined the meaning of the war.

The Union cause in the Civil War had been at a low ebb in the early summer of 1863. Humiliating defeats of the Army of the Potomac at Fredericksburg and Chancellorsville during the previous seven months had caused Northern morale to plummet. The failure of the Union Navy's attack on the Charleston, S.C., forts in April intensified a sense of defeatism that boosted the antiwar Copperhead movement in the North. In the West, after months of frustration in his efforts to capture the Confederate bastion of Vicksburg on the Mississippi River, General Ulysses S. Grant finally seemed to be making progress, but Confederates remained confident that they would defeat him.

General Robert E. Lee believed that June 1863 was

McPherson, an emeritus professor of U.S. history at Princeton University, is the author of the Pulitzer-prizewinning Civil War study Battle Cry of Freedom *(1988). His most recent work is* War on the Waters: The Union and Confederate Navies, 1861-1865 *(2012)*

the time to strike a blow for final victory in the war. He persuaded President Jefferson Davis to endorse an invasion of Pennsylvania with the goal of winning another major Confederate victory, this time on Northern soil. Lee maintained that such an invasion would force Grant to loosen his hold on Vicksburg and would so demoralize the Northern people as to force the Lincoln Administration to sue for peace or be thrown out of office. "If successful this year," Lee wrote in April 1863, "next fall there will be a great change in public opinion at the North. The Republicans will be destroyed & I think the friends of peace will become so strong as that the next administration will go in on that basis." Lee's principal lieutenant, General James Longstreet, believed that the invasion of Pennsylvania offered the best opportunity "either to destroy the Yankees or bring them to terms."

As Lee prepared to lead the 75,000 men of his Army of Northern Virginia into Pennsylvania, he expressed confidence in these "invincible" troops. "There never were such men in an army before. They will go anywhere and do anything if properly led." At the same time, the Army of the Potomac was disorganized by its defeat at Chancellorsville and disillusioned with its commander, General Joseph Hooker. Bickering between the general and the Lincoln Administration led to Hooker's removal and the appointment of General George G. Meade to command the army on June 28.

Three days later and three miles west of Gettysburg, a Union officer in charge of cavalry pickets spotted Confederate infantry marching toward him out of the early-morning mist. He rested a carbine on a fence rail and fired. It was the first shot in what became the largest battle in the history of the western hemisphere. But instead of winning Confederate independence, the Battle of Gettysburg became a crucial turning point toward completion of "the unfinished work which they who fought here have thus far so nobly advanced"—the survival of the United States as one nation, indivisible, with liberty for all. ∎

The Sergeant

The noted chronicler of U.S. military history explores the thoughts of a fictional Confederate fighter as he prepares his troops for Pickett's Charge

By Jeff Shaara

JULY 3, 1863 They had marched most of the night, the early morning spent in whatever sleep the men could find. As the noonday sun slid overhead, they were moved forward, ordered to gather close within a thicket of tall trees. The sergeant did as he always did, cursed his way through the men in his squad, keeping them in tight quarters, with an eye on those few who might slip away to scrounge for something to eat. Through the trees, he could see the other squads of G Company and, beyond them, the entire 9th Virginia. He had no pocket watch, knew only it was early afternoon, knew that very soon the orders

would come from the captain that the great plan was to begin, the strategy plotted by generals to be carried forward on the backs of the men with the muskets. The captain had told them all it was to be a glorious day, repeating words passed down from George Pickett himself. The sergeant could feel an odd sense of presence: far beyond where he could see, a great many more men were spread all through this wide tree line, perhaps the entire division, perhaps the entire army, an enormous force ordered into stillness, waiting, knowing that when the bugles sounded, the command was simple: Rise, fall into line, and move forward. One more glorious fight.

Colonel Owens had spent much of the morning farther back in the woods with his company commanders, a cluster of brass that the sergeant avoided. Too many of those men were younger than he was, some of them yet to face the enemy at all. But there were the others, the good ones, the men you wanted to follow, his own lieutenant for one. There was no friendship between them, just that unspoken obedience that had to be earned, no matter what the manuals said, what had been taught back in the training camps. But the lieutenant had been unflinching, had led them straight into the worst hell the sergeant had ever seen, a fight on the Virginia Peninsula at a place called Seven Pines. Those who survived that were more than just veterans. They were the iron in this regiment, and whether or not those men wore the stripes on their sleeves, the sergeant knew they were just as capable as he was of pulling the shirkers into line. This morning, as they reached the camps near this Pennsylvania town, it was the veterans who carried the grim enthusiasm, the talk flowing through the column so that when the bugles sounded, it would be serious and deadly and would give them victory.

Shaara is one of the world's best-selling historical novelists. His next novel, A Chain of Thunder, *is based on U.S. Grant's Vicksburg Campaign and will be published in May 2013*

The sergeant had been through the fights since the peninsula, the second brawl at Manassas Junction, the gut-churning slaughter of the Yankees at Fredericksburg. All the men who had marched out of those fights were prepared for this one, and when the captain told them what they were to do, there was no confusion. The enemy they would face was a mile away, and if they won the day, they could end the war. All they had to do was make it through the Yankee lines, drive the bluebellies away, and have enough strength left to hold the ground.

Sure, he thought. Why not? If it will end the war ...

He scanned them, the veterans easiest to spot, most sitting alone with their muskets resting against them, a kind of partnership only veterans understand. But there were others too, the replacements, green and stupid, big talkers, those who still believed in the adventure of it all. He looked them over, one at a time, boys who thought they were soldiers, who had never seen the enemy, never sighted down the musket at a target, at a man, that soldier in blue who might be aiming back at you. Unlike the veterans, they were excited, babbling nervous chatter, sitting in clusters, imagining, predicting, anticipating the order, gripping the muskets tight against their chests. They will run, he thought. Some of them. Some won't. Some will stand tall and not flinch, and so they will be the first ones to die. Or, if they survive this day, they'll have changed, be just like these veterans, the men who know of blood and wounds and killing. And the boys will be men.

He glanced up, a hard breeze rustling the tree limbs, green leaves holding away the blanket of heat from a blistering sun. Cooler here, he thought. Out there ... wide open grass, rolling ground. We'll be hidden for a while, maybe. The canteens are filled, but there won't be time for that, not in the wide open. The Yankees will see us soon enough ... and then it will start. He rubbed his beard with a rough hand, nervous himself now, tried to hide it. He couldn't stay still, saw the lieutenant pacing behind them, and he moved that way, the officer so much younger than he was, sweating, hands in motion, lips moving, and the sergeant backed away, thought, Let him be. He's in his own place, prayers I guess, maybe just trying to remember what an officer is supposed to do. My job's easier. Walk out behind these boys and keep them in line, and when they start to go down, fill the gaps. Nothing complicated about it. Might even get to shoot a Yankee myself. Only thing for certain: when it begins, I won't be the first one to go down. Men in front of me.

Now, there's somebody's really good idea. Put the sergeants in back. Some general figured that out, and sure as the dickens, he used to be a sergeant.

Far to one side, a sharp clap of thunder punched the air, jolting him, a stab at the cold fear he tried to ignore. More now, an eruption of sounds from both directions, what had to be dozens of guns, and he tried to see, as they all did. But there was nothing in view, just the terrifying roar, like nothing he had ever heard, a hundred cannons, his brain telling him it was every gun in the army. He felt the power of it all, marvelous artillery, what it would do out there, blasting and obliterating Yankee cannons, killing men, terrifying the rest, driving them away. He inched forward, the tree line ending a few yards to the front, but the colonel was there now, saw him, shook his head, a silent order, motioning him back. Not yet.

The smoke drifted through the trees now, hard stink of sulfur, tearing the eyes, but he fought through that, actually enjoyed the smell. His own men were reacting with coughing, wiping of eyes, some, like him, knowing that those guns had a purpose, opening the way for all these men, knowing that out there, the Yankees were suffering a brutal destruction, guns and wagons and the men themselves.

He moved slowly through them, some lying flat, some against trees, the calm and the terrified. He saw tears on a man's face, but it wasn't the sulfur. The man was staring out with wide-eyed animal fear and, the sergeant saw now, a wad of letters in his hand. The sergeant knelt, put a hand on his shoulder, steel in his grip. The man was shaking, more tears, and he reached out to the sergeant, handed him the letters, mouthed the words, something about ... home. The sergeant stuffed the papers in his pocket, a sharp nod. He had done this before. It was the one piece of gentleness he could offer them, the one pause in the cursing toughness they expected from him. He studied the man's eyes, saw a change, a strange acceptance, the perfect certainty that death was very close, very soon, and the sergeant knew there was no argument, no order that could erase that.

He stood, backed away, looked over them all, their surprise from so much artillery fire starting to pass. Many had their heads down, nothing else to do, the veterans knowing that when the guns stopped, the order would come. He looked for the lieutenant, saw him kneeling, checking his pistol, one hand moving the sword out of the scabbard. Good, he thought. Be ready. Do your job.

The first incoming shell whistled far overhead, exploding in the woods behind him, a burst of fiery smoke. Now more, shrieks that tore through the air to one side, a scattering of blasts in the trees. He cursed, dropped to one knee, felt the familiar anger, knew it was the answer, the Yankees' role in the duel. They're aiming at our guns and overshooting. Damn fools. Killing men who haven't even started moving.

The ground jumped with each incoming shell, some of the new men squirming with fear, but there was nowhere to go, no other place to be. A sharp scream blew through a tree he could see, and he flinched, unavoidable. Through the ongoing roars of the guns came a man's cry, a different kind of scream. Eyes stared that way, and he held up his hand, a furious glare they knew well, held them in place. The heads dropped again, many of the men pulling themselves into a tighter ball, becoming smaller, the only protection.

The artillery fire was numbing now, long minutes, maybe an hour, his lungs growing used to the smoke, the stink absorbed all through him, the impacts in a soft rhythm that made him sleepy. His eyes drifted shut, his shoulders slumped, the musket leaning up across one leg, his brain drifting off, thoughts of home, Virginia, his wife, tears and pleading, and finally, her surrender. He had marched away from her breathing the dust of 200 others, following the colonel's horse, proud, energized men, filled with the spirit of this magnificent adventure, manufactured hatred for the Yankees, those dastardly devils, an army off to fight a war that no one really believed would happen. There were reasons why it did, of course, the most pronounced coming from the men who would stay home.

On the march, they had been swallowed by fury and dedication, officers inspiring them with raucous boasts of the weakness of the men in blue. The generals had come, great gatherings in open fields where men with clean uniforms told them of the honor of Virginia, as though some of the men might forget just why they had volunteered. Now, two years later, the energy remained, strengthened this time by the march into Pennsylvania, treading on Yankee soil. The generals came again, Pickett himself, rousing enthusiasm, so much talk of victory. He thought again of her, drying her eyes, and he missed her painfully. I will be home soon ...

The artillery stopped.

He jolted awake, saw officers hustling to the front, the colonel, the company commanders, a horseman riding past, a staff, flags, the lieutenant rushing past him, call-

ing out, the men standing up. The drums began now, punching the ice in his chest, and he added to the shouts, pulling the men into formation, the annoyance from the parade ground replaced by the urgency to get it done right. He stepped up close, men in two lines in front of him, jerked one man's shoulder, closing the gap, straightening the line. He shivered, couldn't avoid that, angry at himself, distracted himself by staring down the lines, rows of men stretching far out into the woods, drums all around, nervous talk, more shouted orders. The drums seemed to grow louder, filling him, and he fought to keep control, to keep them in control, his sweating fist gripping the musket tight by his side. Farther out front he saw the captain, motioning them forward, slowly, more focus on the lines, the formation. He looked to the side, other sergeants down the line, a quick glance, a nod, fire in the eyes, and now the new sound,

felt a surge of relief ... and panic. It was the bugle.

Out front, the officers watched as they stepped out from the woods. His own men cleared the trees, the lines perfect, and he looked to the left, saw entire brigades and much more, endless formations, more men than he had seen before. He felt his hands shaking, gripped the musket, shouted out something, angry words, needless, the men feeling their part in what he could see, this glorious unstoppable wave. He stared out past the men in front of him, the vast open field, the breeze rippling through tall grass, the enemy so very far away.

The drums pushed them forward, farther into the sunlight, the heat, the rhythm of the march, the sergeants doing what he did, keeping the men together. Now, from far to the front the first streaks of fire came toward him, and he knew it was Yankee artillery, all those guns that were supposed to be obliterated, wiped away. But they were there, and now, the Yankee gunners had targets. Far across the field, up the sloping hill, he could see motion, traces of blue, lines of men, the enemy peering up over their low stone walls, their protection, waiting. ∎

The Road to
Gettysburg

History by accident
*The small town (pop. 2,400)
of Gettysburg, Pa., boasted
no great strategic advantage
in the Civil War. But it was a
place where many roadways
came together, and along those
avenues, more than 160,000
Federal and Confederate
soldiers converged early in July
1863. Here these brave men
fought the greatest battle of
the war—and shaped the
future of their nation*

Division and Secession Touch Off a Civil War

The road to Gettysburg stretches back to the days when
the British colonies in America first won their independence

TO UNDERSTAND THE POISONOUS CON-
coction of passionate hatred and growing
division that consumed the U.S. in the
years before the Civil War, the best place
to start is with the words of the most perceptive observer of the American scene at the time. This
voice of clarity and reason was not that of an academic,
a novelist or a preacher; rather, it belonged to a circuit-
riding lawyer in Springfield, Ill., who had served a term
in the U.S. House of Representatives in the 1840s, until,
disgusted with politics, he returned to Illinois to resume
his legal career. Casting his eye over his fevered nation,
Abraham Lincoln quoted the Bible as he declared, in
1858, "'A house divided against itself cannot stand.' I believe this government cannot endure, permanently half
slave and half free. I do not expect the Union to be dissolved—I do not expect the house to fall—but I do expect
it will cease to be divided. It will become all one thing or
all the other."

Seven years later, in his Second Inaugural Address,
Lincoln recalled the origins of the great Civil War that
his election in 1860 had provoked. Looking back to the
1850s, he observed, "One-eighth of the whole population were colored slaves, not distributed generally over
the Union, but localized in the southern part of it. These
slaves constituted a peculiar and powerful interest. All
knew that this interest was somehow the cause of the
war. To strengthen, perpetuate, and extend this interest
was the object for which the insurgents would rend the
Union even by war, while the Government claimed no
right to do more than to restrict the territorial enlarge-
ment of it."

No better explanation has been offered for the root
cause of the Civil War. In fact, many of the soldiers who
served in the Union Army may not have favored the abolition of slavery, and many who served in the Confederate
States Army may have hated the "peculiar institution"
that defined the life of the South. But that unavoidable
fact remained: the war was fought over the future of the
U.S., and the issue at hand was whether slavery would
be abolished throughout the entire nation or the Union
would dissolve and be re-formed as two separate nations.
Yet the issue was so complex, and the institution of human bondage was so deeply embedded in the cultural
and economic life of the nation, that only a great convulsion could root it out. The Civil War was that convulsion.
The Battle of Gettysburg, the most important single battle in the war, was the turning point that ensured that

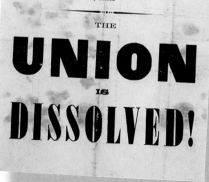

the Union would prevail in the contest. And when Lincoln visited the site of the battle, four months after the guns fell silent, he put forth a compelling vision of the nation's future in words so memorable that Gettysburg became one of the shrines of American democracy, the equal of Concord, Boston, Philadelphia and Yorktown.

All Men Are Created Equal—More or Less

The divisions that led to secession and war were apparent from the first days of American independence. "We hold these truth to be self-evident," declared the rebel Thomas Jefferson, "that all men are created equal, that they are endowed by their Creator with certain unalienable Rights, that among these are Life, Liberty, and the Pursuit of Happiness." Fine words indeed—but Jefferson himself was a slaveholder whose livelihood depended on

CHARLESTON

MERCURY

EXTRA:

Passed unanimously at 1.15 o'clock, P. M. December 20th, 1860.

AN ORDINANCE

To dissolve the Union between the State of South Carolina and other States united with her under the compact entitled "The Constitution of the United States of America."

We, the People of the State of South Carolina, in Convention assembled, do declare and ordain, and it is hereby declared and ordained,

That the Ordinance adopted by us in Convention, on the twenty-third day of May, in the year of our Lord one thousand seven hundred and eighty-eight, whereby the Constitution of the United States of America was ratified, and also, all Acts and parts of Acts of the General Assembly of this State, ratifying amendments of the said Constitution, are hereby repealed; and that the union now subsisting between South Carolina and other States, under the name of "The United States of America," is hereby dissolved.

THE

UNION

IS

DISSOLVED!

The first shots *Shells fired by Confederate troops descend on Fort Sumter, a U.S. government facility in Charleston, S.C., on April 12, 1861.*

At left, in December 1860, a newspaper announced the state's secession

9

MAP OF THE
UNITED STATES
1861
The heavy black line shows the greatest
extent of territory held by the Confederates.

Dividing lines *The map above shows the U.S. in 1861, after 11 Southern states had seceded, and Lincoln, terming their acts a rebellion, went to war to restore the Union. Vast expanses of land on the Western frontier were still territories rather than states, and it was the debate over the future of slavery in these regions that helped drive a wedge between the largely pro-slavery Southern states and largely anti-slavery Northern states*

human bondage. Slavery was much older than the nation itself: the first African slaves landed on American soil in 1619, and cheap labor enabled the growth of the plantation culture that arose in the southern colonies. Just as slavery divided humans along racial lines, it divided the colonies along regional lines. Slavery prospered in the South, but the Northern colonies had little need for slaves, and many Northerners joined the abolition movement, led by Briton William Wilberforce, that helped ban slavery across most of the British Empire by 1833.

Fractions of humans and factions of states

After the 13 colonies won their independence, they established a loose federation, with a weak central government, to order their affairs. For most Americans at the time, loyalty to region and state was much stronger than loyalty to the post-colonial federation. When the Arti-

cles of Confederation, the first iteration of a U.S. government, proved too weak a union, leaders of the states met to create a new constitution. The issue of slavery proved so divisive at this 1787 conclave that human bondage was only mentioned in the U.S. Constitution for purposes of determining the slave states' political representation in Congress: each African-American slave would be counted as representing three-fifths of a human being. In 1790 members of Congress, aware of the divisions between Northern and Southern states, voted to locate the seat of the new Federal Government on land donated to the nation by the state of Maryland, balanced on the dividing line between slave and free states.

In the following decades, many in the Northern states agitated for a national ban on slavery, without success. In 1820, under the Missouri Compromise, leaders in Washington addressed the controversies over the future of

slavery in new states by admitting Maine as a free state and Missouri as a slave state, while forever prohibiting slavery in future states emerging in the Louisiana Territory north of the 36° 30´ latitude line.

This compromise papered over the divisions born of slavery, divisions that were becoming more extreme, rather than less, as the two sections of the nation grew apart. As "King Cotton" became the prime crop in the South, those states became more agrarian and more reliant on slaves to operate their plantations. In the North, the culture was heading in the opposite direction: more and more young people were leaving their parents' farms for the rapidly growing cities that were creating a new, bustling style of life that was defined by business and busy-ness—precisely the opposite of the genteel, slower-paced and highly sociable planter culture of the South.

A Nation Careening out of Control

In the 1840s, the tensions undermining national unity were obscured by the sheer restless momentum of the times. New technologies like the railroad and the tele-graph wrought rapid changes in daily affairs, accelerating the pace of urban life and binding citizens together more tightly than ever before. Massive immigration from Europe swelled the size of U.S. cities and bred a nativist movement, the Know-Nothings, who detested the new immigrants. The settlement of the frontier accelerated, and Americans began to speak of the nation's "Manifest Destiny" to stretch across the continent from the Atlantic to the Pacific.

Under President James Polk, the U.S. went to war with Mexico in 1846. Abraham Lincoln opposed the conflict as little more than a trumped-up land grab. His constituents did not agree, and that's why the Illinois lawyer did not stand for re-election to the House of Representatives in 1848. The new lands wrested from Mexico, the Gold Rush of 1849 and Polk's successful diplomacy with Britain that brought vast territories in the Northwest under U.S. sway—all focused more attention on the West.

It was this new energy along the Western frontier, far from Boston and Savannah, Richmond and Philadelphia, that would once again place the issue of slavery on

Dueling inaugurations
At left above, Lincoln takes the oath of office as President on March 4, 1861, at the still unfinished U.S. Capitol Building. Seven states had already seceded from the Union, and four more would follow.

At right, spectators gather outside the state-house in Montgomery, Ala., the first capital of the Confederate States of America, as Jefferson Davis becomes President on Feb. 18, 1861

Chancellorsville *Fought in early May 1863, this battle was a triumph for Lee and his top lieutenant, Stonewall Jackson. The victory turned back Joseph Hooker's Union invasion of Virginia and gave Lee the chance to launch his own invasion.*

But Jackson was shot by mistake by his own troops on May 2, and he died eight days later, in a major setback for the Confederate cause

the nation's front burner. Debate raged over whether the new territories emerging on the frontier would enter the Union as free or slave states. In Washington, congressional leaders finally reached a grand bargain known as the Compromise of 1850, which consisted of five separate laws that ushered in a new era in U.S. life. Among them was one long desired by the South: a new, much stronger version of the Fugitive Slave Act of 1793, which allowed slaveholders to track and take possession of any slaves who had made their way to free states.

The Fugitive Slave Act electrified abolitionists in the North, where the sight of slave-drivers and bloodhounds in the streets, as well as broadsheets promising rewards for the capture of escaped slaves, brought the inhumanity of slavery into sharp relief. It was the first of a steady drumbeat of events in the 1850s through which the profound divisions in American life were expressed.

One such event was cultural rather than political. The 1852 publication of Harriet Beecher Stowe's *Uncle Tom's Cabin*—essentially an antislavery tract in the form of a

tearjerking novel—galvanized and swelled the ranks of the abolitionist movement. Stowe, who had lived in Cincinnati, along the dividing line between slave and free states, brought to life the growing movement in the North to shelter and assist runaway slaves, the Underground Railroad.

In 1854, pro-slavery forces in Congress succeeded in passing the Kansas-Nebraska Act, which declared that the status of slavery in these emerging territories would be determined by the votes of their citizens. This new power of "popular sovereignty" rendered invalid the Missouri Compromise of 1820 and its limits on the spread of human bondage, infuriating slavery's foes. In "Bleeding Kansas," supporters and enemies of slavery began waging guerrilla warfare over the territory's future.

As the political and cultural battles intensified, the bonds that once united Americans no longer held sway. The nation endured an age that, for sheer divisiveness, hateful rhetoric and poisonous demonization, makes the culture wars of the 1960s and recent decades seem tame by comparison. It was an age of passionate intensity, when the moderate center could not hold.

The War Begins, with the South Ascendant

The insanity reached a peak when a fanatical white abolitionist, John Brown, a veteran of the wars in Kansas, and his associates raided a U.S. Army armory in Harpers Ferry, Va., on Oct. 17, 1859. Barricading themselves inside, Brown and his followers called for a slave insurrection. No slaves rose up to join them, but U.S. forces, led by the respected Colonel Robert E. Lee, apprehended Brown. He was sentenced to death by hanging, and his execution on Dec. 2, 1859, further polarized Americans.

By then, the debate over slavery had reshaped the American political landscape. The Whigs, a progressive party that had supported an active Federal Government, split over the issue of slavery. A new antislavery party, the Republicans, was formed, and it ran a candidate for the presidency in 1856. Lincoln, once a Whig, joined the new party and emerged as one of its strongest voices in his 1858 race against Stephen A. Douglas for the U.S. Senate. In 1860 the Democrats, the party of Andrew Jackson, also divided into two branches, North and South.

That year the Republican Party nominated Lincoln, an outspoken foe of slavery, as its candidate for President. The Democrats ran two candidates: Douglas represented moderate Northern Democrats prepared to allow slavery to continue; incumbent Vice President John

Breckenridge led the stridently pro-slavery Southern Democrats. John Bell, a moderate, ran under the banner of the fledgling Constitutional Union Party.

When Lincoln won election on Nov. 6, 1860, Southern states despaired. Only six weeks after the election, South Carolina became the first state to secede from the Union. When Lincoln took office on March 4, 1861, seven states had seceded. Virginia, the most prominent and powerful Southern state, voted to secede in April and three other states followed. On April 12, the Civil War began in earnest, when Confederate artillery batteries fired on Fort Sumter, a U.S. fortress in Charleston Harbor.

Just as the states had faced a choice of whether or not to leave the Union, the nation's military leaders now faced a choice of loyalties: Would they support their state or their Union? At a time when devotion to region often surpassed devotion to nation, the majority of Southern officers chose to join the secessionists—including many officers who opposed slavery, like Robert E. Lee and Thomas (later "Stonewall") Jackson of Virginia.

The South had always placed a higher value on military service than did the North, and in the first two years of the war, Union forces suffered a series of humiliating defeats, especially in the conflict's Eastern Theater. Time after time, Southern generals proved more professional, more adept and more creative than their foes, and Southern troops, fighting on their native soil, proved more committed and more capable than the Union troops.

On the war's Eastern front, where Washington and Richmond, Va., the Confederate capital, were only 107 miles apart, the years 1861 and 1862 saw a succession of Southern victories, despite the North's advantage in men, supplies and railroads. The string of triumphs emboldened Lee, the gifted commander of the Army of Northern Virginia, to invade Union territory in September 1862. His gambit ended in a bloody battle along Antietam Creek near Sharpsburg, Md., and Lee withdrew. But he still held the upper hand in the conflict in the East, and as Lincoln shuffled commanders of the Union's Army of the Potomac, the Union suffered two more major defeats, at Fredericksburg and Chancellorsville.

In the weeks after his smashing victory at Chancellorsville, Lee decided to embark on a second invasion of the North, one that would lead him to Gettysburg—where, according to the most perceptive observer of the American scene in the land, men would do battle to settle the issue of whether a nation dedicated to the proposition that all men are created equal could long endure. ■

Firing line
This stone wall along Marye's Heights outside Fredericksburg, Va., played important roles in the battles of both Fredericksburg and Chancellorsville

Major Battles Before Gettysburg

April 12-13, 1861 • SIEGE OF FORT SUMTER
Eastern Theater; Confederate victory. Rebels under General P.G.T. Beauregard lay siege to a U.S. fort on an island in the harbor of Charleston, S.C., and win control of it.

July 21, 1861 • FIRST BATTLE OF BULL RUN (MANASSAS)
Eastern Theater; Confederate victory. Union forces under Irwin McDowell attack Confederates in northern Virginia and are first rebuffed, then thoroughly routed.

April 6-7, 1862 • BATTLE OF SHILOH
Western Theater; Union victory. Confederates under A.S. Johnston and Beauregard surprise U.S. Grant in eastern Tennessee with initial success but are beaten when reinforcements arrive. Johnston is killed, a blow to the Confederates.

March 17–July 1, 1862 • PENINSULA CAMPAIGN
Eastern Theater; Confederate victory. Union troops under George McClellan invade northern Virginia, but Robert E. Lee drives the Federals back north in a series of conflicts culminating in the Seven Days Battles.

Aug. 28-30, 1862 • SECOND BATTLE OF BULL RUN (MANASSAS)
Eastern Theater; Confederate victory. Lee, Jackson and the Confederates whip John Pope and the Federals at the site of the first major battle of the war.

Sept. 17, 1862 • BATTLE OF ANTIETAM
Eastern Theater; Union victory. Lee invades Maryland and the two sides battle to a bloody stalemate, but it is the Confederates who withdraw and return to Virginia.

Dec. 13, 1862 • BATTLE OF FREDERICKSBURG
Eastern Theater; Confederate victory. Union forces attack rebels whose artillery is entrenched in uphill fortifications, losing the battle at great loss of life.

April 30–May 6, 1863 • BATTLE OF CHANCELLORSVILLE
Eastern Theater; Confederate victory. As Union troops under Joseph Hooker again invade northern Virginia, Lee and Stonewall Jackson divide their forces and launch a surprise attack that routs the Federals. But Jackson is slain.

Robert E. Lee

GENERAL, ARMY OF NORTHERN VIRGINIA

★

IN SEPTEMBER 1863, THE COMMANDING OFF-icer of the Army of Northern Virginia, Robert E. Lee, looked back at perhaps his greatest victory in the Civil War, the May 1863 Battle of Chancellorsville, as he prepared to file his official battle report, standard practice in any military organization. "The conduct of our troops cannot be too highly praised," he wrote. "Attacking largely superior numbers in strongly entrenched positions, their heroic courage overcame every obstacle of nature and art, and achieved a triumph most honorable to our arms."

That simple paragraph offers one reason why Lee was revered by his troops: in a conflict in which many generals seemed more interested in their own advancement rather than the survival of the troops they commanded, Lee's first thoughts were often with his soldiers. And they loved him in return. "Marse Robert" he was called by these young men, many of them not yet out of their teens. As accounts cited in this book testify, they removed their hats in respect when he rode by.

Under Lee, the Army of Northern Virginia became one of the greatest fighting units in history, sustained by its own sense of invincibility. That expectation of victory radiated from the top down in Lee's army. Could General J.E.B. ("Jeb") Stuart's cavalry troopers run rings around their hapless Federal foes? Yes, indeed. Could Confederates battle the Yankees to a standstill at Antietam Creek in Maryland, even though the Federal commanders were handed Lee's battle plan in advance of combat? Yes, indeed. Could Lee divide his army in the face of a stronger force, send an entire corps on a long flanking march and then launch a surprise attack that smashed the enemy? Yes, indeed—that's how Chancellorsville was won.

And could Lee's invincible troops attack a larger force in a fortified position and still overcome it? Yes, indeed, it must have seemed to Lee; after all, his own life was a long, uphill battle in which he overcame his family's bad fortune by exercising discipline, resolve and willpower. In Lee's homeland, the Commonwealth of Virginia, family, tradition and heritage were the foundations of culture and society. Lee had experienced both the glory and the despair to be found in such a society: born the son of a great Revolutionary War hero who had tasted greatness only to fall on hard times and die in disgrace, Robert had devoted his life to restoring his family's honor.

An Early Fall from Grace

Robert E. Lee's father Henry Lee III was the scion of a great commonwealth family (the "three sticks" after his name are the telltale signs of dynastic ambition). The Lee name ran deep in American history, long preceding the revolution. And when the revolution came, Henry Lee, a graduate of Princeton University, won fame as the leader of "Lee's Legion," a mixed corps of cavalry and infantry troops. A superb horseman, he earned a special citation for valor from the Continental Congress—and picked up a wonderful nickname, "Light-Horse Harry." In the climactic days of the Revolutionary War, Lee played an instrumental role in the southern campaigns that drove the British to surrender at Yorktown.

Henry left the army shortly after the surrender to pursue a flourishing career in law and politics, but in 1794, when President George Washington found himself in need of a general to lead an army of almost 13,000 men to fight citizens engaging in the Whiskey Rebellion, he asked Light-Horse Harry to put on his uniform again and lead U.S. troops against the rebels. By that time, Lee had risen to become Governor of Virginia, but he obliged Washington and quickly dispersed the farmers who were up in arms over a federal tax on homemade spirits.

Henry's political career had flourished after the Revolutionary War: he had served in the Continental Congress in the late 1780s, was elected Governor in 1791 and served until 1794, when he helped quell the rebellion. He held down an alternate major general's post in the U.S. Army for several years afterward. In 1799, he was elected to the U.S. House of Representatives; it was that year he spoke at the funeral of George Washington, famously eulogizing him as "first in war, first in peace, and first in the hearts of his countrymen." But a much more significant event in his life took place earlier, when he lost much of

his family fortune amid the national Panic of 1796-97. He was never adept at business matters, and his financial travails became so severe that he was forced to spend a year in debtors' prison in 1809. No greater horror could be imagined for the standard-bearer of the Lee family.

There were two marriages for him. He and his first wife, Matilda, had three children before her death in 1790. He married Anne Hill Carter, in 1793, and they had six children; Robert E. Lee, born in 1807, was the fifth. He was only 2 when his father went to prison.

Henry's decline continued: he was badly beaten during a political riot in Baltimore over the brewing War of 1812. He would never recover his full health, and his speech was affected. At this time he essentially deserted his family and traveled to the West Indies, where he hoped to recover his health. He never did so, and he died in Georgia in 1818, when Robert was 11 years old.

Growing up amid such charged circumstances, Robert E. Lee resembles a Dickens character, cast out of a state of grace and forced to rely upon the kindness of friends and family to survive. There is no blacking factory in

Two veterans *Lee posed for a formal portrait after the war with his celebrated mount, Traveller. Lee served as president of Washington College (now Washington and Lee University), from 1865 until his death from a massive stroke in 1870.*

Lee strongly supported efforts to reconcile North and South, and, if heartbroken in private, he refused to entertain in public the bitterness that consumed many former Confederates

15

Lee's youth, but it was a transient life, as he and his family traveled from the home of one relative to another, living on familial charity. But his family connections were strong enough to earn his admission to the U.S. Military Academy at West Point, where he matriculated in 1825 and first met some of those with whom he would later serve in the Mexican War and the Civil War.

The Young Lee Rises

Lee was an outstanding cadet with a commanding bearing. After graduating from West Point in 1829, his prospects were promising enough that he snagged a wealthy wife from another great Virginia dynasty, Mary Anna Randolph Custis. She was the great-granddaughter of Martha Washington, and her father originally opposed the marriage, due to the downfall of Lee's father. After their marriage in 1831, the couple would have seven children, three of whom would fight on their father's side during the Civil War. Ultimately, Robert and Mary would settle in the Custis estate in Arlington, Va., today a historic monument at Arlington National Cemetery.

Through the 1830s and early '40s, Lee's service in the U.S. Army primarily consisted of supervising large engineering projects. Helping build federal forts in swampy ground in the Carolinas and making the Mississippi River more navigable for shipping, Lee acquired skills that would serve him well in the Civil War, when the difficult logistics of moving, supplying and protecting troops

would emerge as critical elements in winning battles.

In 1846 Lee participated in that great rehearsal for the Civil War, the Mexican War. After long years of engineering, he seemed to thrive in combat. He excelled in reconnaissance, served as an aide to General Winfield Scott and made a positive impression on that legendary fighter as well as on officers of his own generation.

After the war ended, Lee was offered the position of superintendent of West Point. He was not eager for the management position, but he took the post, and in his three years of service at the academy, he encountered many young men who would serve under him later, including Stuart. He was thrilled when his term ended and he was assigned to cavalry duty in Texas, where U.S. Army forces were tangling with Native American tribes.

Otherwise, the 1850s turned out to be difficult years for Lee. His wife Mary became increasingly ill, and when her father died, Lee was forced to oversee the management of the estate—which included some 200 slaves and a host of debt. At age 50 in 1857, Lee must have felt old pains returning, as he faced the sort of financial woes that had felled his father and left the family reeling.

By sheer chance, Lee soon found himself at the center of two of the most significant events that prefigured the Civil War. In 1859, he was dispatched to Harpers Ferry to arrest the fanatical abolitionist John Brown, who had captured a U.S. Army armory. Lee achieved that task with little fuss, but after he returned to his station in

Texas early in 1861, the state seceded from the Union. Like every officer in the U.S. Army, Lee was now faced with a choice that he had never asked for: to choose between his state or his nation when war broke out.

A Time to Choose

Lee returned to Washington, where he was promoted to full colonel and was offered command of the U.S. Army. For two full days, he agonized over whether he should serve as a top commander in the army of Abraham Lincoln's diminished Union or take up arms to fight for a Southern rebellion he had strongly hoped would never come. But he recoiled at the notion of leading a Union army in an invasion of Virginia.

Lee felt deep ties to the Union cause, and as a slaveholder, he had few illusions about the institution; he despised what it had done to the South, and he believed it harmed whites just as much as blacks. But he could not envision an America in which whites and blacks lived in harmony as equals. Like Lincoln, he supported fanciful schemes to deport African Americans to new lands where they could form their own societies. In the end, Lee chose region over nation, and he resigned his commission and joined the Confederates. He was named commander of the Virginia state forces on April 23.

Surprisingly, Lee's debut as a field commander was inauspicious: he lost the first battle he took part in, at Cheat Mountain in western Virginia, and his later efforts at shoring up the defenses of Savannah were unsuccessful. Even so, he was respected enough that President Jefferson Davis invited him to serve as his top military adviser. Lee proved so able at this position that when Union commander General George B. McClellan launched his Peninsula Campaign in the spring of 1862 and Confederate General Joseph E. Johnston was wounded in the Battle of Seven Pines, Davis asked Lee to take over.

Within days, Lee reversed the flow of the campaign, going on the offensive in the series of clashes known as the Seven Days Battles and driving the Yankees from Confederate soil. Within weeks, he defeated another large Union army at the Second Battle of Bull Run (Manassas). Emboldened, he took the offensive and invaded the North, only to be driven back at Antietam; even so, Lee outgeneraled McClellan throughout the battle to win a draw. Two smashing victories over the Army of the Potomac followed, at Fredericksburg and Chancellorsville.

Small wonder that in the weeks that followed Chancellorsville, Lee again began to ponder an invasion of Union territory. And small wonder that, when that invasion reached its climax, and Lee pondered the odds of victory as he assigned his beloved troops the task of attacking largely superior numbers in strongly entrenched uphill positions outside a small town in southeast Pennsylvania, he never doubted that their heroic courage would overcome every obstacle of nature and art and achieve a triumph most honorable to Confederate arms. ∎

Lee Invades The North

Rolling the dice, the Confederate commander enters Union territory

THE CONFEDERACY'S INVASION OF THE North in June and July 1863 began in pageantry and ended in tragedy. The pageantry was delivered courtesy of the spirited, celebrated cavalry commander, Major General J.E.B. ("Jeb") Stuart, who had long cultivated a dream of holding a grand cavalry review to celebrate—well, to celebrate himself and sing himself, as well as his daring band of mounted soldiers. Stage it he did, and then he staged it again three days later, after the primary intended viewer of the show, Confederate commander Robert E. Lee, missed the premiere. The tragedy came 25 days later, when Lee sent more than 12,000 brave men marching directly into a storm of Union artillery fire in a desperate final attempt to achieve a breakthrough against Federal forces entrenched in the rocky hills outside Gettysburg, Pa. The men died, in droves, and the survivors were forced to retreat back to Virginia, never again to mount an offensive threat against their foes.

On the crisp morning of June 8, 1863, about a month after his smashing victory at Chancellorsville, Lee arrived in the vicinity of Brandy Station, a whistle-stop on the Orange & Alexandria Railroad a few miles northeast of Culpeper, Va., where most of his Army of Northern Virginia was concentrating. There Lee was greeted by Stuart, who was resplendent in a brand-new

Calm before the storm *A Confederate cavalry trooper and his steed enjoy a quiet moment at Brandy Station, Va., where the largest cavalry battle of the war began Lee's invasion of the North*

uniform topped by a long, black ostrich plume fastened to his slouch hat with a golden clasp. He sat astride a horse bedecked with garlands of flowers. As the amused Lee later wrote to his wife, "Stuart was in all his glory."

Stuart had good reason for pride: yes, he loved a show, but his command—now five brigades comprising 9,536 officers and men—had repeatedly demonstrated its ability to ride rings around the Federal cavalry. This day Stuart would put his superb force on display for Lee.

The horsemen were arrayed in double ranks on a plain just west of the Rappahannock River. Lee rode the three-mile line at a brisk trot. Then, his inspection complete, Lee stationed himself on a nearby hillock. In response to a signal from Stuart, bugles blared, and the 22 cavalry regiments wheeled into a column of fours. With horses prancing to the airs of three bands, the troopers moved out beneath rippling flags. As Stuart led the parade past the admiring Lee, an immense cloud of dust arose from the churned-up ground.

The dust cloud was seen by a large Federal force—three cavalry divisions supported by two infantry brigades—that was at that moment descending on the Rappahannock from the east, bent on destroying Stuart's corps.

The mission had been ordered by the commander of the Army of the Potomac, General Joseph Hooker, whose intelligence service had reported Stuart's recent move from Fredericksburg to the Culpeper area. Fearing that Lee planned to strike northward, Hooker directed his cavalry commander, Brigadier General Alfred Pleasonton, to "disperse and destroy the rebel force."

As twilight fell and Stuart's troopers were walking their horses back to their encampments after the grand review, Pleasonton's command of about 11,000 men moved silently into the woods on the opposite side of the river. At dawn they would attack, launching the largest cavalry engagement ever fought on American soil.

This battle would be the opening clash of a campaign that would reach a climax at Gettysburg. To that community of about 2,400 inhabitants, the armies of the Union and the Confederacy would be inexorably drawn in long and toilsome marches, as if by a directing destiny. And there, on 25 square miles of countryside, 160,000 Americans would fight in a terrible battle for which neither commander was prepared. Begun almost by accident, the struggle would intensify across three desperate days, rising uncontrolled and uncontrollable to a crescendo of violence. Gettysburg was Lee's desperate gamble, his bid to achieve the climactic victory that would win both the war and independence for the South. But when a deathly silence finally fell upon the blood-soaked battleground, Lee had been beaten, and the recession of Confederate hopes had begun.

Lee Devises His Battle Plan

The campaign that would lead to Gettysburg was dictated by the logic of Confederate circumstances. For all the glory of Lee's brilliant victory at Chancellorsville early in May, he had managed only to put off the day when the Army of the Potomac would again press his outnumbered and undersupplied army back toward Richmond. The problem of what do next, Lee later said, "resolved itself into a choice of one of two things: either to retire to Richmond and stand a siege, which must ultimately have ended in surrender, or to invade Pennsylvania."

The considerations that had prompted Lee's march into Maryland in September 1862—a drive that was blocked at Antietam—remained valid nine months later. A successful invasion might encourage peace-seeking Democrats in the North, or Copperheads, in their agitation to end the war under terms reasonably favorable to the Confederacy, including the preservation of slavery. And it might sway the European powers of Britain and France to recognize the independence of the Confederacy, one of the major goals of President Jefferson Davis.

A more immediate impetus was provided by the chronic shortage of supplies in the South. Hampered by an inadequate and inefficient railroad system, and operating in a war-ravaged region partly occupied by the enemy, Lee was unable to provide adequate food and clothing for his army or forage for its horses. An invasion of Pennsylvania would provide his soldiers access to the rich farmlands of that state and allow the people of Virginia time to stockpile supplies.

On May 14, 1863, Lee had traveled to Richmond to confer with Davis and his Cabinet. For three days, Lee argued his invasion plan before a fretful, skeptical audience. Yet such was the power of Lee's magisterial presence that the group approved his proposal by a vote of 5 to 1. Before setting out on the march north, however, Lee reorganized his army, using the sad imperative of replacing Stonewall Jackson to make some long-needed changes. The Army of Northern Virginia's 60,000 troops had been organized in two corps, one under Jackson and the other under Lieutenant General James Longstreet. Now Lee decided to add a third corps.

The I Corps would remain under the command of

Stonewall Jackson
At Gettysburg, Lee was deprived of the services of his most able colleague, the brilliant, eccentric, highly religious Thomas ("Stonewall") Jackson. The Virginia-born West Point graduate, 39 in 1863, served in the Mexican War, then became a professor at the Virginia Military Institute.

Jackson received his nickname when he and his troops stood tall at the First Battle of Bull Run (Manassas). But he was slain at the moment of his greatest triumph, hit by friendly fire following his surprise flank attack that led to a Confederate triumph at the Battle of Chancellorsville

Longstreet, the solid Georgian whom Lee fondly called his "Old War Horse." Lieutenant General Richard S. Ewell, who had served well under Jackson, would take Jackson's place as head of II Corps. To lead the new III Corps, Lee chose a man he judged "the best soldier of his grade with me," Lieutenant General Ambrose Powell ("A.P.") Hill. Lee augmented Stuart's cavalry by placing under his command four cavalry brigades that had been operating independently—including that of Brigadier General William E. Jones, whose quarrelsome, complaining ways had earned him the nickname of "Grumble." On June 4, Lee's infantry began moving up the Rappahannock toward Culpeper, first stop on the way north.

The Battle for Brandy Station

Across the river, meanwhile, the sorely perplexed commander of the Union's Army of the Potomac pondered his situation. On May 27, Hooker's intelligence chief had reported that "the Confederate army is under march-

ing orders" and would probably "move forward upon or above our right flank." On June 4, Hooker learned from observers in balloons that some of the enemy's camps around Fredericksburg had been abandoned. Hooker proposed to Lincoln that he cross the Rappahannock and "pitch into" the troops Lee had left behind.

The President scotched that notion, which would have left the Union capital largely undefended and vulnerable to attack. Baffled and frustrated, Hooker sought more information, and a few days later he learned that Confederate cavalry had concentrated in the Culpeper area. It was then that Hooker dispatched Pleasonton's cavalry corps toward Brandy Station.

On June 8, forbidden to light fires, Pleasonton's troopers on the banks of the Rappahannock ate a cold supper, then slept with the reins of their still-bridled horses looped around their wrists. Four miles northeast of Brandy Station, at Beverly Ford, Brigadier General John Buford was preparing to lead the attack of the right

The grand mounted review
Don Troiani's painting of Stuart's cavalry review at Brandy Station captures a moment that, in terms of sheer pageantry and spectacle, was among the war's high points. But even as Stuart and Lee received the salute of the horse soldiers, Federal cavalrymen were in the area, and the war's largest mounted battle began the next day, June 9

wing—three brigades of cavalry supported by one of infantry. More than five miles downstream, southeast of
Brandy Station, an even larger Federal force—a division
under Brigadier General David McMurtrie Gregg and
another commanded by French-born Colonel Alfred
Duffié—was moving into position at Kelly's Ford.

According to Pleasonton's plan, Buford would make a
frontal assault on the Confederate camps north of Brandy Station, while Duffié, and then Gregg, would swing
around and strike the enemy's right flank and rear. But
as it neared time to attack, Duffié's men got lost in the
darkness, and Gregg delayed his crossing of the river to
wait for them. Thus, from the start, Pleasonton's carefully synchronized attack was thrown out of kilter.

At daylight General Buford's leading brigade, con-
sisting of three regiments under Colonel Benjamin
("Grimes") Davis, splashed across the Rappahannock
and swiftly broke through the thin Confederate picket
line. Spearheaded by the 8th New York Cavalry, the Federal horsemen galloped hard, four abreast, down the narrow country road to Brandy Station.

Roused from their sleep, the Confederates hastened
to mount up. Twenty-two-year-old Major Cabell E.
Flournoy of the 6th Virginia gathered about 100 men
and charged headlong at the oncoming Federals. Badly
outmatched, Flournoy soon withdrew—but only after
gaining some precious time for the Confederates.

Jeb Stuart had heard the deadly rattle of small-arms
fire while he was drinking his morning coffee in his
headquarters on Fleetwood Hill, a long and commanding north-south ridge that rose about a half-mile northeast of Brandy Station. Alarmed, he issued orders for reinforcements to move toward Beverly Ford.

As Buford's Federals advanced farther, they came up
against Brigadier General Wade Hampton's brigade,
formed in line of battle at the edge of a wood near St.
James Episcopal Church. Major Robert Morris, a Philadelphia blue blood who commanded the 6th Pennsylvania Cavalry, was ordered to clear the enemy from his
front. Morris deployed his men and charged.

"We flew along—our men yelling like demons," recalled Captain Henry Whelan of the 6th unit. "Grape
and canister were poured into our left flank and a storm
of rifle bullets on our front. We had to leap three wide,
deep ditches, and many of our horses and men piled up
in a writhing mass in those ditches and were ridden
over." The charge faltered, and the Confederates rapidly counterattacked, capturing Major Morris and driv-

ing his troopers back in savage hand-to-hand fighting.

Buford's troopers began to fall back toward the Rappahannock. Now, just as the Confederate regiments were
gathering for a decisive charge, Grumble Jones received
bad news from his scouts. A column of dust had been
seen rising from the direction of Kelly's Ford: the Federal flanking force under Duffié and Gregg had found its
bearings and was coming on fast. At a crossroads three
miles beyond Kelly's Ford, the force split: Duffié continued westward toward Stevensburg, a village about five
miles south of Brandy Station, to menace the Confederate rear; Gregg's column turned north on a road heading
straight for Brandy Station. The way was wide open for
Gregg, and Fleetwood Hill, which commanded the approach, was virtually undefended.

Hurrying off toward the fight near Beverly Ford with
three brigades, Stuart had left behind at Fleetwood Hill
only his adjutant, Major Henry McClellan, and a few

couriers. As he saw the Federals about to take control of the railroad station, McClellan commandeered a single 6-lb. howitzer left by chance near the foot of Fleetwood Hill and managed to hold off the Federals, while he sent a courier galloping to Stuart to warn of the threat. Stuart was inclined not to believe the courier's story, until the sound of guns from the hill dispelled his doubt.

Now Stuart acted fast, dispatching four more artillery pieces to Fleetwood Hill and pulling two of Grumble Jones' regiments out of the line and sending them rearward up the ridge. "Not 50 yards below," Major McClellan recalled, "Colonel Percy Wyndham was advancing the 1st New Jersey Cavalry in magnificent order, in column of squadrons, with flags and guidons flying."

Without pausing, Jones' troopers galloped over the crest and down the far slope, headlong into Wyndham's charging horsemen. The opposing ranks met with what one trooper remembered as a "dead, heavy crash," and

it was the Confederates who gave ground. "They broke like a wave on the bow of a ship," recalled Adjutant Marcus Kitchen of the 1st New Jersey, "and over and through them we rode, sabering as we went." Wyndham had taken a bullet in the leg, but he led his men up the slope, overrunning the rebel artillery pieces. Just as the Federal momentum ebbed, fresh Confederate units entered the fray, driving Wyndham's regiments back down the hill.

With the tide of battle turning against him, General Gregg sent an urgent appeal to Colonel Duffié to ride to the sound of the guns. To the northeast, meanwhile, Buford was again attacking the Confederate position near the Episcopal Church. Yet even his veterans of the Regular Army were unable to effect a breakthrough, and eventually they were pushed back.

Off to the southeast, Duffié had hooked around to Brandy Station from Stevensburg, but he arrived too late to present any real threat. In the end, General Stu-

Firepower *Federal artillery companies assemble on the south bank of the Rappahannock River on June 4, 1863, where the Battle of Brandy Station launched Lee's second invasion of the North. The first was rebuffed at Antietam in Maryland in September 1862*

art and his Confederates held Fleetwood Hill. At 4:30 p.m., Pleasonton began pulling his men back across the Rappahannock in good order. The Federals had suffered 866 men killed, wounded or missing, compared with 532 Confederate casualties. But the fine performance of Pleasonton's troopers against the legendary Stuart had given them a new sense of confidence that would sustain them through the rest of the war. The Battle of Brandy Station, wrote Henry McClellan, *"made* the Federal Cavalry."

A Desperate Battle for Winchester

The conflict at Brandy Station required Stuart to rest and refit his battered regiments, thereby delaying his northward movement by a full week. But Lee was not waiting for anyone, and on the afternoon of June 10, the day following the cavalry clash, he put Ewell's II Corps on the road. With the disabled Ewell traveling in a buggy, the corps crossed the Blue Ridge Mountains at Chester Gap, and by June 13 the divisions of Major Generals Edward Johnson and Jubal A. Early were moving into position near Winchester. That crossroads and rail terminus of 3,500 inhabitants in the northern Shenandoah Valley lay directly athwart the Confederate invasion route, and Lee did not intend to leave its garrison of 5,100 Federals behind him as he marched north into Pennsylvania.

For the past week, Union General in Chief Henry W. Halleck had been trying to get his commander at Winchester, Major General Robert H. Milroy, to move from that exposed position to the relative safety of Harpers Ferry, 30 miles to the northeast. But Milroy had insisted that he could hold Winchester "against any force the rebels could afford to bring against it."

On June 13, Early's vanguard attacked outlying Federal detachments south of Winchester. After a sharp skirmish, Milroy ordered his men to withdraw to three forts north and west of the town. The next day President Lincoln wired Milroy's department commander, Major General Robert C. Schenck: "Get Milroy from Winchester to Harpers Ferry if possible. If he remains he will get gobbled up, if he is not already past salvation."

It was too late. That very morning, at dawn, Ewell had seen that the key to Winchester lay in its three forts, the westernmost of which, or West Fort, dominated the other two. He ordered part of Early's division to advance through the woods and launch an assault on it. Meanwhile, Brigadier General John B. Gordon's brigade of Early's division would demonstrate against Milroy from the south, and Johnson's division would threaten

Winchester from the east. Early's movements went undetected, and shortly after 5 p.m. the Confederates suddenly emerged from the woods, unlimbered 20 guns and opened fire on the West Fort. At about 6:30, there came the keening of the rebel yell as soldiers of Brigadier General Harry T. Hays' Louisiana Brigade descended headlong on the West Fort, took possession of it and turned its guns on the routed, fleeing defenders.

At about 10 o'clock that night, General Milroy, thinking himself surrounded, ordered an evacuation to Harpers Ferry. But Ewell, correctly predicting Milroy's reaction, already had ordered Johnson's division on the march to intercept the fleeing Federals.

At about 3:30 a.m., Johnson arrived at a bridge that spanned a deep railroad cut near Stephenson's Depot, four miles northeast of Winchester on the turnpike to Harpers Ferry. There, in a battle that raged through the night, Milroy threw his 6,000 men against Johnson's 3,500 soldiers, attacking repeatedly until the Confederates were nearly out of ammunition. And then, with the first gray streaks of dawn, Brigadier General James Walker's Confederates came out of the south and threw themselves into the fight. The Federal formation broke, and men fled in all directions, great numbers of them falling into the hands of the enemy.

Ewell's victory was sweet. At Winchester and at Stephenson's Depot, the Confederate II Corps had inflicted 443 casualties and captured 3,358 prisoners, 23 guns and 300 wagons, at a cost of only 269 casualties. Ewell had passed his first test as a corps commander in grand style.

Stuart Heads for Greener Pastures

On June 15, as Ewell's corps was still rounding up prisoners, Lee ordered his other two commanders—Longstreet at Culpeper and Hill at Fredericksburg—to move up in a hurry. Laboring beneath a scorching sun, more than 500 of Longstreet's men dropped out of the first day's march, some dying by the roadway. But the troops crossed the Blue Ridge Mountains through Ashby's and Snicker's gaps on June 19 and entered the Shenandoah Valley. Longstreet hoped to turn north toward the Potomac, but Lee ordered him back into the mountains. Stuart, who had moved north from Brandy Station on June 16, was having trouble preventing the Federal cavalry from breaking through his screen east of the Blue Ridge area. Longstreet would have to help plug the mountain gaps until Hill, who was following the route previously taken by Ewell, could traverse the Shenandoah Valley.

Robert H. Milroy
Unlike many other Civil War generals, Milroy, 47 in 1863, was not a West Point graduate. A lawyer and judge, he recruited a company of volunteers in Indiana and rose quickly in Union ranks. But his defeat at Winchester as Lee invaded the North in 1863 tarnished his reputation, and he was sent to the Western Theater, where he finished out the war

Fight for the Standard
Troopers clash at Brandy Station over a prized possession, a regimental flag, in this 19th century painting by an unknown artist. According to an account related by a member of the 1st New Jersey Cavalry, one such guidon is said to have changed hands six times during the battle, ending up in Federal hands

Stuart had left Brandy Station in a resentful mood; criticism of his handling of the battle there had been severe. Accurately insisting that Stuart and his generals had been caught by surprise, the Richmond *Examiner* blamed it on "vain and empty-headed officers." Intoned the Richmond *Sentinel:* "Vigilance, vigilance, more vigilance, is the lesson taught us by the Brandy surprise. Let all learn it, from the Major General down to the picket." Those who knew Stuart well suspected he might now seek to restore his reputation with one of his patented forays against the Federals. But for the present, Stuart had to content himself with the hard, thankless job of preventing Pleasonton's cavalry from learning what the Confederate infantry was doing west of the Blue Ridge. Between June 17 and 21, in series of vicious cavalry skirmishes on the Loudoun Valley roads leading westward to the Blue Ridge gaps, Pleasonton pushed Stuart back as far as Ashby's Gap but could go no farther. The Federal troopers were exhausted, and their horses were exhausted and breaking down.

Stuart had cause for satisfaction in having prevented the enemy from penetrating his screen. But he had grander ideas, and he soon put them before Lee at the commander's headquarters in the village of Paris, urging that he be allowed to harass Hooker and delay the Federal army's pursuit. Lee agreed, but he stipulated that as soon as Hooker crossed the Potomac, Stuart must take position on the right flank of the Confederate infantry. But when he received Lee's written order confirming this plan on the rainy night of June 23, Stuart believed its discretionary clauses contained just enough wiggle room to allow him to embark on an adventure that promised to make up for his embarrassment at Brandy Station.

Early the next morning, Stuart issued his orders. His two largest brigades—those of generals Beverly Robertson and Grumble Jones, with a total of about 3,000 men—would remain behind to guard the Blue Ridge passes, then protect the rebels' supply line as the infantry passed through Maryland on the way to Pennsylvania. Three other brigades would assemble at Salem and prepare to move on. Around 1 a.m. on June 25, Stuart's column trotted out of Salem, heading east. For the next eight days, Lee' cavalry chief—upon whom he relied for information about enemy movements—might as well have been on another planet.

Of Speeches and Bouquets

Meanwhile, the long, undulating gray lines moved north from Winchester, with Ewell's divisions under Johnson, Early and Major General Robert Rodes crossing the Potomac near Shepherdstown between June 15 and 18. Spirits were high, especially among the soldiers from Maryland. When General George ("Maryland") Steuart reached the far bank, he leaped from his horse and kissed the ground of his native state in joy.

On June 19, Ewell sent his lead division under Rodes up the Cumberland Valley toward Chambersburg, 20 miles beyond the Maryland-Pennsylvania border. On June 22, Lee ordered Ewell to advance along a broad front. If the Pennsylvania capital of Harrisburg "comes within your means," Lee declared, "capture it."

Two days later Rodes entered Chambersburg. Johnson's division was following, and Early's was pushing north on a parallel road 10 miles to the east. That same day, Hill's and Longstreet's corps began crossing the Potomac at Shepherdstown and Williamsport. The Confederates were moving fast; one soldier wrote that in a single day he had savored "breakfast in Virginia, whisky in Maryland, and supper in Pennsylvania."

On June 25, Ewell organized the next phase of his advance. He would accompany Rodes and two of Johnson's brigades as they drove northeast through Carlisle

to Harrisburg. Johnson's third brigade would head west to forage, while Early's division would march eastward to York and from there to Wrightsville, a town on the Susquehanna River. This route would take him directly through the prosperous farming center of Gettysburg.

Late on the afternoon of June 26, Early's division approached Gettysburg, which was defended by a regiment of raw Pennsylvania militiamen mustered into government service only four days previously and who promptly scattered when they got a look at Early's veterans. Early now demanded that the people of Gettysburg turn over to him the equivalent of $10,000 in goods and produce, but the town's merchants and farmers had already removed or hidden most of their commodities. Early, in a hurry to get on to York, took time for no more than a fast search. York, 30 miles from Gettysburg, surrendered to Early's leading brigade on the evening of June 27.

As the Confederate troops rode through York the next morning, they were in high spirits. Brigadier General William ("Extra Billy") Smith took it upon himself to make a humorous speech, but General Early ordered him to desist. Another orator fared better. The gallant General Gordon assured the town's womenfolk that his troops meant no harm. When he had concluded, a young girl ran out and thrust into his hand a bouquet of flowers—in which was hidden a note, in a woman's handwriting, describing the locations of the 1,400 Federal militia men defending Wrightsville, Early's next destination.

Upon reaching Wrightsville later that day, Gordon found the information to be accurate in every respect. But before he could seize a long covered bridge that crossed the Susquehanna from Wrightsville to the town of Columbia, withdrawing Federal troops set it afire. Early was thereby frustrated in an impromptu plan to swing left from Columbia and assail Harrisburg from the southeast while Ewell, coming up from Carlisle, attacked the capital from the southwest. With the bridge gone, Early had little choice but to recall his corps to York and await instructions from Ewell.

When those orders came, they were hardly what Early expected. On June 27 Rodes' troops had entered Carlisle after an uneventful march from Chambersburg. Ewell had raised the Confederate flag over the U.S. Army cavalry barracks where he had been stationed before the war broke out, and he sent a cavalry brigade under Brigadier General Albert Gallatin Jenkins on toward Harrisburg. On the night of June 28, Jenkins camped on a hill four miles from the Pennsylvania capital. It was the north-

The Gettysburg Campaign
June-July, 1863

Union movements
Confederate movements

Battles
✸ *Union victory*
✸ *Confederate victory*
✸ *Inconclusive*

PENNSYLVANIA

Carlisle
July 1

Harrisburg

Ewell

July 1

Wrightsville
June 28

Shippensburg

Dover

Susquehanna River

Chambersburg
June 28

York

Early

Gettysburg
July 1-3

Cumberland

Hagerstown

Taneytown

June 30

Hanover
June 30

Manchester

Martinsburg

Buford

Sharpsburg

Westminster
June 29

MARYLAND

WEST VIRGINIA
Joined the Union as a free state during the Gettysburg Campaign, June 20, 1863

Frederick

Eldersburg

Baltimore

Harpers
Ferry

MEADE takes command
June 28

Winchester
June 14

Stuart

Strasburg

Shenandoah River

Poolesville

Leesburg

Rockville

Annapolis

Front
Royal

Upperville
June 21

June 28

Aldie
June 17

Mount Jackson

Gainesville

Fairfax

Washington

Stuart

Warrenton

Manassas
Junction

Alexandria

Chesapeake Bay

Sperryville

Harrisonburg

Brandy Station
June 9

Dumfries

HOOKER begins pursuit
June 14

Culpeper

Kelly's
Ford

Pleasonton

LEE heads north
June 3

VIRGINIA

Orange
Court
House

Chancellorsville
May 1-4

Fredericksburg

Potomac River

Scale
0   10   20   30
miles

N

To Richmond

Rappahannock River

Charlottesville

27

Burning their bridges
When General Gordon's troops rode into Wrightsville, Pa., on the night of June 28, 1863, Federal troops withdrew from the town and set fire to the long bridge spanning the Susquehanna River, sending plumes of smoke into the sky. The Confederates tried to save the bridge but were unsuccessful

ernmost penetration made by any Confederate army unit during the war.

After some sharp skirmishes with Federal troops west of the Susquehanna, Jenkins reported that Harrisburg looked like easy pickings, and Ewell made plans for an attack. But then, on June 29, urgent word came from Lee. Ewell's entire corps was ordered to withdraw immediately and march south to Gettysburg. The Army of Northern Virginia was concentrating for battle.

A Spy's Story

Behind Lee's surprising order lay one of the war's stranger stories. Back in Virginia before the campaign had begun, Longstreet had sent a spy to Washington to learn what he could about the Army of the Potomac's movements. The agent was a slim, stooped man with a brown beard and hazel eyes who went only by the name of Harrison. On the night of June 28, Longstreet's chief of staff, Lieutenant Colonel G. Moxley Sorrel, was awakened, in his words, by "a detail of the provost guard bringing up a suspicious prisoner. It was Harrison, the scout, filthy and ragged, showing some rough work and exposure."

Taken to Lee, Harrison reported that he had learned

that Hooker's army was moving north. In fact, he had followed it to Frederick, Md., where at least two Federal corps were already encamped. Somehow procuring a horse and buggy, Harrison had hurried on to Chambersburg; on the way he had seen other Federal troops heading toward South Mountain, beyond which lay the Cumberland Valley and Lee's vital supply line.

"I have no confidence in any scout," Lee had said, and certainly Harrison was no sight to inspire trust. But with Stuart gone no one knew where, Lee had no other source of information, and Longstreet vouched for Harrison's reliability. Before the night was over, Lee accepted Harrison's report and ordered the army to concentrate in order to prevent the Federals "from advancing farther west, and intercepting our communications with Virginia."

Upon leaving Lee's presence, Harrison remarked, almost incidentally, that Hooker had been relieved of command and that the Army of the Potomac was now led by a little-known general named George G. Meade.

The new commander of the Army of the Potomac faced an arduous task. Hooker had left Major General Meade with no plan at all—not even a precise idea of his army's disposition. Yet by late on the afternoon of June

28, Meade had determined that all the corps were within easy range of Frederick and developed a strategy. "I must move toward the Susquehanna," he wired to Halleck, "keeping Washington and Baltimore well covered, and if the enemy is checked in his attempt to cross the Susquehanna, or if he turns toward Baltimore, give him battle."

By evening Meade had issued orders for the troops to "be ready to march at daylight tomorrow." By nightfall the next day, June 29, the soldiers in blue had marched nearly 25 miles and were arrayed along a 20-mile front extending southeast from Emmitsburg, Md., near the Pennsylvania border, to Westminster.

On learning that Hill and Longstreet were camped east of Chambersburg on the road to Gettysburg, Meade strengthened the wing closer to the enemy by ordering Major General Daniel E. Sickles' III Corps to close on John Reynolds' I Corps and Major General Oliver O. Howard's XI Corps near Emmitsburg. Buford's cavalry division, ranging ahead, entered Gettysburg at about 11 a.m. on June 30. The troopers found the townsfolk wildly excited about the sudden approach and withdrawal, just a few minutes before, of a Confederate infantry brigade.

This force was commanded by Brigadier General James Johnston Pettigrew of A.P. Hill's corps. On nearing the town, Pettigrew had ridden ahead to reconnoiter. Pausing on a ridge, he swept his field glasses across the landscape. Gettysburg seemed empty of enemy troops—but then he saw a long column of Federal cavalry, coming fast up the road from Emmitsburg.

Since Pettigrew had been instructed to avoid a fight for now, he withdrew to the west, halting his brigade nearly four miles from Gettysburg. That afternoon, he rode back to Cashtown to tell Heth what he had seen. Just then, Hill came up and listened to the conversation. But he placed no stock in Pettigrew's story, insisting that "the enemy are still at Middleburg, and have not yet struck their tents." When Heth declared his intention to lead his men into Gettysburg the next day to survey the scene, Hill consented to his plan.

That night at Gettysburg, Buford listened quietly as one of his brigadiers opined that the Confederates, last seen heading the other way, would not return—and that if they did, he would easily beat them off. Despite his avuncular way, Buford was as tough and hardheaded a man as any in the Army, and he knew better. "No, you won't," he said. "They will attack you in the morning and they will come booming—skirmishers three deep. You will have to fight like the devil until supports arrive." ■

★ A Worn-Out Tale Loses Traction

Over the course of many generations, Americans have been struck by the fact that the largest battle in the Civil War was started simply because a unit of General Lee's Army of Northern Virginia was searching around for badly needed shoes in the small town of Gettysburg. The disparity between cause and effect is indeed delicious—but more and more, modern scholars are agreeing that this tale is no more than a charming legend. In fact, the story of the shoes can apparently be walked back to a Confederate commander's desire not to shoe his men's aching feet but rather to cover his own posterior.

The story of the shoes can be traced back to Major General Henry Heth, a division commander in General A.P. Hill's III Corps. In an 1877 Philadelphia newspaper story, Heth first told the tale of how he led his 7,000-man strong infantry division into Gettysburg on the morning of July 1, 1863, in search of a shoe factory said to operate in the town. According to Heth's account: "Hearing [on June 30] that a supply of shoes was to be obtained in Gettysburg, eight miles distant from Cashtown, and greatly needing shoes for my men, I directed General Pettigrew [one of his four brigade commanders] to go to Gettysburg and get these supplies … About this time Gen. Hill rode up … I then said, 'If there is no objection, I will take my division tomorrow and go to Gettysburg and get those shoes!' Hill replied, 'None in the world.'"

So the stage was set for battle, according to Heth. And generations of historians embraced the tale—until the story began to be debunked, beginning with the publication of scholar Edward Coddington's 1968 book, *Gettysburg: A Study in Command.* Coddington questioned the validity of Heth's claim, and today the story is increasingly believed to be false. For one thing, there was no shoe factory in Gettysburg; a cadre of local independent cobblers attended to the town's footwear needs. However, as National Park Service Gettysburg historian John Heiser points out, there were rumors among Union soldiers that a large supply of shoes had been sent to Gettysburg to be picked up by Federal quartermasters. Perhaps this yarn may have reached Confederate ears.

But why would Heth go to the trouble to fabricate this account? Simple: as of late June, Robert E. Lee had ordered, in the strongest terms, that no Confederate unit was to engage with Union troops until the widely dispersed Army of Northern Virginia could be concentrated for battle. Defying orders, Heth went looking for Union troops—rather than shoes—in Gettysburg on July 1, and he bumped right into them, touching off hostilities well before either side was ready to do battle. Small wonder he concocted the tale of the shoes, absolving himself from blame. But give Heth credit for knowing that his fabricated tale was just charming enough to have legs.

J.E.B. Stuart

MAJOR GENERAL, CAVALRY CORPS, ARMY OF NORTHERN VIRGINIA

★

LONG BEFORE HIS DEATH IN 1864, CON-federate cavalry commander James Ewell Brown ("Jeb") Stuart had become the stuff of legend. His deeds were so daring and his style and dash so appealing that he became the beau ideal of the Southern warrior. It helped that in Stuart's day the cavalryman was the single most exciting figure in uniform, filling the role of today's fighter pilots or Navy SEALs. It helped that Stuart basked in his role and helped cultivate his reputation as the master of the surprise attack, the daring deception, the stirring gambit. And it helped that many Southerners had long been enjoying a giddy love affair with the romantic novels of Walter Scott, and Stuart seemed to spring to life direct-ly from the pages of the beloved writer. (Mark Twain charged that "Sir Walter had so large a hand in making Southern character, as it existed before the war, that he is in great measure responsible for the war.")

When Stuart died, at 31, on May 12, 1864, after being shot in the Battle of Yellow Tavern in the Overland Cam-paign, the legend subsumed the man. For those needing a refresher course in that legend, the quotation from *Confederate Military History* on the facing page distills it for us. The laughing cavalier, the happy warrior with the knightly face, the dandy who could sport an ostrich plume in his hat "without exciting a suspicion of unfit-ness"—the gears of Stuart's fame have been lovingly lu-bricated across the decades.

The problem with such legendary status is not that Stuart's fame is undeserved—there is no doubt he was a brilliant and courageous leader, an inspiring com-mander and a larger-than-life figure. It is that the main-tenance of the legend often demands that he be seen, as Robert E. Lee so often is, as incapable of error.

Yet he was only human, and his flaws rode in tandem with his virtues, especially so in Lee's invasion of the North in 1863. Stuart's insistence on staging a grand cavalry review to impress Lee early in June was a self-serving stunt that sapped time and energy from the deadly serious business of the campaign (and kicked up so much dust it helped Federal cavalrymen find Stuart's position). And his long absence in the course of the cam-paign, driven in part by his attempt to pull off one of his dazzling triumphs that made mockery of his Federal foes, prevented his cavalry corps from operating as Lee's reconnaissance unit and keeping Lee informed of the enemy's movements. The confusion and improvisation that marked the Confederates' first day of battle at Get-tysburg is directly attributable to the officers' ignorance regarding the current location of Federal troops, the sort of information that had contributed to so many major victories in the past.

But enough caviling about the cavalier: equal time must be given to his celebrated deeds. Born in Patrick County, Va., in 1833 to an upper-crust family, he matricu-lated at West Point in 1850, where he was popular and a good student, if 10th in his class in cavalry tactics. There he met the superintendent, Lee, who would become his great mentor. In the 1850s Stuart served in the West, tangling with Native Americans and with zealots of

His characteristics were such as to make him a popular hero. Personally he was the embodiment of reckless courage, splendid manhood, and unconquerable gayety. He could wear, without exciting a suspicion of unfitness, all the warlike adornments of an old-time cavalier. His black plume, and hat caught up with a golden star, seemed the proper frame for a knightly face. A laugh was always at his lips, and a song behind it. He would lead a march with his banjo-player thrumming at his side.

—*Confederate Military History*, 1899

all stripes in "Bleeding Kansas." There he also met and married Flora Cooke, daughter of a U.S. Army officer.

Stuart thus found himself enmeshed in the incendiary national struggles with slavery and secession even before the war began. When the abolitionist firebrand John Brown occupied the Federal artillery depot at Harpers Ferry, Va., in 1859, Stuart volunteered to serve as an aide to Lee, then a general in the U.S. Army, who had been assigned to quell the uprising. When the war came, two years later, Lee was already familiar with Stuart's capacities. He assigned him to serve under Stonewall Jackson as an infantry officer, but Jackson quickly named Stuart to lead his cavalry corps. Stuart was present when Jackson received his nickname by "standing like a stone wall" at the First Battle of Bull Run (Manassas), and soon Lee summoned Stuart back to lead the cavalry divisions of the Army of Northern Virginia.

Stuart won undying fame in June 1862, in the Peninsula Campaign, when Lee asked his units to reconnoiter Union positions on the rebels' left flank. Stuart's 1,200 horsemen not only performed that task—they kept on riding, completing in three days a complete circumference of the Federal army and returning laden with plunder paid for at Abe Lincoln's expense: horses, mules and wagons, plus 165 prisoners. The feat made Stuart the toast of the South, an equal to Lee and Jackson. It captured the emerging consensus view of the two armies: the rebels were spry, crafty, highly mobile fighters who ran rings around the galumphing, buffoonish Federals, laughing all the way.

Other nifty exploits followed. On Aug. 18, 1862, Stuart was almost captured by Federal cavalrymen who raided a cabin in Virginia where he was staying; he escaped with his life, but his enemies snagged his famed plumed hat and cloak. Four days later, Stuart took his revenge: he led a raid on Union headquarters that yielded not only valuable maps and dispatches but also the dress uniform of Army of the Potomac leader John Pope. Stuart wrote Pope a taunting note: "General. You have my hat and plume. I have your best coat. I have the honor to propose a cartel for the fair exchange of the prisoners." Pope never responded: wit was a stranger to most Union generals.

Stuart may live today as more legend than man, but nations need their legends. And for the record: Stuart was one of the most inspiring military leaders in U.S. history—and Mark Twain was a quitter who once enlisted in a company of Confederate volunteers but lasted only a few weeks before he lit out for the territories. ∎

Hat trick *One of Stuart's signature plumed hats was a gift from the Union's General Sam Crawford, an old friend. Meeting under a flag of truce on Aug. 11, 1862, after the Confederates won the Battle of Cedar Mountain (Va.), the two traded war stories, and Stuart wagered Crawford a new hat that biased Union newspapers would call the Confederate victory a Northern triumph.*

A few days later, Stuart received a package containing a copy of a Northern paper—and a new hat

July 1, 1863

A witness to history

A vintage cannon still stands in the fields around Gettysburg, Pa. The first day of combat there was primarily fought to occupy the best positions for the larger conflict that would follow, as troops on both sides were still marching to reach the battlefields. Yet even so, the battle on July 1 ranks among the 20 bloodiest days of the long war

Battlefield Guide: July 1, 1863

Only a Matter of Time

All times given in this book for events on the battlefield are approximate. Clocks in the U.S. were not set to a uniform standard until the 1880s, when railroad companies led the way in establishing standardized time, and the pocket watches carried by military officers might show significantly different times than those used by other officers, both on their side and on the enemy side.

Military Lexicon

canister: A projectile, shot from a cannon, filled with about 35 iron balls the size of marbles that scattered like the pellets of a shotgun.

echelon attack: An assault launched in a synchronized sequence, not unlike the "wave" seen in modern sports stadiums.

enfilade: To fire from the side of an enemy position, thus striking along the length rather than the front of a line of troops.

flank: Used as a noun, it is either end of a fortified position or a unit of troops. Used as a verb, it is to move to allow an attack upon the side of an enemy's position rather than upon the enemy's front.

front, changing front: The forward-facing aspect of a troop position. When units change front, they are changing the direction in which they are aligned.

ramrod: A long, cylindrical metal rod used to push the cartridge down the barrel of a musket in preparation for firing.

skirmishers: Infantry personnel who led the way as a unit moved forward, probing and reconnoitering enemy positions, with a loose formation and a high degree of mobility.

sponge staff: An artillery implement; a pole with a sponge of wool at one end and a wooden block at the other. The sponge was soaked in water to kill any live sparks remaining in a weapon's barrel after firing; the wooden end was used to force a charge of gunpowder deep into the barrel.

Faces in the Ranks

The "Bucktail Brigade" of Pennsylvania infantry volunteers made a name for itself at the Second Battle of Bull Run (Manassas)—so much so that new units who wore deer tails on their hats were formed. They held their place at McPherson's Ridge early in the combat on July 1.

Timeline

5 a.m. Confederates march to Gettysburg
Heth's troops begin marching toward Gettysburg along the Chambersburg Pike.

7:30 a.m. The first shot ❶
Lieutenant Marcellus E. Jones of the 8th Illinois fires at Heth's troops, in the first shot of the battle.

8-9 a.m. Confederates attack at Herr Ridge
Alabamians and Tennesseans south of Chambersburg Pike and Mississippians and North Carolinians to the north push Federals back across Willoughby Run.

10 a.m. Reynolds is killed ❷
Reynolds and the Iron Brigade reach McPherson's Ridge. Reynolds is shot dead.

11 a.m. A brief silence
During a two-hour lull, each side prepares for a renewal of fighting, as more forces arrive on the scene.

12:30 a.m. Confederates approach Federal right
Howard, now in Union command, learns the Confederate infantry is approaching. Soon, 16 guns start firing from Oak Hill at Cutler's Union brigade.

1:30 p.m. Lee surveys the battle
Joining Hill on Herr Ridge, Lee sees an opportunity and, reversing himself, orders full engagement.

2-2:30 p.m. Rodes attacks ❸
Rodes assaults Union right along Oak Ridge, resulting in high casualties for rebels.

2-3 p.m. Federals are driven back ❹
Federal infantry north of town is overwhelmed. Union troops retreat to high ground south of town.

2:00 p.m. Heth renews attack ❺
Heth launches another thrust on Union left, and the retreat by Federal left to Cemetery Hill continues.

4:30 p.m. Federals dig in ❻
Hancock rallies Federals on Cemetery Hill and begins to form a defensive line in a fishhook shape.

6 p.m. Ewell decides not to attack ❼
Ewell refrains from attacking the Union positions on the high ground south of town, thus allowing Union troops to dig in on the heights around Cemetery Hill.

1-2 a.m. (July 2) Meade arrives ❽
Reaching Gettysburg after midnight, Meade confirms previous orders to buttress fishhook line.

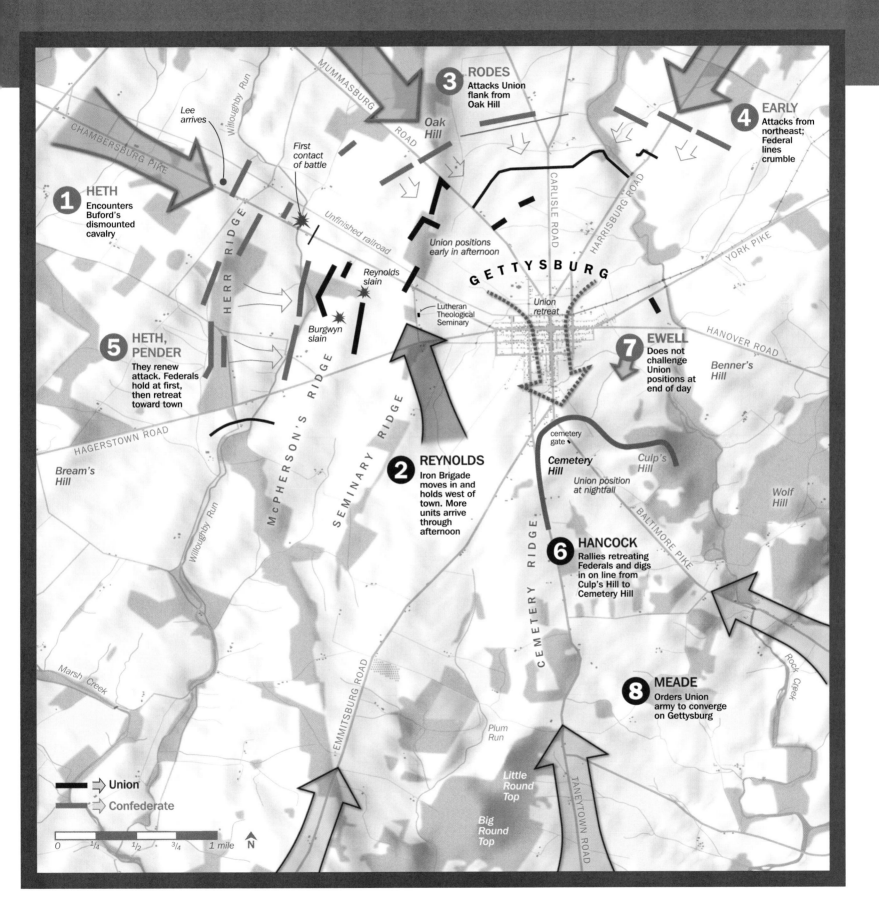

MUMMASBURG ROAD

CHAMBERSBURG PIKE

Lee arrives

First contact of battle

③ RODES
Attacks Union flank from Oak Hill

Oak Hill

④ EARLY
Attacks from northeast; Federal lines crumble

CARLISLE ROAD

HARRISBURG ROAD

YORK PIKE

① HETH
Encounters Buford's dismounted cavalry

Unfinished railroad

Union positions early in afternoon

G E T T Y S B U R G

HERR RIDGE

Reynolds slain

Burgwyn slain

Lutheran Theological Seminary

Union retreat

HANOVER ROAD

⑤ HETH, PENDER
They renew attack. Federals hold at first, then retreat toward town

McPHERSON'S RIDGE

SEMINARY RIDGE

⑦ EWELL
Does not challenge Union positions at end of day

Benner's Hill

HAGERSTOWN ROAD

Willoughby Run

② REYNOLDS
Iron Brigade moves in and holds west of town. More units arrive through afternoon

cemetery gate

Cemetery Hill

Culp's Hill

Wolf Hill

Bream's Hill

Union position at nightfall

BALTIMORE PIKE

CEMETERY RIDGE

⑥ HANCOCK
Rallies retreating Federals and digs in on line from Culp's Hill to Cemetery Hill

Rock Creek

Marsh Creek

EMMITSBURG ROAD

⑧ MEADE
Orders Union army to converge on Gettysburg

Plum Run

TANEYTOWN ROAD

Little Round Top

Big Round Top

➡ Union
➡ Confederate

0   ¼   ½   ¾   1 mile   N

With an Abrupt Reveille, The Great Battle Begins

Improvising on the fly as events outrun strategy, the armies race to Gettysburg and clash. After early Union triumphs, Confederates win the day's main battles, but the Federals control the high ground

T HE BATTLE OF GETTYSBURG TOOK PLACE over a period of three days, each of which has its own story line, principal actors and distinctive settings. The events unfolded as a three-act play, culminating in the grand set piece of the Confederates' last desperate gamble, Pickett's Charge, on the third day. In contrast, the first day of fighting, Wed., July 1, was one of the least-scripted encounters of the war: it was a largely improvised affair, fought on a battlefield that was chosen by neither of the two top commanders, its pace ebbing and flowing as regiments of both Confederate and Federal troops followed the sound of the guns and arrived on the battleground.

The new Federal commander, Major General George Meade, was not even present at Gettysburg on July 1, and Confederate commander General Robert E. Lee didn't arrive on the scene until early afternoon. Time was a crucial factor in the day's struggles: as rival armies raced to reach the scene, the troops were often immediately rushed to the front, however exhausted they were from their lengthy marches. Many of the pivotal events of the following two days of battle were decided in a few game-changing moments on July 1, as the armies seized—or failed to seize—the best ground upon which to fight.

Early Encounters

The Confederate foragers appeared at first as ghostly shapes in the drizzly dawn light. Lieutenant Marcellus E. Jones, in charge of pickets for the 8th Illinois Cavalry, saw them at about 5:30 a.m., marching in a shadowy column down the Chambersburg Pike from Cashtown, approaching the stone bridge across Marsh Creek three miles west of Gettysburg.

From his position on the pike 700 ft. away, Jones saw a mounted Confederate officer pull off to one side to let the infantrymen pass. Borrowing a carbine from one of his sergeants, Jones fired at the enemy horseman without

The road to conflict *The Chambersburg Pike, running northwest from Gettysburg to Cashtown, was the key artery of the first day of battle, and most of the Confederate armies used this route to arrive on the scene. Taken after July 3, this photograph reveals that soldiers have removed wood from the fence to use in their campfires*

"Hold your ground!"

In Don Troiani's painting McPherson's Ridge, *Federal cavalry officer Buford directs a battery of horse artillery and cavalrymen to head off Heth's advancing Confederates until Federal troops under Reynolds can reach the scene*

visible result, then prudently withdrew as the Confederates deployed a line of skirmishers a mile and a half wide.

Jones had fired the first shot in what would begin as a minor skirmish between a few rebel infantry brigades looking for trouble—rather than shoes, as popular legend has long held—and two Federal cavalry brigades tracking enemy movements. But from the moment that hasty shot was fired, events outraced strategy, feeding on capricious circumstance until 70,000 Confederate and 90,000 Federal soldiers were drawn into a monumental battle that is recalled as the turning point of the war.

Neither army was ready to give battle on July 1. Gen-

eral Lee, unfamiliar with the terrain and ignorant of the Federal strength in the area due to the absence of his cavalry unit, insisted that no large engagement be started until his army was concentrated between Cashtown and Gettysburg. Lieutenant General Richard S. Ewell was several hours away to the north, and Lieutenant General James Longstreet's corps almost a day's march to the west. As for the Federals, General Meade was inclined to let Lee make the first move: he had directed his engineers to lay out a defensive line at his current headquarters, 20 miles southeast of Gettysburg, along Pipe Creek near Taneytown, Md. Earlier that morning he had told his corps commanders to be prepared to fall back to it. But the choice of a battlefield was already slipping out of the generals' hands; a desperate struggle had begun in the ridges west of Gettysburg.

Those ridges ran generally north-south. A mile and a half north of the town, Major General Henry Heth's advancing Confederates first encountered Herr Ridge, named for a tavern on its crest. Nine hundred yards to the east, across a swale through which meandered a little stream called Willoughby Run, was McPherson's Ridge, where a farm family of that name lived. Adjoining their farm, a few hundred yards to the south of the Chambersburg Pike, stood the 17-acre patch of McPherson's Woods (the grove was in fact owned by John Herbst and is also referred to as Herbst's Woods).

Another 500 yds. to the east, about three-quarters of a mile from Gettysburg, lay Seminary Ridge; crowned by the three-story brick Lutheran Theological Seminary, it rose gently 40 ft. above the surrounding fields. A short distance north of the pike, Seminary Ridge merged with McPherson's Ridge; from there a single promontory, Oak Ridge, ran north to an 80-ft.-high knob named Oak Hill that dominated the area northwest of Gettysburg.

The Chambersburg Pike, which traversed these ridges from the northwest, was paralleled about 200 yds. to the north by a railbed as deep as 20 ft. in places, in which no track had yet been laid. Nine other roads radiated from Gettysburg to all points on the compass: clockwise from the Chambersburg Pike these led to Mummasburg, Carlisle (to the north), Heidlersburg (and thence to Harrisburg), York, Hanover, Baltimore, Taneytown (to the south), Emmitsburg and Hagerstown.

Skirmish at Willoughby Run

When Heth reached the crest of Herr Ridge at about 8 a.m., he saw Federal troops ahead and realized that he would not get to McPherson's Ridge without a fight. Deploying his two leading brigades, Heth ordered them to move forward and occupy the town. North of the turnpike was a brigade commanded by Brigadier General Joseph R. Davis, a nephew of the Confederate President. Davis was untried in brigade command, and his four regiments had never fought together. South of the pike was a veteran brigade of Alabama and Tennessee troops under Brigadier General James J. Archer, a Princeton graduate, lawyer and veteran of the Regular Army.

The Federal cavalry officer who had so accurately predicted this day's events, Brigadier General John Buford,

★ Brigadier General John Buford

John Buford's fingerprints are all over the Federal response to Robert E. Lee's invasion of Union territory in 1863. The cavalry officer played a pivotal role when the Confederate campaign began, as one of the leaders of the successful Federal surprise attack at Brandy Station on the previously untouchable Confederate cavalry led by Major General Jeb Stuart. Farther north, on June 30, it was Buford who rode into Gettysburg, observed the highly defensible positions along Cemetery Ridge and decided to stake out the elevated ground for the Federal position in the battle to come.

When the fighting began the next morning, Buford's cavalrymen, though outnumbered 3 to 1, stood their ground against Confederate Major General Henry Heth's divisions along Willoughby Run for two crucial hours, until the divisions led by Major General John F. Reynolds could reach the scene. After the three days of battle, as Lee's beaten soldiers conducted their retreat back to Virginia, Buford's cavalry constantly harassed them. Under Buford, his superior, Brigadier General Alfred Pleasonton and other gritty officers, the Federals at last possessed a cavalry command that could hold its ground against Stuart's celebrated horse soldiers.

Buford, 37 in 1863, was a West Point graduate. Historian Shelby Foote describes him as "a tough, Kentucky-born regular with a fondness for hard fighting and the skill to back it up." Buford was cast in the mold of Ulysses S. Grant; he cared little for the spit-and-polish show of such leaders as General George B. McClellan, preferring combat to dress parades. The cavalry officer fell ill in the autumn of 1863, only months after the Battle of Gettysburg; he died Dec. 16, 1863, most likely of typhoid fever. In the hours before his death, President Lincoln promoted him to the rank of major general, in recognition of his service at Gettysburg.

Wisconsin's pride
Soldiers of the 2nd Wisconsin Infantry Regiment, a unit of the Iron Brigade, charge to relieve Buford's cavalrymen at McPherson's Ridge in this painting by Don Troiani, For God's Sake Forward.

At right, a member of the unit, wearing the brigade's distinctive black hat, loads his weapon

was ready for Heth's advance. As Buford later wrote, "My arrangements were made for entertaining him until Reynolds [Major General John F. Reynolds] could reach the scene." Buford placed the dismounted troopers of Colonel William Gamble's 1st Brigade along the east bank of Willoughby Run in a 1,000-yd. line extending from the railbed south across the Chambersburg Pike. North of the railbed, Colonel Thomas Devin's 2nd Brigade reached to the base of Oak Hill. But the Federal line was woefully thin: against Heth's 7,461 men, Buford counted only 2,748 troopers, with 1 in every 4 holding horses for his comrades. Buford knew he was outnum-

bered and sent word urgently for reinforcements to General Reynolds, commanding the Federal left wing.

As Heth's skirmishers came confidently down Herr Ridge toward Willoughby Run, their muskets gleaming as the sun broke through the overcast skies, they were staggered by a burst of fire from Gamble's men and salvos from Lieutenant John Calef's battery of horse artillery. Firing furiously with their seven-shot breech-loading Spencer carbines, which fired 20 rounds a minute, as opposed to the Confederate muskets' four per minute, the Federals held up Heth's advance for a full hour. But by about 9 a.m. Buford could see from his observation post atop the Lutheran Theological Seminary building that Gamble's troopers were being pushed back across Willoughby Run.

Just then General Reynolds rode up. "The devil's to pay!" exclaimed Buford. But when Reynolds asked if he could hold out a while longer, until his reinforcements arrived, Buford replied simply, "I reckon I can." That was good enough for Reynolds. The battle was at hand. "The enemy is advancing in strong force," he wrote to Meade at Taneytown. "I will fight him inch by inch, and if driven into the town I will barricade the streets and hold him back as long as possible." Though still unsure about where to make his stand, Meade was delighted when he received the message. "Good!" he exclaimed. "That is just like Reynolds, he will hold out to the bitter end."

Reynolds Seizes the Offensive

Meade's high opinion of Reynolds was widely shared: a West Pointer, Reynolds was a crisply professional soldier who went about his business with little fuss. At 42, he had been with the Army of the Potomac from the beginning and had repeatedly demonstrated that he could be relied upon. Moreover, he was a Pennsylvanian determined to rid his home state of the Confederates.

Reynolds had decided the evening before to hold Gettysburg. Before riding off at dawn on July 1 from his camp at Emmitsburg, 12 miles to the southwest, he had set his forces in motion: Brigadier General James S. Wadsworth was told to put his 1st Division of I Corps on the road to Gettysburg at once; Major General Abner Doubleday—in charge of I Corps while Reynolds served as overall commander of the Federal left wing—was assigned to bring up the rest of the corps. Reynolds also left orders for XI Corps to follow and recommended that III Corps move toward Gettysburg in support. Doubleday was slow to get his troops moving—a typical showing by a general who seldom did anything poorly enough to warrant criticism or well enough to attract applause.

About a mile short of Gettysburg, the men at the head of Wadsworth's column saw a rider approaching fast. It was Reynolds, returning from his meeting with Buford. He ordered the two leading brigades to advance across the fields directly toward the ridges west of town. Off they went, shucking their knapsacks and loading their muskets as they trotted toward McPherson's Ridge.

They reached the crest at about 10 a.m. and rushed into battle. Brigadier General Solomon Meredith's 1st

★ The Iron Brigade

There are those damned black-hatted fellows again!" shouted a Confederate soldier who had the misfortune to bump into the Union Army's famed Iron Brigade amid McPherson's Woods early on the morning of July 1. "Tain't no militia! It's the Army of the Potomac!" He had encountered one of the proudest and hardest-fighting units of that Federal force, its soldiers distinguished by the tall black Hardee hats they wore, which resembled a frontiersman's hat more than the blue kepis that were worn by most Federal units.

These tough troops did hail from the frontier—the frontier as of the 1850s and 1860s, that is. The first three units that formed the Iron Brigade were the 2nd, 6th and 7th infantry volunteers from Wisconsin. They were joined by a light artillery company from Indiana and later by another regiment of infantry volunteers, the 24th Michigan. After winning praise in 1862 for their strong stand against Stonewall Jackson's troops at the Second Battle of Bull Run (Manassas), the rugged men from the Western frontier were supposedly christened by General George B. McClellan at the Battle of South Mountain in September 1862. Legend has it that McClellan praised the unit's valor and that of their commanding officer, General John Gibbon, saying, "They must be made of iron."

It makes for a good story, but the tale is perhaps apocryphal: many units sought to characterize themselves as being as impregnable as iron, and early in the war these units from today's Midwest were known as the "Iron Brigade of the West," to distinguish them from the units from New York and Pennsylvania who called themselves the "Iron Brigade of the East."

The soldiers of the Iron Brigade of the West fought with valor not only at Gettysburg but also at Antietam, Chancellorsville and other battles. By war's end, there was no longer a need for the directional tag: the Iron Brigade was one of the most widely known and respected units in the Army of the Potomac, and its men took pride in calling themselves the "first brigade of the first division of the first corps of the first army of the Republic."

On July 1 at Gettysburg, the Iron Brigade held off the Confederate attack at McPherson's Ridge, drove the rebel troops back across the creek called Willoughby Run, collared Confederate General James J. Archer, captured the flag of a Mississippi division and took scores of Confederates prisoner at the unfinished railroad cut. When the three days of fighting ended, some 63% of the Iron Brigade (1,153 out of 1,829 men) were casualties. Small wonder that 150 years after Gettysburg, the name "Iron Brigade" is still employed with pride by several active infantry and armored divisions of the U.S. Army.

The fallen *The photograph above, taken after July 3, was captioned by its photographers as showing Federal soldiers who died on July 1 near McPherson's Woods. However, most modern scholars believe the image shows members of the Union III Corps who died on July 2 near the Rose farm. The bodies are barefoot, indicating the men's shoes were likely stolen after they died*

Brigade—known as the Iron Brigade for its exploits at Groveton, South Mountain and Antietam—was on his left, extending through McPherson's Woods and on toward the south; the five regiments of Brigadier General Lysander Cutler's 2nd Brigade were to Meredith's right, two just south of the Chambersburg Pike and three to the north. Gamble's hard-pressed cavalrymen, who were falling back to a reserve position, shouted encouragement as the soldiers moved through their ranks: "We have got them now. Go in and give them hell!"

Reynolds, seizing the offensive, placed Captain James A. Hall's 2nd Maine Battery astride the turnpike and rode south to join the Iron Brigade in McPherson's Woods. As he turned in his saddle to urge on the 2nd Wisconsin, a Minié ball took him behind the ear, and

Reynolds fell dead from his horse. Historians are uncertain as to who fired the bullet that killed Reynolds: the prime suspect is a Confederate sharpshooter. Doubleday, who had arrived on McPherson's Ridge only a few minutes before, was now the senior officer on the field.

South of the turnpike, the Confederates had advanced with little notion of what lay ahead of them. Archer's brigade crossed Willoughby Run and attacked recklessly through McPherson's Woods, the troops thinking their foes were cavalrymen, who would quickly flee under a determined rebel infantry assault. But they soon saw, amid the smoke and flame in the woods, that their enemy wore the Iron Brigade's distinctive black felt hats, with wide brims turned up on the left side. "There are those damned black-hatted fellows again!" shouted one Confederate. "Tain't no militia. It's the Army of the Potomac!"

The Iron Brigade soon seized the advantage in the fray. The Federal line extended farther south than that of the Confederates, and in the brigade's advance the 19th Indiana and the 24th Michigan surged ahead, turned Archer's right flank and caught his men in a murderous enfilade. Unable to withstand such fire from both front and flank, Archer's Confederates made a hasty retreat back across Willoughby Run.

The Iron Brigade came surging after them, scooping up prisoners—among them Archer, who was collared by the burly Private Patrick Maloney of the 2nd Wisconsin. Archer, the first of General Lee's staff officers ever to be taken prisoner in battle, was led to General Doubleday, a former comrade in the Regular Army, who greeted him with a certain lack of sensitivity. "Good morning, Archer," said Doubleday, "I am glad to see you." Replied Archer: "Well, I am not glad to see you by a damned sight."

Trapped in the Railroad Cut

All this while, on the Federal right, north of the railroad grading, Cutler's 2nd Brigade had been furiously engaged. There, the tactical situation was reversed; Cutler's line was shorter than that of General Davis' Confederate brigade. Overlapping Cutler's right, the inexperienced 55th North Carolina wheeled with surprising precision to the south and struck hard at the Federal flank and rear. From his position in Cutler's line, just north of the railbed, Captain J.V. Pierce of the 147th New York heard the dreaded cry: "They are flanking us on the right!"

With a disaster in the making, Wadsworth was forced to order Cutler's three regiments north of the pike to pull back to Seminary Ridge. Two of them obeyed at once. But Lieutenant Colonel Francis C. Miller, commanding the 147th New York, fell with a bullet in his throat before he could repeat the order to withdraw. The New Yorkers, alone, unknowing and under assault from front and flank, fought on in a wheat field adjacent to the railbed before breaking for the rear.

Seeing the peril to their right, the red-trousered 14th Brooklyn and the 95th New York—the two Cutler regiments that had been posted south of the Chambersburg Pike—now faced to the north, marched to the road and began firing at the flank of Davis' Confederates as they ran in pursuit of Wadsworth's retreating regiments. The New Yorkers were soon joined by Doubleday's only reserve unit, the 6th Wisconsin of the Iron Brigade. The Wisconsin men rested their muskets on the fence along-

★ Major General John F. Reynolds

The sketch below was drawn from life by professional illustrator Alfred Waud, who witnessed the death of Union General John F. Reynolds on the morning of July 1. The death of Reynolds was one of the pivotal moments of the first day's fighting, for he was widely considered one of the most capable generals in the Federal ranks. A native of Lancaster, Pa., Reynolds graduated from West Point in 1841 and, like many of the top commanders of the Civil War, earned his spurs as a young officer during the Mexican War, where he distinguished himself at the battles of Monterey and Buena Vista. After serving in the South and on the Western frontier in the late 1840s and '50s, Reynolds became Commandant of Cadets at West Point in 1860 and was serving in that role when the war broke out. Named a brigadier general, he commanded a brigade of Pennsylvania Reserve troops during the Union's Peninsula Campaign of 1862, where he was captured after the Battle of Gaines' Mill but was exchanged for a Confederate officer six weeks later.

Only two weeks after his return to duty, Reynolds commanded a full division of Pennsylvania troops in the Second Battle of Bull Run (Manassas), where he led a stalwart stand at Henry House Hill, amid a chaotic defeat for the Federals, that earned him wide respect in the Union ranks.

Thoughtful, decisive and opinionated, Reynolds was frequently critical of the leaders of the Army of the Potomac, faulting General Ambrose Burnside after Fredericksburg and General Joseph Hooker after Chancellorsville. President Lincoln met in private with Reynolds on June 2, a month before Gettysburg, and offered him the leadership of the Army of the Potomac, but Reynolds refused, fearing interference from Washington. In rushing to join General Buford's cavalry troops on the morning of July 1, Reynolds played a key role in determining the location of the decisive battle in Lee's 1863 invasion of the North.

side the pike and opened an enfilading fire into the 2nd Mississippi. The Confederates slowed, stopped, then broke for the only available cover—the banks of the railroad cut. Some of the Confederates milled around in the bottom of the 20-ft. cut; others crawled up the side and started shooting.

From the protection of the cut, the Confederates were now able to direct a lethal fire into the ranks of the New York and Wisconsin men. As the Federals began to fall, Lieutenant Colonel Rufus Dawes of the 6th Wisconsin ran to Major Edward Pye of the 95th New York. "We must charge!" Dawes cried. "Charge it is," replied Pye, and the two regiments headed across a field toward the cut, followed by the 14th Brooklyn. In the attack, 180 men of the 6th Wisconsin went down. But the Federals reached their objective, driving the Confederates from the rim of the cut in a brief, brutal exchange of gun butts and bayonets, and capturing the flag of the 2nd Mississippi Regiment. Soon the Confederates in the cut were surrounded, bottled up like a child's fireflies in a jar.

Amid the heat of battle, the Federal troops lining the rim could have conducted a frightful slaughter. Instead, a merciful impulse prevailed, and from the length of the Union line there arose a loud chorus: "Throw down your muskets. Down with your muskets!"

So many troops surrendered that Dawes found himself encumbered by an "awkward bundle" of swords taken from captured officers. Davis had lost more than half of his 2,300 men, most as prisoners. The remnants of Davis' command retired to Herr Ridge, joining Archer's shattered brigade. As General Heth would later report, the enemy "had now been felt, and found to be in heavy force in and around Gettysburg."

A Brief Respite

Late in the morning, an uneasy quiet fell over the battlefield, one that would last for more than two hours, punctuated occasionally by the sharp crack of muskets as skirmishers sniped at one another or by the deeper roar of cannon searching at long range for enemy artillery positions. During the lull, the ridges and fields outside Gettysburg swarmed with soldiers moving from place to place in preparation for a renewal of the fighting; men in blue and in butternut marched for all they were worth in what had become a race between reinforcements.

The first phase of the first day's battle was over; as additional troops surged onto the scene, an entirely different battle, with new forces in play, was taking shape.

When the fighting resumed, it would be waged by much larger armies: some 24,000 Confederates would launch assaults against 19,000 Federal soldiers along a semicircular front that ran for three miles along the ridges, slopes and valleys north and west of Gettysburg.

General Heth was still determined to occupy the town. He was encouraged by his corps commander, Lieutenant General A.P. Hill, who, although ill that day and still back in Cashtown, sent word that Major General William Dorsey Pender was moving up to support Heth. Meanwhile, the Federals realigned their defenses. The Iron Brigade was recalled to its former line in McPherson's Woods and along the ridge to the south. Cutler's battered brigade moved from Seminary Ridge back to McPherson's Ridge north of the turnpike.

As these movements were under way, a new Union commander—the fourth of the day—relieved Doubleday. He was Major General Oliver O. Howard, who had arrived in Gettysburg at about 10:30 a.m., in advance of his XI Corps. Howard had climbed to the top of one of the town's taller buildings just in time to see Cutler's men breaking for the rear. Jumping to the wrong conclusion, he sent a courier galloping to Meade at Taneytown with what Doubleday later described as "the baleful intelligence that the First Corps had fled from the field at the first contact with the enemy." A few minutes later, Howard was informed that Reynolds had been killed; as the senior officer present, he assumed command.

Howard was given little time to contemplate his new responsibilities. At about 12:30 p.m. there came the ominous news that a large body of Confederate infantry was approaching the exposed Federal right from the north. Moments later the Confederates ran 16 guns out of the woods onto Oak Hill and began firing at Cutler's line from a range of 800 yds. A Federal brigade under Brigadier General Henry Baxter was sent racing to deploy on Oak Ridge on Cutler's right.

These men were part of the veteran division commanded by Brigadier General John C. Robinson, an old Army Regular and a tough customer—who looked the part. "In a much-bearded army," wrote a Federal officer, "he was the hairiest general I ever saw." Robinson placed Baxter's brigade behind a stone wall along a section of the Mummasburg Road that faced generally north.

With only about 1,400 men, Baxter's brigade could hardly be expected to do more than briefly blunt a major enemy drive from the north. But just then, as luck would have it, the leading elements of Howard's own XI Corps,

Firepower *Early in the fighting on July 1, Buford's Federal cavalry troops were able to hold off the larger force led by General Heth, thanks to superior weaponry. The Spencer repeating carbine, above, fired rounds much more quickly than a standard musket*

First Person

Elizabeth Masser Thorn
Gettysburg resident

Thorn's husband Peter served as the caretaker of Gettysburg's Evergreen Cemetery on Cemetery Hill, but she assumed his job when he enlisted in the Union Army. The mother of three was six months pregnant at the time of the battle, yet still helped bury some of the dead. She is shown in her later years in the photograph below.

The battle was on Wednesday, the 1st of July, and it was on the Friday before that I first saw the rebels. As the rebels came to Gettysburg, we were all scared and wished for them to go.

Six of them came up the Baltimore Pike. Before they came into the Cemetery they fired off their revolvers to scare the people. They chased the people out and the men ran and jumped over fences ... I was a piece away from the house ... When they rode into the Cemetery I was scared, as I was afraid they had fired after my mother. I fainted from fright, but finally reached the house ... They said we should not be afraid of them, they were not going to hurt us like the yankeys [sic] did their ladies.

Soon they went to different places where they destroyed the telegraph and the railroads. Evening came on and they had destroyed a good many of the cars, and burned the bridge and seven cars on it. This was the Rock Creek Bridge. We could see the cars drop down from Cemetery Hill. Next morning we heard that there was a small battle at York. Everywhere they destroyed all they could.

We were trying to feed them all we could. I had baked in the morning and had the bread in the oven. They were hungry and smelled the bread. I took a butcher knife and stood before the oven and cut this hot bread for them as fast as I could. When I had six loaves cut up I said I would have to keep one loaf for my family, but as they still begged for more I cut up every loaf for them.

Tillie Pierce
Gettysburg resident

Fifteen years old during the battle, Pierce wrote a memoir of her experiences decades later.

We were having our literary exercises on Friday afternoon, at our Seminary, when the cry reached our ears. Rushing to the door, and standing on the front portico, we beheld in the direction of the Theological Seminary a dark, dense mass, moving toward town. Our teacher, Mrs. Eyster, at once said, "Children, run home as quickly as you can."

It did not require repeating. I am satisfied some of the girls did not reach their homes before the Rebels were in the streets.

As for myself, I had scarcely reached the front door, when, on looking up the street, I saw some of the men on horseback. I scrambled in, slammed shut the door, and hastening to the sitting room, peeped out between the shutters.

What a horrible sight! There they were, human beings! Clad almost in rags, covered with dust, riding wildly, pell-mell down the hill toward our home! Shouting, yelling most unearthly cursing, brandishing their revolvers, and firing right and left. I was fully persuaded that the Rebels had actually come at last. What they would do with us was a fearful question to my young mind.

Soon the town was filled with infantry, and then the searching and ransacking began in earnest. They wanted horses, clothing, anything and almost everything they could conveniently carry away. Nor were they particular about asking. Whatever suited them they took. They did, however, make a formal demand of the town authorities, for a large supply of flour, meat, groceries, shoes, hats and (doubtless, not least in their estimations) 10 barrels of whisky; or, in lieu of this, $5,000.

But our merchants and bankers had too often heard of their coming, and had already shipped their wealth to places of safety. Thus it was, that a few days after, the citizens of York were compelled to make up our proportion of the Rebel requisition ...

At last we reached Mr. Weikert's and were gladly welcomed to their home. [The Weikert home, south of Gettysburg, served as a refuge for Pierce and others.]

It was not long after our arrival until Union artillery came hurrying by. It was indeed a thrilling sight. How the men impelled their horses! How the officers urged the men as they all flew past toward the sound of the battle! Now the road is getting all cut up; they take to the fields, and all is in anxious, eager hurry! Shouting, lashing the horses, cheering the men, they all rush madly on.

Suddenly we behold an explosion; it is that of a caisson. We see a man thrown high in the air and come down in a wheat field close by. He is picked up and carried into the house. As they pass by I see his eyes are blown out and his whole person seems to be one black mass. The first words I hear him say are: "Oh dear! I forgot to read my Bible today! What will my poor wife and children say?"

came panting and sweating into Gettysburg on the run.

With commendable foresight, Howard left a division under Brigadier General Adolph von Steinwehr, along with some artillery units, on the commanding heights of Cemetery Hill, about half a mile south of the Gettysburg town square. "Boys," Howard told the troops, "I want you to hold this position at all hazards." With this single command, Howard helped shape the flow of the battle over the course of the next two days. Then Howard ordered Major General Carl Schurz, who had temporarily succeeded him in command of the corps, to rush northward the divisions of Brigadier Generals Alexander Schimmelfennig and Francis C. Barlow, to meet the menace from that direction.

Unsure of where the Confederate infantry would attack, Schurz established a thin, mile-long, east-west line that failed by a full quarter of a mile to hook up with the right flank of I Corps. Scarcely had Schurz completed his deployment than out of the woods to his left appeared Confederates in battle line. They belonged to the 7,983-man division of Major General Robert E. Rodes, in Ewell's corps, and they clearly meant business.

Battle on Oak Ridge

In a rare bow to caution, early that morning Hill had notified Ewell, who was on the march from Carlisle, that Heth's division was on its way to Gettysburg. Ewell, in turn, had ordered the divisions of Rodes and Lieutenant General Jubal Early to head directly for Gettysburg, rather than their scheduled rendezvous with Lee near Cashtown. Later, Ewell received a message from Lee approving the change but warning that a general engagement was not to be brought on till the rest of the army came up.

Rodes and his troops approached Gettysburg from the northeast along the Heidlersburg Road, followed at a distance by Early's division. About two miles from the town, Rodes turned west, toward the Mummasburg Road and Oak Hill. There, stretching away to the south along Oak Ridge, Rodes saw the right flank of the Federal I Corps line—Cutler's brigade—and realized that it was open to assault from the north. As far as he could see, Rodes said later, the enemy "had no troops facing me at all."

Rodes, a lean 34-year-old with a tawny mustache and hard blue eyes, was an aggressive commander; despite Lee's warning against a general engagement, he decided to attack. To preoccupy the Federals while his infantry was deploying, he posted his artillery battalion on Oak Hill, where its flanking fire startled the exposed Federal

Abner Doubleday
Doubleday served capably when he was thrust into a Federal leadership role early on July 1, after Reynolds was slain. His units held off a far larger Confederate force for hours, but when Howard reported to Meade that all Doubleday's soldiers had fled the battlefield, Meade replaced Doubleday, launching a controversy that would last for decades

line—and drew the quick response of General Robinson.

By the time Rodes had deployed his five brigades, the situation had changed. The men of Baxter's brigade were scurrying into their blocking position astride Oak Ridge, and the men of Howard's XI Corps were hurrying out of Gettysburg onto the plain east of the ridge; Rodes' advantage was rapidly evaporating. Shortly after 2 p.m., without further reconnaissance, without even bothering to throw out a line of skirmishers, Rodes attacked.

The general's haste soon exacted a heavy penalty. On his left was a brigade of Georgians led by Brigadier General George Doles; the men were veterans, and the quiet 33-year-old Doles was a fine officer. Moreover he was directly in front of the inviting quarter-mile gap between the Federal XI Corps and Robinson, on the I Corps's right. But Doles' brigade was held out of the initial assault, in part to contain the XI Corps and in part to provide a link with Early's division, which was expected to arrive from the northeast momentarily.

To Doles' right was a brigade of Alabamians under Colonel Edward A. O'Neal, who had performed clumsily at Chancellorsville. Beyond O'Neal was the North Carolina brigade of Brigadier General Alfred Iverson Jr., whose advancement in the army was widely considered to be the result of family influence. In support of Iverson's right rear was a large brigade under Brigadier General Junius Daniel, a West Pointer who had just come to Lee's army from the North Carolina coast and who had an excellent reputation. Held in reserve was the small but formidable brigade of Brigadier General Stephen Dodson Ramseur, who at age 26 was already known as one of the Army of Northern Virginia's toughest fighters.

Rodes' dispositions placed the heaviest burden on O'Neal and Iverson, his two weakest commanders—and the whole affair was botched from the beginning. Iverson's brigade, assigned to attack abreast of O'Neal's, delayed to allow more time for the rebel batteries on Oak Hill to clear the way. O'Neal's brigade therefore went forward alone—using only three of its five regiments.

Attacking on a narrow front down the eastern slope of Oak Ridge, the brigade ran headlong into a storm of musket fire from behind the stone wall along the Mummasburg Road, where Baxter's brigade had only minutes before taken its position. Soon 696 of O'Neal's 1,688 men were casualties. As Rodes later described it, with considerable understatement, "The whole brigade was repulsed quickly and with loss." And Rodes was enraged to find that O'Neal had chosen to remain with a reserve

regiment rather than go into battle with his men. Iverson also had not accompanied his men when they began to move. Instead, he merely told his troops to "give 'em hell." With those words, as one of the embittered North Carolina soldiers later wrote, Iverson's part "in the heroic struggle of this brigade seems to have begun and ended."

Iverson's Brigade Destroyed

The collapse of O'Neal's attack left Iverson's left flank wide open, and so as the brigade moved down the western slope of Oak Ridge, it began drifting toward the left. In its path was another stone wall, which ran south from the Mummasburg Road. There, the Federals waited: soon after sending O'Neal's regiments reeling back, Baxter had changed front, and his men now crouched, hidden behind the wall Iverson's troops were approaching.

Baxter and his men waited until the nearest Confederates were less than 80 yds. away. Then they arose and delivered a volley that scythed down the Carolinians. More than 500 of the attackers fell in what a Confederate officer later described as a "line as straight as a dress parade." The Confederate formation, wrote Captain Isaac Hall of Baxter's 97th New York, "staggered, halted, and was swept back as by an irresistible current." Baxter's men now counterattacked, taking nearly 400 prisoners and destroying Iverson's brigade. The 23rd North Carolina alone lost 236 men, including all but one of its officers.

Watching the carnage from his position of relative safety, General Iverson became completely undone, hysterically reporting to Rodes that his entire regiment had changed its allegiance and gone over to the enemy. What Iverson had seen was a few of the survivors pitifully waving their handkerchiefs in surrender amid the ranks of the dead. Iverson had sent 1,384 men into a fight that lasted 15 minutes; no more than 400 were present when the brigade was reassembled. Iverson was so distraught

The decider *In this Bradley Schmehl painting,* Lee Deliberates Heth's Advance, *Lee arrives where the Cashtown Road crosses Herr Ridge, around 3:30 p.m., and meets Heth and his top officers. Although he had vowed to avoid a general engagement on this day, Lee changed his mind when he saw that the Confederates were poised to win a major victory, and he ordered further attacks*

that one of his staff officers, Captain Donald P. Halsey, had to assume command of what was left of the brigade.

Confederates Turn the Tide

As Iverson's few survivors were making their way to the rear, Daniel and Ramseur launched their brigades into the battle. Daniel took his 2,162 men to the right, southward down McPherson's Ridge, beyond the effective range of Robinson's and Cutler's infantry on his left. Daniel's aim was to get onto the Chambersburg Pike, then push down the road to strike Cutler's left flank. It was a good idea, but Daniel was entirely unaware of the railroad cut that lay in his way.

Awaiting Daniel on the other side of the cut was the 149th Pennsylvania, one of three regiments in Colonel Roy Stone's Bucktail Brigade, whose men wore deer tails

on their caps. The 149th, commanded by Lieutenant Colonel Walton Dwight, leveled a savage volley as Daniel's brigade approached. The Confederates fell back, and the Bucktails charged through the railroad cut.

Even as they closed on the Confederates, the Bucktails were enfiladed by Hill's guns to the west and forced to fall back to the cut. There, with smoke swirling about them, they waited until Daniel's advancing men were a mere 20 paces away, then let fly another murderous volley. Daniel's troops fell back only to come on again. The fight seesawed back and forth. Stone went down, severely wounded; so did his successor; so did Dwight. In all, the Bucktail Brigade lost two-thirds of its men before the day ended. But they held Daniel at the railroad cut in a lethal stalemate.

At the same time Ramseur's brigade was having its

own troubles against the stubborn troops of Robinson's division. Robinson had sent a brigade under Brigadier General Gabriel René Paul to join Baxter's men near the Mummasburg Road. Rodes, for his part, had neglected to alert Ramseur that Iverson had been ambushed there, and Ramseur's 1,027 men almost met the same fate. Warned at the last minute by two of Iverson's surviving officers, Ramseur adjusted his line of march to the east to strike the right flank of Paul's brigade. But nothing came easily to the Confederates on this afternoon—the Federals fought like Furies.

In the struggle, Paul suffered a head wound that left him blind and partly deaf. The officer who took over from him soon fell, and then others went down. Paul's brigade was led by five successive commanders. Baxter's brigade exhausted its ammunition and was forced to retire; when Paul's brigade in turn ran low, Robinson went around scrounging cartridges from the dead and wounded. Finally, Paul's brigade was forced to give ground foot by foot in the face of overwhelming pressure. The 16th Maine remained as a rear guard—at terrible cost, with 232 of its 298 men killed, wounded or missing. As the Confederates closed in, the men tore their regimental flag to shreds rather than let it fall into enemy hands.

On Herr Ridge, a gray-bearded general on a gray horse was watching the spectacle. Robert E. Lee had arrived on the battlefield.

Lee had been cheerful that morning when he set out toward Cashtown from Chambersburg, accompanied by Longstreet and his I Corps. But before long they heard the rumble of artillery to the east; Lee grew anxious and rode ahead. About three miles from Gettysburg, Lee passed through Pender's division of Hill's corps, deployed for battle. Farther on, at Herr Ridge, Lee found Heth still trying to re-form his shaken division after its earlier trial. To his front, the commanding general could see the brigades of Daniel and Ramseur fiercely engaged. Heth, eager to redeem himself, asked permission to attack. "No," replied Lee, "I am not prepared to bring on a general engagement today—Longstreet is not up."

But Lee's repeated assertions that he was not prepared for a large battle were overridden by the events unfolding around him. From his perch on Herr Ridge, the rebel general soon saw a cloud of dust beyond the right flank of the Federal XI Corps; Early and his division had arrived on the battlefield. Here was opportunity indeed. The long, thin, discontinuous Federal line was bent at a right angle, with XI Corps stretching from east to west

and I Corps from north to south. Early was now assailing the Federal right, and Rodes was hammering at the vertex of the angle. If Hill could renew the assault against the Federal left, the enemy would be caught as if in the jaws of a nutcracker. Lee saw that it must be done. He ordered Heth, supported by Pender's division, to attack.

A Hectic Union Retreat

East of Oak Hill, General Doles had bided his time while Rodes fed the division's other brigades piecemeal into the battle. Expecting Early at any moment, Doles extended his line to meet him, sending skirmishers to seize a hillock near the Adams County Alms House, just to the west of the Heidlersburg Road. On the far right of the Federal XI Corps, Barlow thought that same small prominence on the otherwise featureless plain looked like a good place to anchor his right flank. Quickly, Barlow's division of 2,459 men shouldered Doles' skirmishers off the hillock—which would thereafter be known as Barlow's Knoll.

In attacking, however, Barlow moved well ahead of the adjacent Federal division under Schimmelfennig. In order to correct the XI Corps alignment, General Schurz ordered Schimmelfennig forward. Inevitably, the movement triggered fighting, which swiftly grew in intensity. Doles' single brigade of 1,323 men was soon engaged with two Federal divisions that totaled 5,530 troops, and his effort seemed doomed—until Early announced his arrival with a devastating explosion of cannon fire.

On Early's right, Brigadier General John B. Gordon's brigade struck Barlow's line from the front. The dashing Gordon led his men, waving his hat and standing in his stirrups on a coal-black stallion whose warlike appearance impressed a Confederate artillerist, even in the midst of chaos: "I never saw a horse's neck so arched, his eyes so fierce, his nostrils so dilated." Meanwhile brigades commanded by Brigadier General Harry T. Hays and Colonel Isaac E. Avery attacked down both sides of the Heidlersburg road, turning Barlow's right flank.

Barlow's position was utterly untenable. Moreover, his troops proved unreliable. "The enemy's skirmishers had hardly attacked us before my men began to run," Barlow later wrote. And back toward Gettysburg they went.

Riding after the retreating Federals, Gordon came upon an enemy officer lying badly wounded with a Minié ball in his chest. Gordon dismounted, knelt to give him water and asked his name. "Francis C. Barlow," said the man, requesting that Gordon send word to Mrs. Barlow that

I remember the still trees in the heat, and the bullets whistling over us, and the stone wall bristling with muskets, and the line of our men, sweating and grimy, firing and loading and firing again, and here a man suddenly lying still, and there another rising all bloody and cursing and starting for the surgeon.

—*Captain Abner Small, 16th Maine Infantry*

Rally to the colors

Don Troiani's painting The Boy Colonel *captures the moment when Henry Burgwyn of the 26th North Carolina regiment seized the unit's battle flag to lead the charge up McPherson's Ridge. He died moments later.*

The photo of Burgwyn on this page was taken during his cadet days at the Virginia Military Institute

her husband's dying thoughts had been of her. Gordon scribbled the note and sent it into Gettysburg under a white flag. Then, after having Barlow carried to the shade of a tree, Gordon went back to the fighting.

Barlow survived—and he and Gordon became fast friends after the war—but the collapse of his division sent shock waves along the entire Federal line; one by one the other units of XI Corps gave way to the Confederates and streamed toward Gettysburg. Watching, one of Early's officers sensed a triumph beyond reckoning: "It looked indeed as if the end of the war had come." Yet over on the Federal left, against all expectation, the men of Doubleday's I Corps still clung to McPherson's Ridge.

Rallying to the Flag

Moments after Lee had granted permission for the attack, Heth's infantry moved down the long incline of Herr Ridge toward General Doubleday's lines. On the left, near the turnpike, was a Confederate brigade led by Colonel John M. Brockenbrough; in the center, facing the difficult task of clearing the Iron Brigade out of McPherson's Woods, were the men of Brigadier General J. Johnston Pettigrew's brigade; and on the right was Archer's badly bruised brigade, now commanded by Colonel Birkett D. Fry. The remnants of Davis' battered brigade remained in the rear.

Although Heth was known for his bad luck, on this afternoon he was fortunate indeed. His clerk had adapted a civilian hat to Heth's use by rolling a dozen or so sheets of paper into the sweatband to achieve a proper fit. Just after crossing Willoughby Run, Heth was struck in the head by a Minié ball that fractured his skull and knocked him unconcious briefly; but for the rolled-paper padding, he might well have been killed.

With Pettigrew assuming command, the gray line pressed on toward McPherson's Ridge under heavy artillery and musket fire. From the woods, Colonel Henry A. Morrow of the Iron Brigade's 24th Michigan saw the men of the 26th North Carolina coming toward him, "yelling like demons."

"The fighting was terrible," reported Confederate Major J.T. Jones. "The two lines were pouring volleys into each other at a distance not greater than 20 paces." The North Carolina color-bearers were particularly hard hit.

The brigade's assistant inspector general, Captain W.W. McCreery, seized the flag from a dying soldier and ran forward; he was shot through the heart and died instantly. Lieutenant George Wilcox of Company H picked up the bloody banner; he was killed seconds later.

Next, 21-year-old Henry King Burgwyn Jr., the youngest colonel in the Confederate armies, raised the bullet-riddled flag. Knowing his commander risked certain death, Private Frank Honeycutt broke from the ranks and asked Burgwyn for the flag. At that moment both men went down, fatally wounded. Seeing them fall, the second-in-command of the 26th, Lieutenant Colonel John R. Lane, sprinted through the hail of fire and picked up the flag. When one of his Lieutenants tried to stop him, Lane said, "It is my time to take them now." Shouting "Twenty-sixth, follow me!" he led the cheering Carolinians into the ranks of the Iron Brigade, which gave way before them. At the moment of victory, Lane too went down, severely wounded in the head. He was the 14th color-bearer in the regiment to fall that day.

Flanked on the left, the I Corps line fell back, fighting savagely before retiring to Seminary Ridge. Behind them in McPherson's Woods the bodies of men in blue and in gray lay intermingled. The toll for both sides was staggering. During its day-long defense of McPherson's Ridge, the 1,829-man Iron Brigade had suffered 1,153 casualties; Heth's 7,500-man division had lost nearly 1,500. At the center of the cauldron, Morrow's 24th Michigan had suffered 397 casualties, or just over 80% of its 496 men. In the 26th North Carolina, only 212 of 800 men survived unwounded—a casualty rate of nearly 75%—and every one of the 90 officers and men of its Company F had fallen.

Back on Seminary Ridge, the Federals of I Corps reformed behind some crude breastworks that had been thrown up earlier. But before the exhausted men could catch their breath, Pender's division—a crack outfit led by one of the Confederacy's most promising young generals—was upon them.

Battery B of the 4th U.S. Artillery, under the command of Lieutenant James Stewart, managed to check the assault for a few minutes with double charges of canister. But then the Confederates came on again, charging over the bleeding bodies of their comrades. In a trickle

and then in a flood, I Corps broke again and fled from Seminary Ridge. Many of the soldiers mingled with the XI Corps throng in the streets of Gettysburg; others slanted to the southeast and the crest of Cemetery Hill, where Von Steinwehr had been erecting defenses since his arrival.

Hancock Rallies the Federals

At Cemetery Hill, the fleeing Federals learned that yet another general had assumed command of the battle-field—and unlike Doubleday or Howard, this one was an inspiration to all. At 39, Winfield Scott Hancock was an officer of magnetic presence. Meade shared the high regard in which Hancock was held; on receiving the news of Reynolds' death, the Federal commanding general had ordered Hancock to hurry north from Taneytown and take command of the field.

Arriving around 4:30 p.m., Hancock saw the Federal troops stampeding south out of Gettysburg toward Cemetery Hill. "Wreck, disaster, disorder," one of his subordinates wrote later, "the panic that precedes disorganization, defeat and retreat were everywhere." At the gate of the Evergreen Cemetery, Hancock met Howard, who was trying furiously to stop the rout. Howard was senior to Hancock, and their confrontation was awkward. Hancock explained that Meade had sent him to take charge, but Howard wouldn't yield. "You cannot give orders here," he said. "I am in command and I rank you."

Somehow, the two worked out a way of sharing command. Surveying the terrain, Hancock said carefully, "I think this is the strongest position by nature on which to fight a battle that I ever saw, and if it meets with your approbation I will select this as the battlefield." Howard agreed, and Hancock declared, "Very well, sir. I select this as the battlefield."

The field was in fact a topographic complex of which Cemetery Hill, rising about 80 ft. above the town, was only a part. Just to the east stood Culp's Hill, about 100 ft. higher, strewn with boulders and thick with woods. Stretching southward from Cemetery Hill for about two miles was the low Cemetery Ridge, dipping in places almost to ground level. At the southern end of Cemetery Ridge loomed two more hills—Little Round Top and, beyond it, Big Round Top.

Hancock was right: it was indeed a strong position. But it was also a long one, extending for nearly three miles; reinforcements would be needed to hold it. Major General Daniel E. Sickles' III Corps and Major General Henry W.

Slocum's XII Corps were in fact on the way; whether they would arrive on time was another question.

Pending their arrival, Hancock set up a defensive line on Cemetery Hill facing to the north and west. Then he ordered Doubleday to send part of I Corps over to Culp's Hill. Doubleday protested that his men had been fighting all day and were completely done in. "Sir!" roared Hancock, rising in his stirrups, "I am in command on this field. Send every man you have!" Doubleday complied, with the battered Iron Brigade. Having done all he could until reinforcements arrived, Hancock sat down on a stone fence and gazed through his field glasses at Seminary Ridge—where General Lee was beset by problems.

A Confederate Opportunity Lost

Following Pender's attacking division, Lee had stopped on Seminary Ridge to watch the Federal retreat to Cemetery Hill. Lee recognized immediately the value of possessing that high ground and urged Hill to renew his attack. For all his combativeness, Hill declined; his troops were bloodied, tired and almost out of ammunition. That left the matter up to Ewell. Without taking time for written orders, Lee sent an aide, Major Walter H. Taylor, to tell Ewell that, with the Federals in headlong flight, it "was only necessary to press those people in order to secure possession of the heights." It was the commanding general's wish that Ewell should do so "if practicable."

While Lee was waiting for his orders to bring results, General Longstreet arrived, well in advance of his troops. Like Lee, he surveyed the scene—but he perceived a vastly different opportunity. This was the perfect chance, he asserted, to initiate the sort of tactical defensive strategy that he thought Lee had agreed upon. The army must swing around the Federal left, Longstreet said, and deploy south of them, thus interposing itself between the Army of the Potomac and Washington. The Confederates could then take up a strong defensive position and confidently await the attack that must surely result from the threat posed to the Federal capital. "No," Lee said, gesturing toward Cemetery Hill, "the enemy is there, and I am going to attack him there." Longstreet argued, "If he is there, it is because he is anxious that we should attack him—a good reason, in my judgment, for not doing so." But Lee replied, "I am going to whip them, or they are going to whip me." Lee had invaded Union territory in search of a decisive battle that would lead to a negotiated peace, and he was determined to take on the Federals in a winner-take-all clash.

Carl Schurz *One of the "Hessians" of the Union Army, the German-born Schurz came to the U.S. after the failed revolution of 1848. Settling in Wisconsin, he helped deliver German-American votes for Lincoln in 1860, and was rewarded with his high rank. He proved a better politician than a general, eventually serving in the U.S. Senate and as Secretary of the Interior*

★ A County Seat and Its Elderly Constable Enter the History Books

Like Concord, Mass., Waterloo, Verdun and Bastogne, Gettysburg is an inconspicuous, sleepy town that was plucked from obscurity and rendered immortal by the great forces of history. Nestled in the rolling hills of the eastern Appalachian Mountains, whose wooded heights are punctuated by rocky outcroppings like Devil's Den, the seat of Adams County numbered some 2,400 citizens in the summer of 1863, although almost all its young men were serving in the Union Army.

The reason Gettysburg became the final battleground of Lee's 1863 invasion of Union territory could be seen from the heights made famous over the three days of battle: from Seminary Ridge, Cemetery Hill and other elevated land around Gettysburg, observers could see 10 different roads converging on the town from every direction, like spokes on a wheel. Over these roads, during the last days of June and first three days of July, some 160,000 soldiers from both sides marched and rode into the cauldron of the war's largest single combat.

A few of the local townspeople were caught up in the battle on July 1, when Union troops controlled Gettysburg early on but were driven through its streets in retreat later that afternoon, giving way to Confederate occupiers. Remarkably, given the ferocity of the fighting, only one civilian, Ginnie Wade, 20, was killed during the battle. She died on the morning of July 1 after being struck by a Minié ball, apparently fired from a Confederate weapon, while baking bread at her sister's house on Baltimore Street.

One local resident found fame in the battle. John L. Burns, at right above, a veteran of the War of 1812, was 69 years old in 1863. He had volunteered to serve in the Union Army when the war broke out, but he had been rejected because of his age and was sent to Gettysburg to serve as the town's constable. On July 1, he picked up his ancient musket and powder horn, donned a laughably antique "uniform," and headed for the front lines,

where he fought alongside the young soldiers of the 7th Wisconsin unit of the Iron Brigade in McPherson's Woods. Burns was hit several times by enemy fire and was left behind when Union troops retreated and advancing Confederate troops rushed by him. Had he been taken prisoner, Burns could have been legally executed for serving as a combatant out of uniform; such irregulars, or bushwhackers, were subject to summary execution on the battlefield if captured.

Burns crawled to a nearby home filled with wounded Confederates, where he was treated by a sympathetic Confederate physician. He was later taken back to his home. He survived and posed with his antique musket and crutches for photographer Timothy H. O'Sullivan shortly after the battle. Hailed as a hero by the Union press, he became a celebrity in the North. When President Lincoln visited Gettysburg for the dedication of the national cemetery in November 1863, he asked to meet with Burns.

The old-timer's celebrity was further enhanced by popular author Bret Harte, who wrote a poem that portrayed the young Union soldiers' amused reactions to Burns' outdated get-up turning into admiration: "Until, as they gazed, there crept an awe/ Through the ranks in whispers, and some men saw,/ In the antique vestments and long white hair,/ The Past of the Nation in battle there." John Burns, veteran of both the War of 1812 and the Civil War, died in 1872.

Lay of the land *These two photos were taken after the battle atop Seminary Ridge, held by the Confederates at the end of July 1, looking south to Gettysburg. The unfinished railroad cut is on the left; at right is the Chambersburg Pike. Rising beyond the town are Culp's Hill and Cemetery Ridge, high ground where Union troops built a stronghold after retreating through the town*

It was about 5:30 p.m. as Lee nervously awaited Ewell's assault, and at least three hours of fighting time remained before darkness. A half hour passed, then another and yet another. At last, his patience gone, Lee rode off toward Ewell's headquarters on the Carlisle Road north of Gettysburg. Ewell had been gripped that day by a curious mental inertia. Arriving at the front during Rodes' attack, he had been little more than a spectator. Then, as the Federals retreated, both Early and Gordon had urged him to push his corps past Gettysburg and onto the hills. Ewell declined, telling Gordon, "General Lee told me to come to Gettysburg and gave me no orders to go farther." Later, fierce old Brigadier General Isaac Trimble, who was serving temporarily as an aide to Ewell, begged per-

mission to lead a force against Culp's Hill. When Ewell brushed him aside, Trimble stomped away in a rage.

Late in the afternoon, Taylor arrived with General Lee's oral order to seize the high ground south of Gettysburg "if practicable"—a discretionary phrase that only further puzzled Ewell. This was the first engagement in which Ewell had served directly under Lee; before, he had always answered to Stonewall Jackson, whose orders always left him with no leeway at all.

At any rate, Ewell failed to act. By the time Lee arrived at Ewell's headquarters, Federal reinforcements—the corps of Slocum and Sickles—were streaming onto Cemetery Ridge. The opportunity had passed.

The Federal commander was as worried as Lee, even

though General Meade was only hearing second-hand reports of the fast-moving events taking place north of his headquarters in Taneytown. As the entanglement around Gettysburg worsened, Meade thought about ordering the divisions around Gettysburg to fall back to the defensive line his engineers had laid out along Pipe Creek. But Hancock arrived at Meade's headquarters at about 9 p.m. and assured him that Gettysburg was the place to fight the next day's battle. Shortly after 10 p.m., the untried commander of the Army of the Potomac rode north, along roads congested by troops and wagons.

A few hours after midnight, Meade reached the little graveyard on Cemetery Hill and summoned ranking officers to the gatekeeper's living quarters. Turning to a trusted subordinate, General Howard, he asked, "Well, Howard, what do you think? Is this the place to fight the battle?" Howard responded: "I am confident we can hold this position." The other officers agreed. "I am glad to hear you say so, gentlemen," said Meade. "I have already ordered the other corps to concentrate here—and it is too late to change." All night long, the roads into Gettysburg were busy, as the remaining divisions of both sides converged on the scene of the battle.

However improvised, the conflict on July 1 was one of the 20 bloodiest days of the war, engaging some 18,000 Federals and 30,000 Confederates and resulting in 9,000 casualties on the Union side and 7,000 on the Confederate side. Even so, there was worse to come. ■

The Commanders

A.P. HILL

Ambrose Powell Hill found himself in a new position of power at Gettysburg. Prior to the Southern invasion of the North, Lee had reorganized the Army of Northern Virginia after the death of Stonewall Jackson at Chancellorsville, and Lieutenant General Hill was named to lead the III Corps, joining I Corps commander James Longstreet and II Corps commander Richard S. Ewell as Lee's top lieutenants.

Hill, a Virginian who was 37 in 1863, graduated from West Point and served in the Mexican War. He and Longstreet became bitter enemies following a dustup during the Peninsula Campaign of 1862. Impatient and impulsive, Hill often seemed to act before he thought. At Antietam, Hill and his quick-stepping Light Division arrived just in time to prevent a Union rout of the rebels, but he was criticized for poor leadership at Fredericksburg. He was shot and killed by a Union soldier only a few days before Lee surrendered at Appomattox.

JUBAL EARLY

In the decades before the war, Early had been a progressive Whig, and he strongly opposed secession. But the Virginia-born lawyer chose region over nation when war came—and he rose quickly through the ranks after he stood tall at the First Battle of Bull Run. The West Point graduate, 47 in 1863, served with honor under Stonewall Jackson at Malvern Hill, Second Bull Run, Fredericksburg and Chancellorsville, though he was known for losing his sense of direction when under fire.

Intense and driven, Early had a short fuse; Robert E. Lee, who admired his spirit, called him a "Bad Old Man." Many of his subordinate officers found him a nitpicking martinet.

Early and his soldiers helped drive Federal troops from Winchester, Va., at the beginning of the Gettysburg Campaign, then routed Union troops under Brigadier General Francis Barlow on July 1. On July 2 and 3 he directed his troops as they assaulted the Union right flank at Cemetery Hill and Culp's Hill. After the war, Early became one of the most prominent voices in the Lost Cause movement, as he publicly attacked General James Longstreet and other old colleagues.

HENRY HETH

An 1847 graduate of West Point, Heth, 37 in 1863, won the esteem of Robert E. Lee when he served briefly as his quartermaster as the war began. After serving in Kentucky, Heth joined the Army of Northern Virginia at Lee's request in February 1863, where he served under A.P. Hill, and he assumed Hill's command briefly when the senior officer was wounded at Chancellorsville. Heth touched off the Battle of Gettysburg when he led his men from Cashtown into Gettysburg on the morning of July 1. In his memoirs he claimed he was looking for shoes in the crossroads town, but while it makes for a wonderful story, an increasing number of modern historians argue that Heth was looking for Yankees, not footwear, on that morning.

Whatever the truth, Heth's men definitely launched the fighting at Gettysburg on July 1, where they were routed by the Iron Brigade and other Union troops. But Heth's men regrouped to help drive the Federals out of Gettysburg late in the afternoon, when Heth received a head wound. After Gettysburg, Hill fought with Lee through the last campaigns of the war and in the Siege of Petersburg. He died in 1899.

RICHARD S. EWELL

The 1840 graduate of West Point thrived when he served as one of Stonewall Jackson's chief subordinates, although Ewell was very profane and Jackson very pious. Ewell was wounded in the Battle of Groveton in August 1862 and lost part of one leg. On May 26, 1863, only weeks after Jackson was killed at Chancellorsville, Ewell, at 46, married the widow who nursed him back to health. He was soon given command of most of Jackson's former troops (A.P. Hill also received some of those divisions), and Gettysburg was his first major battle as a corps commander.

Arriving at Gettysburg late in the afternoon of July 1 after a long, difficult march, Ewell was faced with the choice of whether or not to contest the Federals for control of Cemetery Ridge. Lee had written him to do so only "if practicable." Ewell was less fond of spur-of-the-moment gambits than was Jackson, and he decided not to risk mounting an attack with weary troops so late in the day. His subordinate, Early, agreed with his decision—but generations of Monday-morning quarterbacks have made Ewell a Confederate scapegoat at Gettysburg.

FRANCIS C. BARLOW

The clean-shaven young Harvard graduate, 29 in 1863, was one of the few men to join the Union Army as an enlisted man and leave it a general. He led his troops at some of the most intense scenes of combat in the war, commanding a bayonet charge in the Seven Days Battles in Virginia and holding Bloody Lane for the Union at Antietam, where he was seriously wounded. He survived Stonewall Jackson's surprise flank attack at Chancellorsville and the fighting at the Mule Shoe at Spotsylvania.

At Gettysburg, Barlow was assigned to defend Cemetery Hill on July 1, but he advanced too far in front of the rest of the army and had to defend a salient along Blocher's Knoll, since known as Barlow's Knoll. Georgia troops under John B. Gordon overran the knoll, sending the Union troops into full retreat, and Barlow was shot in the side and left for dead; it was Gordon who found him and took him to a rebel field hospital.

Barlow survived and lived to fight again in the Overland Campaign. After the war, he enjoyed a brilliant career as a lawyer, becoming a founder of the American Bar Association.

SOLOMON MEREDITH

Like Abraham Lincoln, Solomon Meredith was born south of the Mason-Dixon line, in North Carolina, but moved to Indiana at an early age—and, like Lincoln, he worked in a backwoods town's general store in his youth. He served as a county sheriff, a U.S. marshal and in the Indiana legislature, then formed a company of volunteers when the war broke out. At 6 ft. 7 in., "Long Sol" was one of the few Union generals who could look down on his Commander in Chief. He became a colonel when his company joined the Iron Brigade, and was injured on Aug. 28, 1862, in the first day of combat in the Second Battle of Bull Run (Manassas).

Meredith, 53 in 1863, declared himself unfit for service before the Battle of Antietam in September 1862, due to his injuries, and his replacement was killed. Though some generals faulted him, he was promoted to brigadier general. At Gettysburg, Meredith was severely wounded in the afternoon rout of the Federals; he was hit by shrapnel and his horse fell on him. He survived but was no longer fit for action, and he spent the rest of the war behind a desk.

WINFIELD SCOTT HANCOCK

Hancock, born in 1824, had martial greatness thrust upon him: he was named in honor of one of the greatest soldiers in American history, Winfield Scott. Yet he would give Scott a run for his money as a leader of troops. In his memoirs, Ulysses S. Grant described Hancock as "a man of very conspicuous personal appearance ... His genial disposition made him friends, and his personal courage and his presence with his command in the thickest of the fight won for him the confidence of troops serving under him."

Hancock rose in the U.S. Army by following the same path as so many of his fellow West Point graduates: service in Indian Wars ranging from Texas to Florida and duty in the Mexican War. When the Civil War came, he was serving under General Albert Sidney Johnston in Southern California. Hancock chose to join the Union; Johnston became one of the finest Confederate generals before his untimely death at the Battle of Shiloh.

In the Civil War, Hancock distinguished himself at the Battle of Williamsburg, where General George B. McClellan declared, "Hancock was superb today." Without irony, colleagues ever after called him "Hancock the Superb." He made a dramatic appearance on the battlefield at Antietam, holding the Union position at Bloody Lane just as it was about to be overrun. He was the Union's indispensable man at Gettysburg, where he was fighting on home turf (he was born near Philadelphia).

After taking over as a corps commander in place of the slain General John F. Reynolds, Hancock proved a fine leader. Commanding four corps atop Cemetery Ridge on July 2, he directed the flow of Union divisions to the points along the sprawling front where replacements were most needed, often plugging gaps in the Federal lines just as Confederate troops were threatening to break through. He was badly wounded holding off the charging rebels on July 3 and never fully recovered his health, though he fought with distinction in the bloody battles of the Overland Campaign in 1864.

In 1880, the magnetic Hancock ran as the Democratic candidate for President but was defeated by Republican James A. Garfield. Hancock appears as a leading character in two popular Civil War novels, Michael Shaara's *The Killer Angels* and Jeff Shaara's *Gods and Generals*.

George G. Meade

MAJOR GENERAL, ARMY OF THE POTOMAC

★

H E WAS THE COMMANDING GENERAL in the Union victory at Gettysburg, yet George G. Meade is one of the least remembered of the larger-than-life figures who took part in the battle. That's fair, in a sense: summoned to command the Army of the Potomac only four days before the battle began, he rose to the occasion and led the Federal troops to victory on July 3. It was the apex of his military career, but his decline began in the immediate aftermath of the battle, when he allowed Lee's beaten troops to retreat to Virginia, rather than actively engaging them during their escape.

In the fall of 1863, months after Gettysburg, Meade mounted a pair of campaigns in Virginia, where he hoped to deal Lee a shattering blow, but both efforts ended in failure and a Union withdrawal. In March 1864 President Lincoln finally brought in the hero of the Western theater, General Ulysses S. Grant, to command all the Union armies, and Meade was outranked. He finished out the war as a top aide to Grant, who came to respect him but continued to rely on his trusted subordinates from the West as his principal lieutenants.

The problem: even among the often colorless Union commanders, Meade lacked charisma. War chronicler Shelby Foote observed, "He seemed utterly incapable of provoking the sort of personal enthusiasm [George B.] McClellan and [Joseph] Hooker could arouse ... [he] gave an impression of professorial dryness and lack of juice. What he lacked in fact was glamour." Nicknames can be revealing: Southern troops hailed General Thom-

as Jackson as "Stonewall" or "Old Blue Light," because his eyes shone a deep indigo when in battle. Jeb Stuart was "Beauty." Homely Richard Ewell was fondly called "Old Baldy," while on the Union side, Winfield Scott Hancock was "Hancock the Superb" and Hooker was "Fighting Joe." But soldiers took a gander at the dour Meade and christened him, alas, "Old Snapping Turtle."

Meade was among the older commanders to fight in the war. He was born in 1815 in Cádiz, Spain, where his father, a well-to-do Philadelphia merchant, was a naval agent for the U.S. government; he lost his fortune during the Napoleonic Wars and died when Meade was only 12. Meade received an appointment to West Point but did not intend a career in the military; at the time, the curriculum at the military academy was heavily oriented to engineering, and Meade resigned his commission within a year of his graduation to become a full-time engineer. But when work became scarce, he returned to the U.S. Army as a topographical engineer, then took part in the Mexican War, where he performed well and was promoted to first lieutenant.

Meade spent the late 1840s and much of the 1850s as a U.S. Army engineer specializing in the design and construction of lighthouses on the East Coast, many of which can still be seen. When the war broke out, he was promoted to brigadier general in August 1861 and given command of the 2nd Brigade of Pennsylvania Reserves; his first assignment was to help create the fortifications defending Washington. In the campaigns that followed, he served well as leader of first a brigade, then a division,

I tried, as far as possible, to leave General Meade in independent command of the Army of the Potomac. My instructions for that army were all through him, and were general in their nature, leaving all the details and the execution to him. The campaigns that followed proved him to be the right man in the right place.

—Ulysses S. Grant,
Personal Memoirs

then a corps. He was badly wounded during the Peninsula Campaign at the Battle of Glendale, but he recovered and became known as a resolute and reliable battlefield tactician. His men held a key point in the Federals' rout at the Second Battle of Bull Run (Manassas), fought bravely at the Battle of South Mountain in September 1862, and did so again at Antietam. He won increased attention for the strong showing of his troops at Fredericksburg, where his division was the only unit to break through Jackson's line.

Meade was thus rising quickly in the estimation of Lincoln and his overall war chief, General Henry Halleck, back in Washington. But it still came as a surprise when a staff officer awakened Meade at 3 in the morning of June 28, saying, "I'm afraid I've come to make trouble for you." Meade later claimed that he suspected he was going to be relieved of his command—he and General Hooker had quarreled sharply at Chancellorsville, where Meade resented being held in reserve during the battle and questioned both Hooker's tactics and bravery.

Meade knew that Lincoln had been searching for an officer to replace Hooker, and he may have known that Lincoln had offered the command to the much admired John F. Reynolds, only to be refused. Meade likely sus-

pected that Lincoln was yearning to bring Grant east to fight Lee, but Halleck had opposed the move while Grant was so close to capturing Vicksburg.

It's bracing to imagine the weight of "the trouble" Meade now confronted: Lee, Jeb Stuart and the Army of Northern Virginia were loose on Union soil, hoping to invade Washington—and Meade's army of some 88,000 men was so widely scattered across the countryside that he didn't know the whereabouts of many of his divisions. This was not the time for glamour; brisk, active leadership was called for. Meade arrived in Gettysburg just after midnight on July 1, and at first, in counsel with his top aides, he seemed timid, reluctant to stand and fight. But Hancock and others convinced him that the Union position was strong, and in the next two days, the Federals won their greatest victory in the war to date.

Meade's descent from glory was rapid: his dithering allowed Lee to make a clean getaway after the battle. When Meade wrote Halleck to say he was calling a council of war to decide whether or not to attack Lee, Halleck responded, "Act upon your own judgment and make your generals execute your orders. Call no council of war. It is proverbial that councils of war never fight." The attack never came. After all, a turtle likes his shell. ∎

The Great Illuminator
Meade the engineer left his mark on America in the form of lighthouses that still stand, like the Cape May Light, above. Other Meade structures include the Barnegat and Absecon lights in New Jersey and the Jupiter Inlet and Sombrero Key lights in Florida.

At top, Meade strikes a pose in camp in June 1864

Wanted: A Man to Match Robert E. Lee

By David Von Drehle

ABRAHAM LINCOLN WAS, ON BALANCE, an astute judge of character, but now and then he made a mistake. Unfortunately, during the months that led to Gettysburg, those mistakes involved the commanders of the Army of the Potomac. Everyone remarked on what a splendid army it was, well drilled and copiously supplied, yet no one could lead it to a decisive victory. Now it was summer 1863, and Lee's rebels were once again marching northward through the picturesque valleys of western Maryland toward Pennsylvania. Lincoln could not afford another mistake.

Ambrose Burnside had been a doozy. What was it about the Rhode Island inventor with the splendidly feline whiskers? Perhaps it was his winning, and entirely justified, modesty that appealed to Lincoln during the summer and fall of 1862, when the President was besieged by regiments of self-promoters. Burnside had, in the early days of the Civil War, a neat little victory to his name—an innovative amphibious assault on Confederate posts along the North Carolina coast—and few Union generals could claim more than that. He took on a high gloss in Lincoln's eyes; the Commander in Chief pleaded with Burnside to accept command of the Army of the Potomac in place of the maddening, preening George B. McClellan. In November 1862, Lincoln finally turned his request into an order, and Burnside reluctantly embarked on three disastrous months in which he conceived the suicidal plan for the Battle of Fredericksburg, ordered the humiliating and feckless Mud March and provoked a near mutiny among his division commanders.

Even then, Lincoln merely reassigned Burnside to a lesser command in Ohio, where the general's ill-considered crackdown on antiwar protests stirred up a tempest of criticism, leaving Lincoln to ride out the storm. Determined not to repeat his mistake, Lincoln picked his next general with his clear gray eyes wide open. Joseph Hooker was a schemer, and Lincoln knew it. Hooker had a well-founded reputation for backstabbing and loose morals, but as veterans of the carnage at Antietam could

Von Drehle is an editor at large at TIME *magazine. His latest work is* Rise to Greatness: Abraham Lincoln and America's Most Perilous Year, *published in 2012*

Confab *Lincoln visited General McClellan at Antietam days after the battle. A month later, the President removed him from command*

Shuffling Commanders in the War's Eastern Theater

HENRY HALLECK

Halleck, 48 in 1863, became Lincoln's top military adviser in July 1862. He helped Lincoln select the commanders of all the Union armies, was known to play favorites—and was no friend to Grant.

GEORGE B. MCCLELLAN

His men enthusiastically supported the young (37 in 1863) general, but "Little Mac" looked on Lincoln with ill-concealed contempt and proved to be more interested in drilling for battle than in doing battle.

JOHN POPE

Lincoln brought Pope from the West to lead the new Army of Virginia in the East. But Pope, 41 in 1863, first insulted his troops, then was whipped at the Second Battle of Bull Run (Manassas) in 1862.

attest, the man did not dodge a fight. "Fighting Joe" had his foot just about shot off in the opening hours of that battle, and for months afterward he told everyone who would listen that Lee was able to escape from Maryland only because Joe Hooker couldn't chase him. It was this show of aggressive spirit that tipped the balance and earned him the top job, but before Hooker got started, Lincoln wanted the general to know that his President had taken his measure.

So he had handed Hooker a brutally candid letter to go with his new command. "I think it is best for you to know that there are some things in regard to which, I am not quite satisfied with you," Lincoln wrote bluntly. He liked the general's bravery, his skill, his self-confidence, even his ambition. But Hooker's insubordination to Burnside had undermined the morale of the entire army, Lincoln scolded. What's more: "I have heard, in such way as to believe it, of your recently saying that both the Army and the Government needed a Dictator." Scoffing, Lincoln gave Hooker a dose of his own considerable self-confidence. "Only those generals who gain successes, can set up dictators," he warned. "What I now ask of you is military success, and I will risk the dictatorship."

But Lincoln's eyes were trained on the wrong dangers. Hooker devised a lovely plan for trapping Lee and seizing Richmond, and struck a bold tone when he declared,

AMBROSE BURNSIDE

After using troops as cannon fodder at Fredericksburg in December 1862 and then leading them into the ill-conceived Mud March early in 1863, Burnside, 39 in 1863, had to be removed.

JOSEPH HOOKER

The fight seemed to go out of "Fighting Joe," 49 in 1863, when he came to face to face with Lee and Jackson at Chancellorsville. Outgeneraled and outsmarted, he was soon out of command.

GEORGE MEADE

Meade, 48 in 1863, had greatness thrust upon him when he was handed the reins of the Army of the Potomac, even as the biggest battle of the war was starting to take shape in eastern Pennsylvania.

"May God have mercy on General Lee, for I will have none." When the outnumbered rebels launched perhaps the most audacious attack of the war, however, the brave and brash Hooker froze like a charmed snake. Apprised of the fact that Lee's army was scattered through the woods and byways south of the Rappahannock River around Chancellorsville, he lacked the nerve to commit his troops to a decisive battle. Hooker could not even claim credit for the death of Thomas ("Stonewall") Jackson, the Confederate magician who was mortally wounded at dusk on May 2. Jackson was hit by friendly fire.

Such low moments had become all too familiar for Lincoln, but the bright side of failure was that he had mastered the art of staying cool while people around him panicked. When Lee, after regrouping, pointed his troops northward through the green springtime of early June, Hooker rashly proposed a counterthrust to the south. Lincoln quashed the idea. "I would not take any risk of being entangled upon the [Rappahannock] river, like an ox jumped half over a fence," he counseled. Lee could hit the Union army on both sides of the stream, and Hooker's ox was "liable to be torn by dogs, front and rear, without a fair chance to gore one way or kick the other."

Instead, Lincoln advised Hooker to follow Lee toward Maryland, or Pennsylvania, or wherever he was headed. Confederate incursions into the North were occasions

The path to victory, Lincoln had come to understand, lay in breaking up the rebellion and snuffing out its armies. Grant was on the verge of cutting the rebel lifeline to the fertile lands of the West and forcing the surrender of an entire Confederate army for the second time in his short career. Why couldn't the President find such a man for the Eastern Theater?

of fear and trembling for most Americans, but for Lincoln, they were bracing opportunities. Lee was sticking his neck out, just as he had done the previous summer, and this meant that Hooker had a chance to do what McClellan had failed to do in September 1862: cut him off. By mid-June, Lee's Army of Northern Virginia was stretched out from the Rappahannock almost to the Potomac. "The animal must be very slim somewhere," Lincoln urged. "Could you not break him?"

Yet Hooker was slow to turn his own gaze away from Richmond. Lee's column flowed onward as he ripened his plans to strike a series of blows in Pennsylvania to break the will of the Northern voters. Meanwhile, he would feed his troops for a while on Northern crops and livestock, giving his battered Virginia homeland a reprieve. At the same time, Confederate Vice President Alexander Stephens sought permission to deliver a peace overture to Washington, hoping to ratchet up pressure for a truce. He was refused.

By day, Lincoln goaded his general to attack. "Fight him when opportunity offers," he urged Hooker. By night, the President passed short hours of troubled sleep. "Think you better put 'Tad's' pistol away," Lincoln cabled his wife on June 9 at the Philadelphia hotel where she was traveling with their youngest son. "I had an ugly dream about him."

In the Western Theater, a Fighter Rises

How different things were in the West, where the taciturn cigar-chewer Ulysses S. Grant, a onetime quartermaster who never lost the common touch, had spent April and May solving the problem of Vicksburg without troubling Lincoln a bit. The President had seen to the core of Grant's character when he said simply, "He fights." Sure enough, in April Grant ran gunboats down the Mississippi through storms of artillery fire from the Vicksburg bluffs. With the boats as cover, he ferried an army across the river, then launched the most dazzling campaign of the war. "Grant is a copious worker, and fighter, but a very meagre writer, or telegrapher," Lincoln once explained. The first news he received of Grant's exploits came from captured Confederate newspapers, but on May 23, an aide to Grant filled in the details.

Grant's Army of the Tennessee "landed at Bruinsburg on 30th April," the aide telegraphed. "On 1st May, fought battle of Port Gibson; defeated rebels ... On 12th May, at the battle of Raymond, rebels were defeated ... On the 14th, defeated Joseph E. Johnston, captured Jackson ...

On the 16th, fought the bloody and decisive battle of Baker's Creek ... On the 17th, defeated same force at Big Black Bridge ... on the 18th, invested Vicksburg closely." Simple as that. The last Confederate stronghold on the Mississippi was now surrounded, besieged, starving.

The path to victory, Lincoln had come to understand, lay in breaking up the rebellion and snuffing out its armies. Grant was on the verge of cutting the rebel lifeline to the fertile lands of the West and forcing the surrender of an entire Confederate army for the second time in his short career. Why couldn't the President find such a man for the Eastern Theater? Lee continued down the Shenandoah Valley, capturing the Union garrison at Winchester, as Hooker's cavalry tried and failed to break through the Confederate screen. As the head of the rebel column neared Union soil, Lincoln issued a call for 100,000 fresh volunteers, but that was no use in the present emergency. If Lee was to be stopped, the Army of the Potomac would have to stop him.

And Lee was moving rapidly now, sending his vanguard straight through Maryland to the outskirts of Harrisburg, the capital of Pennsylvania. For Lincoln, these were dark hours indeed. There was no word from Grant at Vicksburg. The Democrats of Ohio and New York had issued formal protests against the arrest of leading antiwar activists and draft resisters. Friends in Philadelphia and the governor of New Jersey pleaded with him to call McClellan back to command, for only the ousted general could "rescue" the nation "from the hopelessness now prevailing," they declared.

Hooker Gets the Hook

But Lincoln, still convinced that the rebels were overplaying their hand, had already moved quietly in another direction. On June 28, as Lee began to collect his forces in the rolling countryside west of Harrisburg, the President took the extraordinary step of changing generals in the midst of a crisis. He accepted Hooker's petulant offer to resign and promoted in his place a turtle-eyed Pennsylvanian named George G. Meade. Short-tempered, conservative, an Army man top to toe, Meade was no one's favorite officer—but he proved to be the right man for the moment. Assuming command so abruptly that he didn't even know precisely where his army was, he nevertheless managed to collect his troops and his wits in time to meet Lee three days later.

What followed has been called the turning point of the Civil War, the beginning of the end for the Confederacy,

The man for the job
Even as Lincoln and his top military aide, Halleck, shuffled commanders of the Army of the Potomac, Grant pursued the Confederates in the Western Theater with a fierce, unrelenting urgency. Lincoln finally found success in the East when "Unconditional Surrender" Grant took command

and the making of Lincoln's presidency. There is some truth and a bit of exaggeration in those assessments, but what can be said for sure is that no handful of days in American history was richer in portents or more saturated in blood. Through three days of fighting along the meadows and ridgelines of Gettysburg, Meade's Union defenses often bent but never broke, and Lee's failure in Pennsylvania was quickly followed by news that Grant had captured Vicksburg.

In the immediate aftermath, Lincoln ached to see Meade attack Lee's decimated force, for he imagined that the end of the war was but one more battle away. As the smoke cleared, however, he came to hold a more charitable opinion of the general. When Oliver O. Howard, an experienced division commander in the Army of the Potomac, protested to Lincoln that Meade had managed to

bring harmony to a badly demoralized force, the President agreed. "A few days having passed" since Lee's successful retreat across the Potomac, "I am now profoundly grateful for what was done, without criticism for what was not done" at Gettysburg, Lincoln wrote. "Gen. Meade has my confidence as a brave and skillful officer, and a true man."

Now the pieces were rumbling into place for the ghastly final act of the nation's great drama. Grant was soon on his way to Chattanooga, Tenn., to break the South's main railway and start William T. Sherman down his long road of destruction. From there, Grant would be called to the East to devise the final, crushing campaigns along the path to Appomattox. Lincoln had found his generals at last, in the only way circumstances would allow: by gory trial and error. He made his mistakes, yes, but he learned from them. ■

July 2, 1863

Still standing sentinel
A statue commemorating Major General Gouverneur Kemble Warren crowns Little Round Top, the site where soldiers of both sides reached peaks of valor on July 2. The alert and capable Union officer organized the last-minute defense of the heights, a key to the Federals' victory

Battlefield Guide: July 2, 1863

Infantry, by the Numbers

Corps
Union: 10,000 to 20,000 men
Confederate: 20,000 men (average)

Division
6,000 to 8,000 men

Brigade
1,200 to 4,000 men

Regiment
400 to 1,000 men

Company
40 to 100 men

Platoon
One-half a company

Military Lexicon

battery: The basic unit of an artillery company. Batteries included four or six cannons and the men, horses, ammunition and equipment needed to move and fire them. The term is also used to describe an artillery unit's position on the battlefield.

demonstration: A simulated attack used as a ploy to distract enemy attention from a primary assault.

elevation: The angle at which an artillery gun's barrel is raised above the horizon line; too much elevation, and shells may fly over the enemy position.

field of fire: The area under fire during an assault or artillery barrage; also, the area a gun or artillery piece is able to reach.

limber, unlimber: A limber is a two-wheeled carriage used to move artillery weapons. To unlimber is to disengage the tail of the gun, which is elevated by the limber during movement, and situate the gun on the ground for firing.

oblique, right and left: Changes in the angle of direction by a line of soldiers during a march or infantry advance.

salient: A part of an offensive or defensive line that projects outward beyond the main line toward the enemy and is thus exposed and vulnerable to fire from three sides.

traverse: A type of fortification; a mound of earth raised up to protect gun positions from enemy fire.

Faces in the Ranks
The horse soldiers of the 7th Virginia Cavalry Regiment took part in Stonewall Jackson's famous Shenandoah Valley Campaign of 1862 and fought in the largest mounted engagement of the war, the Battle of Brandy Station, as Lee's army moved north in early June 1863.

Timeline

4:30 a.m. Lee assesses Union position
From Seminary Ridge, Lee evaluates the Federal positions on Cemetery Hill.

6-8 a.m. Culp's Hill is reinforced
Meade sends troops to strengthen Union defenses on Culp's Hill.

10 a.m. Lee issues battle orders
Lee directs Longstreet to attack Federal left flank across Emmitsburg Road. Ewell is to demonstrate in force on Union right flank.

12 noon Union troops are in position
By midday, most Federal troops are on the battlefield. Sedgwick's troops are still on the march.

12 noon Longstreet begins moving ❶
Longstreet delays march to Federal left, waiting for Law's brigade to arrive. He then takes a circuitous route, causing more delay.

12 noon Jeb Stuart reappears
Out of touch since June 25, the cavalry chief arrives to a chilly reception from Lee.

2-3 p.m. Sickles' troops advance
Sickles moves 10,000 Federals close to Emmitsburg Road, far in front of other Union troops and leaving both Round Tops undefended.

4 p.m. The Confederate attack begins ❷
The day's serious fighting begins with Hood's attack on the Federal left. Between 4 and 7 p.m., some 15,000 casualties occur.

5-7 p.m. The attack intensifies ❸❹
McLaws and then Anderson join the Confederate attack on Cemetery Ridge by Hood's troops.

6 p.m. Barksdale's charge
Mississippi troops attack Federals through the Peach Orchard. Barksdale is slain.

7 p.m. Battle on Little Round Top
20th Maine bayonet charge drives Confederates from Little Round Top.

7-11 p.m. Late combat at Culp's Hill ❺❻
Early and Johnson attack Cemetery Hill and Culp's Hill, capturing a few positions at the latter heights.

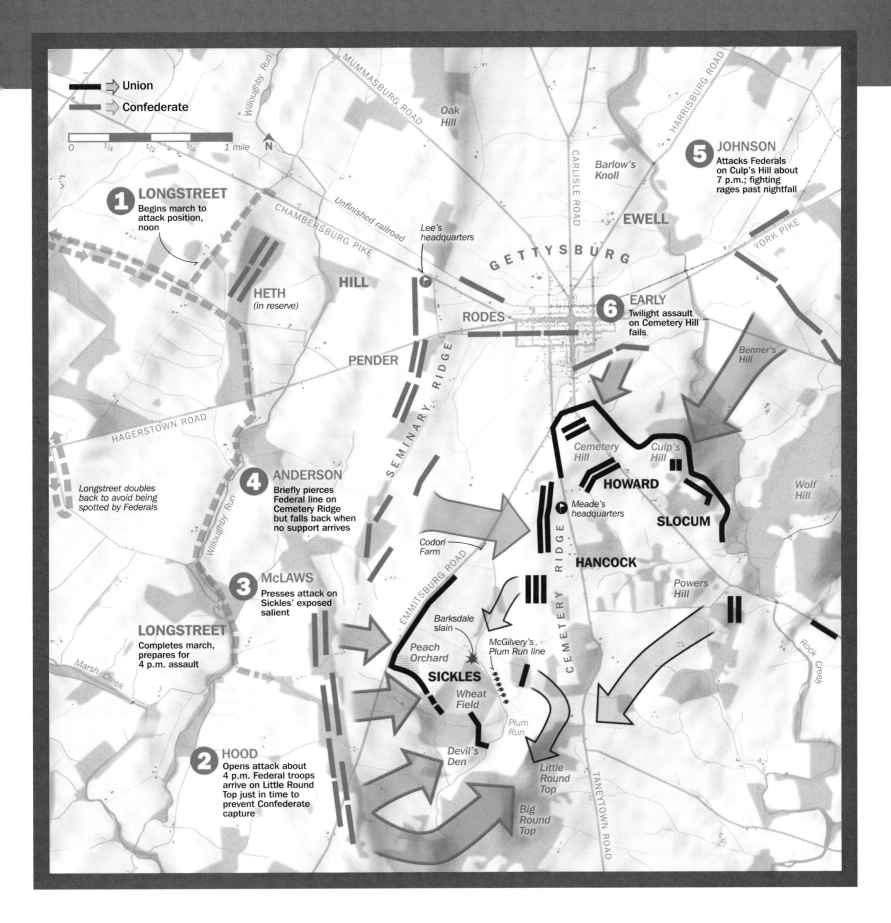

Union
Confederate

0   ¼   ½   ¾   1 mile

N

MUMMASBURG ROAD

Willoughby Run

Oak Hill

CARLISLE ROAD

HARRISBURG ROAD

Barlow's Knoll

⑤ JOHNSON
Attacks Federals
on Culp's Hill about
7 p.m.; fighting
rages past nightfall

EWELL

YORK PIKE

① LONGSTREET
Begins march to
attack position,
noon

Unfinished railroad

CHAMBERSBURG PIKE

*Lee's
headquarters*

G E T T Y S B U R G

⑥ EARLY
Twilight assault
on Cemetery Hill
fails

*Benner's
Hill*

HETH
(in reserve)

HILL

RODES

PENDER

S E M I N A R Y   R I D G E

HAGERSTOWN ROAD

*Longstreet doubles
back to avoid being
spotted by Federals*

*Cemetery
Hill*

*Culp's
Hill*

HOWARD

*Wolf
Hill*

④ ANDERSON
Briefly pierces
Federal line on
Cemetery Ridge
but falls back when
no support arrives

*Meade's
headquarters*

SLOCUM

*Codori
Farm*

HANCOCK

C E M E T E R Y   R I D G E

*Powers
Hill*

③ McLAWS
Presses attack on
Sickles' exposed
salient

EMMITSBURG ROAD

*Barksdale
slain*

*McGilvery's
Plum Run line*

*Rock
Creek*

LONGSTREET
Completes march,
prepares for
4 p.m. assault

Marsh Creek

*Peach
Orchard*

SICKLES

*Wheat
Field*

*Plum
Run*

*Little
Round
Top*

*Devil's
Den*

TANEYTOWN ROAD

② HOOD
Opens attack about
4 p.m. Federal troops
arrive on Little Round
Top just in time to
prevent Confederate
capture

*Big
Round
Top*

A Slow Fuse Ignites A Deadly Uphill Battle

Robert E. Lee's grand plan of attack is foiled by his own officers' delays—and by a Union officer's unauthorized but effective gambit

W HILE THE FIGHTING ON THE first day of battle at Gettysburg was a lengthy exercise in improvisation on both sides, the second day's combat followed a script written by Confederate top commander Robert E. Lee—up to a point. With the Army of the Potomac occupying the high ground south and northeast of town, Lee devised an elegant plan of battle that called for his armies to stage a sequential series of carefully coordinated attacks on the Federal positions. The strategy was fine, in principle. But lengthy delays and failures of coordination on the Confederate side gave the Union forces almost the full day of Thursday, July 2, to improve their fortified positions before the fighting began in earnest.

On this day, the Confederates—who had won so many battles by acting with more dispatch, more dexterity and more discipline than their foes—behaved much as the Federals had in the war's earlier set pieces. Lee's lieutenants dillied and dallied the day away, and when they finally launched their massive uphill attack, they failed to act in unison, allowing the Federals to take advantage of their superior position and closer interior lines to shift troops quickly from one hot spot to another. The theme of the day was that age-old climax to a good war story, the last-minute rescue: time after time, on front after front, a hard-fought battle seemed all but lost only to be resolved in the Federals' favor after the sudden, revitalizing appearance of reinforcements on the battlefield.

The Confederates would fail to achieve their objectives on July 2. Yet despite the chaos and confusion, there were countless moments of heroism on both sides, amid fighting so furious that the names of the individual battlegrounds have entered the American lexicon: Little Round Top, Cemetery Ridge, Devil's Den, the Peach Orchard, the Wheat Field.

Lofty setting, deadly deeds *Big Round Top, in the background, looms over the heights of Little Round Top, foreground. At one point Confederate officer William C. Oates summited Big Round Top, but his division was ordered to descend and attack Little Round Top, where it engaged in a famed battle with Federal troops*

Decision at Dawn
Don Troiani's painting shows Lee conferring early on July 2 with, from left, Hill, Hood and Longstreet. Watching from a tree is British Army observer Arthur Fremantle. Henry Heth, at rear, is bandaged from his July 1 head wound

The day began with little fuss. "The roll was called in low tones," wrote Augustus Buell, a 19-year-old cannoneer whose Federal I Corps battery overlooked the Gettysburg plain from the frowning northern brow of Cemetery Hill. "In the dim light of the daybreak we could see our infantry in front of us astir, and looking a little further out into the gloom we could see the enemy's gray pickets. The stillness of everything was oppressive.

We felt that a few flashes of musketry would be a relief.

"But the daylight came on, the sun rose and mounted up higher and higher, and yet the enemy, though in plain sight, gave no sign of hostility. Our men looked at each other and asked, 'What does it mean?'"

Buell and his comrades would find out soon enough what it meant. For on this sultry morning of July 2, volcanic forces were building toward a colossal eruption.

Lee Devises His Battle Plan

After only about three hours' sleep, Robert E. Lee arose at 3:30 a.m. and immediately dispatched two officers—Captain Samuel R. Johnston of his staff and Major J.J. Clarke of General Longstreet's—to reconnoiter in the direction of the Round Tops. An hour and a half later, the commanding general was on Seminary Ridge, intently surveying the dispositions of the Federals concentrated on Cemetery Hill. Their line did not seem to Lee to extend very far south along Cemetery Ridge, the low spine connecting the hill with the Round Tops.

Meeting outside his headquarters on Seminary Ridge with Generals Longstreet, A.P. Hill, John Bell Hood, Henry Heth and others, Lee pondered his plans. Confederate troops, including the divisions of Brigadier General Evander Law, Major General Lafayette McLaws and Major General George E. Pickett, were still en route to the area, prompting Longstreet to argue that any attack must be delayed until they arrived. Lee disagreed, and then he and Longstreet, so often in accord, quarreled briefly over the correct placement of McLaws' troops.

When Captain Johnston returned from his scouting expedition, he reported that only Federal pickets occupied the southern portion of Cemetery Ridge and that the Round Tops were unoccupied. The news confirmed Lee's sense that the Federals were defending only the northernmost section of the ridge, and helped him complete his plans. Longstreet would march to the south, he said, then advance his two divisions along the Emmitsburg Road to the northeast, toward Cemetery Ridge. After rolling up the Federal left, he would attack Cemetery Hill from the south, while Hill would assault Cemetery Hill from the west with the divisions of Major Generals Richard H. Anderson and William Dorsey Pender.

Lee ordered that the attack be made in echelon, starting on the right flank of the Confederate line and moving toward the left, with one brigade after another striking the Federal line in a series of triphammer blows.

On the rebel left, General Richard S. Ewell's corps, still occupying Gettysburg and facing the Federal positions to the south, would conduct a demonstration in force at the sound of Longstreet's guns, keeping the Federals engaged on that front. If the chance arose, Ewell would make a full-scale assault on Cemetery and Culp's hills.

Lee's arrangements for these complicated operations were incredibly casual. He issued no written orders. At no time during the battle would he bring together his three corps commanders—Longstreet, Hill and Ewell—upon whose understanding and cooperation the entire affair depended. And the commanding general would frequently act as his own courier, riding back and forth between the three corps at considerable cost of time. Lee seemed out of sorts on this day; he was said to be suffering from severe diarrhea, and some historians have suggested that he may have been experiencing signs of the heart disease that would contribute to his death in 1870.

Stuart Arrives at Last

About 10 a.m. Lee rode off to visit Ewell's corps, expecting Longstreet's assault to be under way soon. But after he found Ewell, talked with him briefly and started back toward his own headquarters, Lee found, to his intense exasperation, that Longstreet had not even begun the march to reach his attack position; instead, he was waiting for Law's brigade, which did not arrive for another hour. It was noon when Longstreet's corps finally set off, and it would be another four hours before Longstreet launched the attack Lee had expected around noon.

Shortly after Longstreet began moving his men into position, the long-lost General Jeb Stuart arrived at Gettysburg. He was riding far ahead of his men, who were returning from their wild and pointless forays into Maryland and Pennsylvania, east of Lee's main armies.

According to Stuart's adjutant, Major Henry McClellan, their meeting that day was "painful beyond description." At the sight of Stuart, Lee reddened, raised his hand as if to strike his knight errant and demanded to know where Stuart had been: "I have not heard a word from you for days, and you the eyes and ears of my army."

"I have brought you 125 wagons and their teams, General," replied Stuart. "Yes," said Lee, "and they are an impediment to me now."

Then the commanding general's manner turned from anger to "great tenderness," according to McClellan. "Let me ask your help now," Lee said. "We will not discuss this matter further. Help me fight these people." But it was already too late for Stuart's exhausted, disorganized forces to join the assault that day.

General Longstreet, meanwhile, was meeting with nothing but frustration in trying to move his two divisions to the point of attack. Seeking to avoid detection, he had marched his troops on country back roads, then had to backtrack and take a more distant route along Willoughby Run. Had Stuart's cavalry been on the scene earlier to scout the Federal positions, Longstreet would likely not have wasted this precious time. Delayed by

Lee's presentation sword
Robert E. Lee's formal sword is displayed at the Museum of the Confederacy in Appomattox, Va. The new branch of the museum, whose primary facility is in Richmond, opened in 2012

Lee's headquarters
At top left is the stone Thompson House on Seminary Ridge that served as Lee's command center during the battle. The fence has been stripped of its pickets in this photo, taken shortly after the battle. The structure survived the fighting and is now a museum

nearly two hours, his corps finally began filing into place west of the Emmitsburg Road at about 3:30 p.m., with Hood's division on the right facing the Round Tops and McLaws' division on the left, opposite Cemetery Ridge.

McLaws had been told to expect little or no opposition on his immediate front. But just to make sure, he rode forward, dismounted and walked to the edge of the woods in which his troops were concealed. "The view presented astonished me," he wrote later, "as the enemy was massed in my front, and extended to my right and left as far as I could see."

The large Federal force deployed along the Emmitsburg Road only 600 yds. away was General Daniel Sickles' III Corps—and its presence there was almost as unpleasant a surprise to the commander of the Army of the Potomac as it was to General McLaws.

Daniel Sickles Goes Rogue
General Meade had been up all night, inspecting and arranging his lines. During the night and early morning, the roads from the south had been thronged by hard-

marching Federal troops, many of whom had not slept for two days. By 9 a.m., the majority of the Federal divisions were present, deployed in the shape of a rough horseshoe pointing toward Gettysburg and open to the south. On the Federal right, General Henry W. Slocum's XII Corps held a line along the rocky slope extending southeast from Culp's Hill along Rock Creek. The arc of the horseshoe was manned by General James Wadsworth's battered I Corps division on Culp's Hill and General Oliver O. Howard's shaky XI Corps on Cemetery Hill.

Behind XI Corps on Cemetery Hill were the other two I Corps divisions. At Cemetery Hill, Meade's line bent sharply southward, with General Winfield Scott Hancock's II Corps extending down Cemetery Ridge. Sickles was ordered to position III Corps beyond Hancock on the extreme Federal left. Meade's old V Corps, now under Major General George Sykes, was held in reserve on the Baltimore Pike behind Cemetery Hill, a location that offered easy access to all parts of the battlefield.

Only Major General John Sedgwick's VI Corps—at nearly 14,000 men the army's largest—had yet to arrive.

Around sunset on July 1, his troops were 30 long miles from the scene of the battle, but he had told a Meade courier that "my corps will be at Gettysburg at 4 o'clock tomorrow." It would mean marching all night and most of the next day, but Sedgwick would keep his appointment.

Meade had tasked General Sickles' III Corps with holding the Federal left along Cemetery Ridge, but the two had quarreled over the precise placement of Sickles' troops. Half a mile north of the Round Tops, Cemetery Ridge diminished in height until it was a barely perceptible swell in the countryside. Sickles thought this low place was a dangerous position, rendered even more vulnerable by the fact that it was commanded by higher ground—upon which a peach orchard was situated—about half a mile to the west. Enemy guns on that elevation would imperil the III Corps line, Sickles said, and he requested permission to take control of the position.

Late in the morning, Meade sent the army's artillery chief, Brigadier General Henry J. Hunt, to survey Sickles' situation. To the gunner's keen eye, the elevation out in front of the Federal left—the Peach Orchard, as it would

henceforth be known—was attractive. It was a short, flat-topped ridge, midway between Cemetery and Seminary ridges and traversed diagonally by the Emmitsburg Road. From the orchard another ridge ran off to the southeast, terminating after about 1,100 yds. in a fantastic jumble of huge granite boulders that locals called the Devil's Den. Between the Devil's Den and Little Round Top, 500 yds. to the east, was a marshy, rock-strewn swale that would soon be known as the Valley of Death; through it flowed a little stream named Plum Run.

General Hunt agreed that the Peach Orchard ridge and the one leading to the Devil's Den "constituted a favorable position for the enemy to hold" but he would not authorize Sickles to take it. When Sickles sent a unit to reconnoiter the area, the Federals ran into Confederate resistance. In fact, the rebel troops were a small, isolated group. But Sickles did not know this, and so he determined to advance en masse to the Emmitsburg Road, defying Hunt. At 3 p.m., the 10,000 battle-tested veterans of III Corps pushed forward, skirmishers in front, artillery to the rear, colors flapping, swords and bayonets

Meade's headquarters
The stone fences around the Leister Farm on Cemetery Ridge that was used as a command post by General Meade have been damaged by Confederate artillery fire in this photo taken after the battle, and dead horses lie in the road outside the door.

Meade did not arrive at Gettysburg until the early hours of July 2

gleaming, the drummers beating a steady cadence count.

The unauthorized advance bewildered Sickles' superiors. The II Corps commander, Hancock, realized that Sickles not only was isolating his corps half a mile in front of the rest of the army but also had exposed the left flank of II Corps. When Meade hastily rode to the scene, under heavy artillery fire, he saw the division of Brigadier General Andrew A. Humphreys far out in front of the Federal line with its right flank completely exposed.

On Humphreys' left, Brigadier General David B. Birney's division occupied the Peach Orchard, then angled off on a line southeast, stretching past a wheat field to the Devil's Den and the Plum Run Valley beyond. Thus, the two divisions formed a salient that could be vulnerable to fire from two sides. Yet even as Meade chastised Sickles for his risky advance, Confederate guns began to boom: it was too late for Sickles to withdraw.

Hood Attacks at Devil's Den

The Confederate commanders had been having their own disagreements. Confronted by Sickles' new position, General McLaws immediately realized that it knocked Lee's plan askew. Instead of thrusting along an undefended Emmitsburg Road toward a weak Federal flank on Cemetery Ridge, as Lee had envisioned, McLaws would have to fight every inch of the way. Twice more he protested—and twice more he was told that he must attack the Federals head on when the time came.

General Hood was enduring similar woes on the Confederate far right. From his attack position in the woods, Hood could see Birney's Federals in the Peach Orchard salient to the northeast. And Hood's scouts reported that although the Round Tops were unoccupied, the enemy's line extended all the way to Devil's Den. Three times he proposed to Longstreet that he attempt to swing around the Federals and attack them on their left flank, and three times Longstreet insisted that Lee's orders were to attack up the Emmitsburg Road.

In the end, Hood simply ignored Longstreet. In clear disregard of his superior's orders, Hood faced his division eastward and launched an attack toward the Devil's Den and the Round Tops, hoping to outflank the Federal left. Hood's division advanced in two lines. On the right front was General Law's Alabama brigade, supported about 200 yds. behind by the Georgia brigade of Brigadier General Henry L. Benning. To the left was Hood's old Texas brigade, now commanded by Brigadier General Jerome B. Robertson; it was backed by another Georgia brigade, under Brigadier General George T. Anderson.

As the troops advanced, the 15th Alabama, on the far right of Law's line, came under heavy fire from the 2nd U.S. Sharpshooters on the heavily wooded lower slope of Big Round Top. To clear them out, the 15th Alabama under Colonel William C. Oates, joined by most of the 47th Alabama, charged up the hill, bypassed the sharpshooters and kept climbing all the way to the summit of Big Round Top, 305 ft. above the plain, the highest place for miles around. Oates let his men rest for a few minutes, but a courier soon arrived with news that General Hood had been wounded and that General Law was now in command on this front—and with Law's order that Oates must abandon Big Round Top and seize Little Round Top. Oates and his troops trekked down the slopes of Big Round Top and began to ascend the rugged southeastern slope of Little Round Top, when, without the slightest warning, what Oates would remember as "the most destructive fire I ever saw" erupted from behind a natural row of rocks less than 50 steps in front of them.

The Defense of Little Round Top

The Federals behind the rocks had been there for only 10 minutes—about the same length of time that Oates had rested his men on Big Round Top. Their presence was attributable to the good judgment of Union chief engineer General Gouverneur Kemble Warren, who had been sent by Meade to inspect the Round Tops. Arriving just before the Confederate advance, Warren had found Little Round Top held only by a few signalmen, even as he saw the rebels approaching nearby.

Now, suddenly, every minute was precious. As Federal commanders desperately sought troops to plug the gap, Colonel Strong Vincent, a 26-year-old Harvard graduate and lawyer, volunteered his men to take control of Little Round Top and sent them racing to the scene. The last of Vincent's four regiments to gain the heights was the 20th Maine, a regiment of fishermen and lumberjacks who had learned how to fight, and fight well. As they took their position, Vincent told their commander, Colonel Joshua Lawrence Chamberlain, "This is the left of the Union line." By this he meant the left of the entire Army of the Potomac. "You understand," Vincent told the officer. "You are to hold this ground at all costs."

Colonel Chamberlain understood perfectly—and for his bravery and leadership during the next hour and a half, the 34-year-old former seminarian and professor of rhetoric at Bowdoin College would be awarded the

The crucible *Large boulders formed a natural breastworks on the slopes of Little Round Top, scene of some of the most furious fighting on July 2. In the early-evening hours, a bayonet charge by the 20th Maine division repelled a Confederate attack here*

Medal of Honor. No sooner had Chamberlain's men got their backs to the side of the hill than Oates and his Confederates appeared. From behind their protective rocks, the men of the 20th Maine rose, fired and sent the enemy line staggering back. The Confederates re-formed and rushed again, against a hail of bullets so destructive that, in Oates' words, "my line wavered like a man trying to walk against a strong wind."

When the Alabamians began to lap around his left flank, Chamberlain ordered the left wing to drop back, so that the 20th Maine's formation took the shape of a letter V. Colonel Oates cried, "Forward, my men, to the ledge!" And firing his revolver, he led an uphill surge toward the Federal line 30 yds. away. Nearby, his younger brother, Lieutenant John A. Oates, was hit and fell dying.

Chamberlain's dead lay sprawled grotesquely around him, his soldiers were down to their last cartridges, and the Confederates were rallying for another charge. A desperate Chamberlain decided to fix bayonets and charge first. But his shouted orders could not be heard above the din, and the men didn't move. Then Lieutenant Holman S. Melcher of Company F jumped out in front of the line, yelled "Come on! Come on, boys!" and charged—alone. Moments passed, then a few men followed, then more, and then, with an animal roar, the entire 20th Maine

swept forward, led by Chamberlain with drawn sword.

The shocked Confederates stopped, stumbled back and braced themselves. But suddenly they were hit from behind. The sharpshooters who had earlier opposed Oates' passage to the Round Tops were now firing on his rear; other Federals were on his flanks. Finally, Oates ordered retreat. "When the signal was given," he said, "we ran like a herd of wild cattle."

The 20th Maine, at a cost of 130 of its 386 men, had won its lonely fight. But farther around the hill, on the west slope, the Federal troops were in desperate straits. There, on the far right of Vincent's brigade, the 16th Michigan was beginning to crumble under a savage attack from Robertson's 4th and 5th Texas divisions. As Colonel Vincent tried to rally the Michiganders, he went down mortally wounded, murmuring, "Don't give an inch." But just as all seemed lost for the Michigan men, reinforcements arrived as if on cue, once again thanks to the brisk, decisive actions of General Warren.

The Confederates Take Devil's Den

Chamberlain's men on Little Round Top could see to the immediate west a savage battle for the Devil's Den and the Plum Run Valley. The Devil's Den—a wilderness of huge boulders sheltering a labyrinth of crevices, caves

First Person

Colonel William C. Oates
15th Alabama Infantry Regiment

Oates' regiment fought at Little Round Top against Chamberlain's 20th Maine division.

I saw no enemy until within 40 or 50 steps of an irregular ledge of rocks—a splendid line of natural breastworks … From behind the ledge, unexpectedly to us, because concealed, they poured into us the most destructive fire I ever saw. Our line halted, but did not break … As men fell, their comrades closed the gap, returning the fire most spiritedly. I could see through the smoke men of the 20th Maine in front of my right wing running from tree to tree …

Lieutenant Charles A. Fuller
61st New York Infantry

Fuller fought against General George T. Anderson's divisions at the Wheat Field.

We were in this wheat field and the grain stood almost breast high. The Rebs had their slight protection, but we were in the open, without a thing better than a wheat straw to catch a Minnie [sic] bullet that weighed an ounce. Of course, our men began to tumble. They lay where they fell, or if able, started for the rear. Near to me I saw a man named Daily go down, shot through the neck. I made a movement to get his gun, but at that moment I was struck in the shoulder. It did not hurt and the blow simply caused me to step back. I found that I could not work my arm …

Sometime after this, I felt a blow on the left leg, and it gave way, so that I knew the bone was broken. This stroke did not hurt, and I did not fall, but turned around and made a number of hops to the rear, when my foot caught in the tangled grain and I went down full length. While lying there entirely helpless, and hearing those vicious bullets singing over my head, I suffered from fear …

In a short time I heard a line of battle advancing from the rear. As the men came in sight I sang out, "Don't step on me, boys!" Those in range of me stepped over and rushed forward and fought the enemy in advance of the line we occupied.

After a while I was aware that a skirmish line was coming from the front, and soon discovered that the skirmishers were not clothed in blue. The officer in command was mounted and rode by within a few feet of me … This fighting was not severe and a short time after these gentlemen in gray moved back in the same manner they had advanced, greatly to my relief. I did not fancy remaining their guest for any length of time.

As the Rebs went back, a nice looking young fellow, small of stature, with bright black eyes, whose face was smutted up with powder and smoke, came along where I lay. My sword was on the ground beside me. He picked it up, and said, "Give me that scabbard!" I said, "Johnny, you will have to excuse me, as my arm is broken and I can't unbuckle my belt." He made no comment but went off with my sword.

Sergeant Valerius C. Giles
4th Texas Infantry Regiment

Giles describes the moments before Confederates mounted an attack on Little Round Top.

By this time order and discipline were gone. Every fellow was his own general. Private soldiers gave commands as loud as the officers … To add to this confusion, our artillery on the hill to our rear was cutting its fuse too short. Their shells were bursting behind us, in the

treetops, over our heads, and all around us.

Nothing demoralizes troops quicker than to be fired into by their friends. I saw it occur twice during the war. The first time we ran, but at Gettysburg we couldn't. This mistake was soon corrected and the shells burst high on the mountain or went over it.

Major [Jefferson C.] Rogers, then in command of the 5th Texas Regiment, mounted an old log near my boulder and began a Fourth of July speech. He was a little ahead of time, for that was about 6:30 on the evening of July 2nd. Of course nobody was paying any attention to the oration as he appealed to the men to "stand fast." He and Captain Cousins of the 4th Alabama were the only two men I saw standing. The balance of us had settled down behind rocks, logs and trees.

While the speech was going on, John Haggerty, one of Hood's couriers, then acting for General Law, dashed up the side of the mountain, saluted the major and said: "General Law presents his compliments, and says hold this place at all hazards." The major checked up, glared down at Haggerty from his perch, and shouted: "Compliments, hell! Who wants any compliments in such a damned place as this! Go back and ask General Law if he expects me to hold the world in check with the 5th Texas Regiment?"

Turning point *Don Troiani's painting* Bayonet! *captures one of the emblematic moments of the fighting on July 2, as Joshua Chamberlain leads the soldiers of his 20th Maine division in a bayonet charge that drove Colonel Oates and his Alabama troops from the summit of Little Round Top*

and dank, dark rock-walled passages—formed the base of the ridge that rose up toward the Peach Orchard. Near the crest of that ridge were positioned six guns of the 4th New York Battery and a host of New York, Pennsylvania, Maine and Indiana men. Now, from the Federal ranks, a cry arose: "Here they come! Here they come!" Robertson's Texas and Arkansas regiments, followed by Benning's Georgians, were charging the Federal positions.

In the wild fight that followed, some of the Confederates assailed the Devil's Den, while others flooded into the nearby Valley of Death along Plum Run Creek, where they were hit by the fire of Federal troops on Little Round Top. Men in blue and gray found themselves on opposite sides of the same boulder, reaching around its circumference to fire muzzle to muzzle; others used their bayonets to stab blindly through the corners of crevices. The struggle, recalled a Confederate, was "more like Indian fighting than anything I experienced during the war."

When the engagement sputtered to an end, the Confederates had control of the Devil's Den and the ridge above. The defending Federals of Brigadier General J. Hobart Ward's 2,200-man brigade had suffered 781 casualties. Yet to the north, around the Peach Orchard, another stage of this chaotic battle was erupting—and the Federals' overall superior position was beginning to tell.

On the morning of July 2, while visiting Ewell's front on the rebel right, General Lee had made an observation that revealed his unease. "The enemy have the advantage of us in a shorter and inside line," he said, "And we are too extended." Later calculations would confirm his point. From the Federal right near Culp's Hill to the left on Little Round Top, Meade's hook-shaped line stretched three miles—totaling an average of 17,000 soldiers per mile. Arrayed outside that arc, Lee's Confederate forces formed a line two miles longer and proportionately thinner, averaging a much less dense 10,000 men per mile.

Moreover, the Federal troops could move quickly from one place to another on their line simply by cutting across the arc. In no case was the marching distance between two Federal positions more than two and a half miles. In the fighting that followed the first Confederate assaults on Little Round Top and the Devil's Den, General Meade would use his advantage to the fullest, borrowing from quiet parts of his front to patch his line where it was in danger. His efforts would be aided not only by the topography but also by the unevenness of the Confederate attack, which did not proceed, as Lee had hoped, in an orderly, overpowering succession of trip-hammer blows. Instead, it unfolded in sputtering fits and starts, now fierce and now feeble. The battle quickly slid out of control for the Confederates, and in time Lee's plan would dissolve in confusion.

Man to Man in the Wheat Field

While their comrades had been storming Little Round Top and the Devil's Den, Confederates on Hood's left—General Richard H. Anderson's brigade, along with some of General Benning's Georgians—made little headway against Birney's thin but obstinate Union line along the ridge running from the Devil's Den northwest to the Peach Orchard. Clearly, the rebels needed help, and McLaws' division—poised just to the north—was growing increasingly restless under the restraints imposed by Longstreet, the corps commander. Indeed, Hood's onslaught had passed its fullest fury before Longstreet finally sent McLaws into battle at about 5:30 p.m.

Crossing the Emmitsburg Road, three of Brigadier General Joseph B. Kershaw's South Carolina regiments wheeled north in a vain attempt to breach the Federal line in the Peach Orchard. The remaining two leaped a stone fence and charged eastward to join Anderson's Confederates near what would soon be known simply as the Wheat Field. As the two regiments advanced across the property of a farmer named John P. Rose, they were swept by a flailing fire from a division under 62-year-old Brigadier General James Barnes. Many of Barnes' troops were firing from behind a stone wall that offered substantial protection. An officer in Barnes' division believed his troops could hold their favorable position "against considerable odds till the cows come." They might have, too, had not the cautious Barnes ordered a withdrawal, creating a huge gap in the Federal line.

The Confederate soldiers streamed across the Wheat Field, whooping in exultation, only to collide head on with fresh Federal troops who came in on the double, firing as they charged. These much needed reinforcements were the men of Brigadier General John C. Caldwell's division, which had been shifted from the left flank of II Corps on Cemetery Ridge. General Hancock had dispatched the troops to Sickles' aid at 5:15 p.m.

Caldwell had no time to indulge in elaborate tactics; he simply fed his brigades into the fray as they arrived at the Wheat Field. Leading the way was a unit under a salty old Indian fighter, Colonel Edward E. Cross, who died leading his men into action. Cross's brigade was followed by that of Brigadier General Samuel K. Zook, who

Aftermath *Brady corps member James F. Gibson took this photograph of dead soldiers lying at the foot of Little Round Top. This version was printed as a stereoscopic double image that created a 3-D effect when viewed through a special device, a technology increasingly popular throughout the latter half of the 19th century*

found his way barred by Barnes' retreating troops. The fiery Zook was enraged. "If you can't get out of the way," he roared, "lie down and we will march over you!" In an extraordinary development, Barnes' men did indeed lie down, and Zook's brigade plunged into the Wheat Field over their prone bodies. Zook was among the first to fall. As his horse leaped over a stone wall into the Wheat Field, he was shot in the stomach and mortally wounded.

To the right of Cross's troops marched the 532 men of Colonel Patrick Kelly's Irish Brigade. On being ordered to the Wheat Field, the Irishmen had knelt in prayer as Father William Corby, the brigade chaplain, mounted a rock and blessed them with a general absolution. Advancing into the trampled, corpse-strewn field, the Irishmen plugged the gap between Cross's and Zook's troops and started shooting. Finally, Caldwell threw in his last brigade, under 24-year-old Colonel John R. Brooke. The young officer led a magnificent charge, and the Geor-

gian troops slowed, stopped and began giving ground.

But not for long. Rallying at the Rose Farm, the rebels rushed back on Caldwell's right flank, reinforced by another Georgia brigade, under Brigadier General William T. Wofford. For yet another time the Wheat Field changed hands. Briefly, knots of Federals stood their ground, grappling hand to hand with the Georgians. One Confederate seized the flag of the 4th Michigan Infantry but was shot dead by the regiment's commander, Colonel Harrison Jeffords. As Jeffords snatched up the fallen banner, he was run through by a Confederate bayonet and killed. At last, with the help of a fresh V Corps division, the Federals were able to restore Birney's line between the Wheat Field and the Devil's Den.

Barksdale Charges the Orchard

Preoccupied with the assault against their left flank, both Generals Sickles and Meade had either ignored or been

ignorant of the menace to the Peach Orchard. Yet even as fighting raged in the Wheat Field, the Confederates on McLaws' left had launched an attack from the woods west of the orchard. Leading that assault was Brigadier General William Barksdale, a barrel-chested former U.S. Congressman from Mississippi who had what one of his men called "a thirst for battle glory." Barksdale had pleaded with McLaws and Longstreet to be allowed to enter the fray, and around 6:30 p.m., Longstreet at last ordered Barksdale to advance.

Drums began to roll, and Barksdale rode to the front of his old regiment, the 13th Mississippi, to take his place before its flag. As he turned toward the enemy, an aide saw that his face was "radiant with joy." From 1,600 throats came the rebel yell, and out of the covering woods burst the Mississippians. "At top speed," recalled one of them, "without firing a shot the brigade sped swiftly across the field and literally reached the goal." A Federal

colonel recalled the enemy's urgent lunge as "the grandest charge that was ever made by mortal man." The gray tide bore down on the apex of the Peach Orchard salient, which was held by General Charles K. Graham's men.

The Confederates smashed down the rail fences along both sides of the road and soon were through the Federal line and into the Peach Orchard. Covered by their infantry support, the Federal artillery batteries began pulling back. Graham was wounded; he fought on until his horse fell and threw him heavily to the ground. Then, dazed and bleeding, he was taken prisoner. In only minutes the brigade had lost 740 of its 1,516 men.

In that attack, the Federal III Corps would lose the services of its headstrong leader. On horseback near his headquarters, a farmhouse owned by the Trostle Family about a quarter mile north of the Wheat Field, Sickles was hit by a solid shot that left his right leg dangling below the knee by a few shreds of flesh. He lost the leg—but

Saving the Flag
Don Troiani's painting shows Colonel Harrison Jeffords of the 4th Michigan Infantry, at center, fighting to save a furled Union flag amid desperate hand-to-hand combat in the Wheat Field

he lived to conduct a long feud with Meade over the efficacy of the III Corps' advance to the Peach Orchard.

The rout of Graham's division in the salient now exposed the flank of Caldwell's forces down by the Wheat Field, enabling Wofford's Georgians to push the Federals back there. From the II Corps lines on Cemetery Ridge, Lieutenant Frank A. Haskell, an aide to Brigadier General John Gibbon, watched the Confederate onslaught in despair. "The III Corps is being overpowered," Haskell would recall later. But he was incorrect:

had Haskell looked closer, he would have seen that part of III Corps—the division commanded by Brigadier General Humphreys along the salient's north leg—was retiring in good order, fighting fiercely as it went, under fierce attack from fresh rebel brigades.

With the unleashing of Barksdale and Wofford, Longstreet had put all the available units of his corps into action, and Lee's echelon sequence now passed to Hill's corps—specifically, to the division commanded by General Anderson, who got his right flank into action shortly after Barksdale swept over the Peach Orchard. Attacking in rapid succession across the Emmitsburg Road, Anderson's brigades under the reliable Brigadier General Cadmus M. Wilcox and Colonel David Lang slammed into Humphreys' isolated line at about the same time, overlapping it on both flanks and shoving it back toward Cemetery Ridge.

Yet Humphreys managed to keep his troops more or less in hand, riding up and down his ragged line, steadying the men. "Twenty times," Humphreys recalled, "did I bring my men to a halt and face about." At last he got the survivors to the crest of Cemetery Ridge, where they helped fill at least part of the hole left earlier by the departure of Caldwell's division. Humphreys had lost more than 2,000 of his 5,000 men on the fields between the Emmitsburg Road and Cemetery Ridge. In one regiment, the 120th New York, 17 officers had fallen.

Battles for Cemetery Ridge

Still the Confederate blows continued. Now two more of Anderson's brigades attacked, north of Humphreys' former position. The 1,413 Confederates under Brigadier General Ambrose R. Wright made dramatic progress. At the Emmitsburg Road, Wright's men came up against two Federal regiments posted near the Codori Family farmhouse and barn. Wright swept this opposition aside, then paused before pressing his attack on Cemetery Ridge. The Federal left and center were in mortal danger. But the stubborn resistance in the Wheat Field and on Humphreys' front had gained for the Federal leaders what they needed most—the time to rush reinforcements from the quiet side of their hook-shaped line.

General Meade sent two additional V Corps brigades from Culp's and Cemetery hills to consolidate the shaky position on Little Round Top. And out of reserve came three of Sedgwick's VI Corps brigades, right on time, though exhausted by their marathon overnight march. Meanwhile, Federal artillery chief Hunt was scrounging for guns to defend an improvised line on a low rise just east of Plum Run, between the Peach Orchard and Cemetery Ridge. As the Confederate attack began to develop, General Hancock was skillfully juggling his II Corps units to strengthen the Cemetery Ridge line.

Thus, as the Confederate brigades trotted across the fields south of Gettysburg and flung themselves at the enemy, they were time and again confronted by reinforcements that had arrived only moments before. The Confederates who had broken through at the Wheat

★ Major General Daniel Sickles

Federal commander George Meade was surprised—and then furious—when he heard around 3 p.m. on July 2 that General Daniel Sickles had taken it upon himself to move his 10,000 troops away from the position assigned them atop Cemetery Ridge in order to occupy a more forward position that formed a salient on the Western front of the Union line. Sickles' new line ran south along the Emmitsburg Road, across a crest marked by a peach orchard at the Trostle Farm and angling southeast to join the tumble of boulders known as Devil's Den. Many of the day's most furious encounters were fought along this position. Sickles, a colorful and highly opinionated New York City politician who had served in the U.S. House of Representatives before the war began, was guilty of disregarding his orders.

When he was informed of Sickles' actions, Meade rode in haste to meet him. Finding Sickles near the orchard, the Union commander could barely restrain his temper. "General," said Meade, "I am afraid you are too far out." When Sickles tried to explain that he had gained the advantage of higher ground, Meade ridiculed his argument in front of other officers. By then, Sickles himself was having some second thoughts. But just as he offered to withdraw his corps to its original position, a shell burst nearby. "I wish to God you could [move]," Meade shouted over the din, "but those people will not permit it!" At that moment Meade's horse, Old Baldy, maddened by the shellfire, bolted and galloped off. The battle on this front had begun.

Many scholars and historians argue that Sickles' unauthorized gambit worked in the Union's favor: by introducing a surprise element that disrupted and delayed Longstreet's attack on the Union left, it helped undermine Robert E. Lee's plan for the day's battle. Others simply denounce Sickles as a loose cannon. He was awarded a Medal of Honor, but he paid a steep price: he lost his right leg after being wounded at the Peach Orchard.

Always a larger-than-life figure, Sickles had shot and killed prominent Washington attorney Philip Barton Key in 1859, after Sickles discovered that the son of Francis Scott Key was conducting an affair with his wife. But a jury found Sickles not guilty due to temporary insanity, a first in American jurisprudence. Returning to serve in the House in 1893, Sickles performed a final service for his nation: he helped preserve the Gettysburg battlefield for posterity.

Glancing towards the Peach Orchard on my right, I saw that the Confederates had come through and were forming a line 200 yards distant, extending back ... as far as I could see ... No friendly supports of any kind were in sight, but Johnnie Rebs in great numbers.

—Captain John Bigelow,
9th Massachusetts
Light Artillery

Field, for example, pursued the Federal survivors toward Little Round Top. Later, one Confederate would claim that "nothing but the exhausted condition of the men prevented them from carrying the heights." But in fact it was recently arrived troops of the Pennsylvania Reserve Division who turned the tide, charging down the hill and driving the Confederates back to the Wheat Field.

To the north, Barksdale's strong assault had also run into trouble. After sweeping across the Peach Orchard, Barksdale veered slightly to his left. Waving his sword and still shouting as he urged his men forward, he led his brigade toward the Trostle Farm. There, the Mississippians met surprisingly stiff opposition from some skilled Federal artillerymen.

In their fighting retreat from the Peach Orchard, four Federal batteries had lost so many horses that some of their cannons had to be hauled off by hand. The batteries, commanded by Lieutenant Colonel Freeman McGilvery of Maine, paused near the Trostle Barn and briefly checked the advance of the 21st Mississippi, one of Barksdale's regiments. Then, under pressure on his front and both flanks, McGilvery again hauled his guns back—this time to the rise east of Plum Run—leaving at the Trostle Farm a Massachusetts battery of six 12-pounders under Captain John Bigelow.

In the next moments, Bigelow's tough troops heroically checked Barksdale's advance long enough to allow the enterprising McGilvery to round up more cannons and form a stronger artillery line on a little ridge beyond Plum Run. McGilvery's cannons held off the Confederates until 7:15 p.m., when—once again—Federal reinforcements arrived. Colonel George C. Burling's brigade, detached from Humphreys' command, reached the Plum Run line and set up in position to support McGilvery's guns. In addition, Colonel George L. Willard's brigade of General Alexander Hays' division arrived from the northern end of the II Corps position on Cemetery Ridge.

Willard's brigade, led by General Hancock himself, charged down the slope of the ridge, crashed through the elderberry thickets that lined the stream and struck the center of Barksdale's brigade. Willard went down in the assault, decapitated by a shell. But the Confederates were badly shaken and slowly began to fall back.

Barksdale strove to rally his Mississippians, but then he too was shot from his saddle. According to Battle of Gettysburg lore, a Federal officer ordered an entire company to fire at the burly, inspirational Confederate commander. True or not, Barksdale's chest and legs were rid-

dled with bullets, and he died of his wounds that night.

Even as Barksdale's men broke for the rear, however, General Hancock saw trouble to the north: Wilcox's Confederate brigade was heading straight for the gap on Cemetery Ridge that had been left when Caldwell's division departed for the Wheat Field. As Federal troops raced to the scene, Hancock came upon a small regiment poised for action, the 1st Minnesota under Colonel William Colvill, and ordered them to stop Wilcox's advance. As Lieutenant William Lochren of the 1st Minnesota recalled, "Every man realized in an instant what that order meant: death or wounds to us all, the sacrifice of the regiment to gain a few minutes' time and save the position."

Even so, they charged, one undersized regiment against

"Forward!" *After a series of delays, Confederates led by Barksdale launch their attack against the Union salient near the Peach Orchard in this Edwin Forbes painting. The Trostle Barn was used as a hospital after fighting ceased on this front*

an entire brigade, down the ridge with muskets at a right shoulder shift, their bayonets flashing. Just before they reached the Confederate lines, Colvill shouted, "Charge bayonets," and the muskets were lowered, presenting a solid front of steel. Wrote Lochren: "The men were never made who will stand against leveled bayonets coming with such momentum and evident desperation. The ferocity of our onset seemed to paralyze them for a time."

The Confederate line crumbled. Of the 262 Minnesotans who had so fearlessly hurled themselves at Wilcox's brigade, only 47 men remained fit for combat. This toll, 82% of those engaged, was the highest casualty rate of any Union regiment in the war.

After Barksdale's magnificent advance was finally re-

pelled, two more Confederate divisions—Georgians under General Wright and Mississippians under Brigadier General Carnot Posey—also bogged down under superior Federal energy and manpower, and the aggressive, young Pender lost his life as he tried to rally them.

With these two divisions stalled, Lee's carefully planned but severely disrupted echelon sequence broke down completely around 8 p.m. Surprisingly, several commanding officers—including Generals Richard Anderson, A.P. Hill and Lee himself—had been little more than spectators during the complicated attack on the Federal left. One observer later reported that Lee had sent only one dispatch, and received only one, during the entire battle. A member of Lee's staff said later, "The whole affair was disjointed. There was an utter absence of accord in the movements of the several commands."

Ewell's Tardy Attack Fails

Amid all the glories and horrors of the battle on the rebel right, General Ewell, on the Confederates' extreme left, had frittered away the afternoon hours. Since midmorning, most of Ewell's troops had been in place and ready to accomplish their primary mission—to pin down the Federal forces on Culp's and Cemetery hills and prevent them from going to the aid of Federal units being attacked by Longstreet and Hill. As General Ewell waited his turn to act, he did nothing to prepare for his demonstration in force beyond tinkering with his artillery emplacements, not even discussing plans for the demonstration with his subordinates, Generals Edward ("Allegheny") Johnson, Jubal Early and Robert E. Rodes.

Meanwhile, the men waited, restless and chafing in the hot sun. "Greatly did the officers and men marvel," recalled an officer of Stonewall Jackson's old division, "as morning, noon and afternoon passed in inaction—on our part, not on the enemy's, for, as we well know, he was plying axe and pick and shovel in fortifying a position which was already sufficiently formidable."

Longstreet's late charge should have been the reveille for Ewell's demonstration. Yet when at length Ewell did stir, it was not with a display of infantry might but with an artillery barrage. For more than two hours, while Longstreet's and Hill's divisions were battering themselves into bloody exhaustion, Ewell's guns atop Benner's Hill blasted away fruitlessly at Federal positions on nearby Cemetery and Culp's hills. Finally, the rebel batteries were ground down and withdrew around 6:30 p.m. All this time, Federal troops led by a master engineer, Brigadier General George Sears Greene, a 62-year-old general with the gaunt face of an Old Testament prophet, were erecting strong fortifications atop the slopes.

At that inauspicious moment, Ewell decided to launch not a demonstration but a full-scale infantry attack. He had already failed to do what Lee had asked of him; most of the Federal forces on Culp's Hill and roughly half of the units on Cemetery Hill had gone to bolster the Federal left. Darkness was closing in by the time Johnson's troops—led by General George ("Maryland") Steuart on the left, Brigadier General John M. Jones to the center and Colonel J.M. Williams on the right—got to the eastern foot of Culp's Hill.

On came the Confederates, clambering up the steep, boulder-strewn hill, darting from tree to tree. As the brigades of Williams and Jones neared the Federal works, reinforcements arrived to bolster Greene's line, and the rebels fell back to the base of Culp's Hill. Three times Williams and Jones re-formed and attacked, the flash of their muskets illuminating the pitch-black night, and each time they were repulsed. Steuart's brigade fared somewhat better, occupying several trenches left unmanned by the Federals, but the Confederates in them were pinned down by musket fire through the night.

The rebels weren't finished—yet. Jubal Early had put in motion the Louisiana brigade of General Harry T. Hays and the North Carolina brigade of Colonel Isaac E. Avery. Eager for action, they made some headway against the Federal positions in the low "saddle" between Culp's and Cemetery hills. For pure fighting ferocity, Hays' Louisiana Tigers had few equals in either army, and they seized a Federal gun battery position. But again General Hancock had a response at hand: he sent troops led by the capable 30-year-old Colonel Samuel Sprigg Carroll to the scene, and the Tigers were forced to retreat down Culp's Hill. That ended the day's fighting.

Meade Holds a Council of War

It was then about 10:30 p.m. The uproar of the previous six and a half hours had subsided, although now and then the spiteful crack of a picket's musket could be heard above the moans and sobs of the wounded who lay sprawled by the thousands on the slopes and meadows south of Gettysburg. Yet there was little respite for the ranking generals of the Federal army; Meade had summoned them to a council of war.

That afternoon, watching the sullen Confederate withdrawal from Cemetery Ridge, Meade had been understandably elated. "It is all right now!" he had shouted to the men around him. "It is all right now!" Later, at about 8 p.m., he had sent off a sober message to Washington: "I shall remain in my present position tomorrow."

Meade's council began around 11 p.m., with at least a dozen generals crowded into the 10-ft. by 12-ft. front room of his farmhouse headquarters. Illuminated by the flickering light of a single candle on a small pine table, the little parlor was soon clouded with cigar smoke.

At first the conversation was informal, with the generals trading notes on the day's battles. At length General Daniel Butterfield, Meade's chief of staff, wearied of the rambling talk. He got out a pencil and some paper and suggested that the generals give answers to three ques-

George ("Maryland") Steuart

Why "Maryland"? The nickname helped distinguish in conversation the infantry general from Maryland and the famed cavalry commander from Virginia, Jeb Stuart.

Steuart was badly injured during the Shenandoah Valley campaign of 1862 and rejoined Lee's army just before Gettysburg. He was present when Lee surrendered in 1865

tions: Should the Federal army retreat or remain where it was? If it stayed, should it attack or continue to stand on the defensive? And if the decision were to await an assault by Lee, how long should they wait?

In answer to the first question, the generals were of a single opinion, most forcibly expressed by Slocum: "Stay and fight it out." As for launching an immediate offensive, all were opposed. The third question—how long they should wait for Lee to act—drew a variety of responses, ranging from a few hours to a day. Then Meade, who had remained generally silent, brought the session to a conclusion: The Army of the Potomac would remain in place—and would fight Lee when he attacked.

Would Lee fight again? On July 2, in only eight hours of battle, his losses were some 6,500 killed, missing or wounded, while Meade had lost some 9,000—totals slightly more than those of July 1. As U.S. Naval Academy historian Craig L. Symonds argues in *History of the*

Battle of Gettysburg (2004), "Nowhere else in the war was there such a concentration of death as in the late afternoon and evening of July 2, 1863. Though the one-day Battle at Antietam, fought the previous September, had been bloodier, that battle had begun at dawn and lasted all day. At Gettysburg, the serious fighting on July 2 had not started until four o'clock in the afternoon ... [making] Gettysburg ... by far the bloodiest battle in American history to date, surpassing even Antietam. And, despite that, the outcome was still very much in doubt."

Indeed it was. As his staff meeting broke up, Meade turned to General Gibbon, whose II Corps division had held the center of the Federal line. "If Lee attacks tomorrow," he said, "it will be on your front." Asked why he thought so, Meade replied with a prophetic reading of Robert E. Lee's mind: "Because he has made attacks on both our flanks and failed, and if he concludes to try it again, it will be on our center." ∎

> We steadily advanced, driving the enemy before us until we reached the houses with the trees on the left; the trees proved to be a peach orchard.
>
> —*Major George B. Gerald, 18th Mississippi Infantry*

Wake of the fray *Taken days after the battle, this photograph shows dead horses lying outside the Trostle Farmhouse, home to Abraham and Catherine Trostle and their nine children. The Trostles counted 16 dead horses near the house and some 100 more on the farm grounds.*

The building was purchased by the U.S. government and is still standing at Gettysburg

The Commanders

JOHN BELL HOOD

Hood's destiny seemed written in his long, woebegone face. Poet Stephen Vincent Benét described him as a "Viking shape of a man," while the noted Southern diarist Mary Chesnut, who came to know Hood in Richmond after he was wounded at Gettysburg, wrote of his "sad Quixote face, the face of an old Crusader." Few generals in the war fought as fiercely as Hood, and few who survived surmounted such physical obstacles: he lost the use of his left arm at Gettysburg in an artillery barrage, and his right leg was amputated when he was wounded at the Battle of Chickamauga in September 1863, where he helped lead the Confederates to victory.

Hood was also one of the war's most traveled commanders: in 1862 he fought in the battles of Eltham's Landing and Gaines' Mill in the Peninsula Campaign, as well as at the Second Battle of Bull Run (Manassas), Antietam and Fredericksburg, although he did not see action at Chancellorsville in 1863. He was sent to the Western theater

of war after Gettysburg, where he lost his leg at Chickamauga. Even so, he returned to the saddle to play major roles in the failed Confederate defense against Sherman in Atlanta and then led a campaign against Union forces in Tennessee.

Hood's trajectory in the war traces a perfect bell curve: an unknown when the war began, he gradually ascended in the Confederate ranks, reaching the apex of his career at Chickamauga. Yet when he was entrusted with the all-important defense of Atlanta and then the difficult task of holding Tennessee, his efforts ended in defeat and disgrace.

As the Confederates retreated before Sherman's advance from Chattanooga upon Atlanta in 1864, Hood replaced General Joseph E. Johnston, whom he had criticized as timid. Only 33 at the time, Hood became the youngest Confederate officer to lead an army, but his four headlong assaults on Sherman failed, at the cost of thousands of lives. He was forced to flee, burning the city as Union troops moved in.

Hood fared no better when he led a campaign intended to lure Sherman into battle back in Tennessee. Sherman refused the bait, continuing his March to the Sea and sending General George H. Thomas to lead Federal forces against Hood. At the Battle of Franklin, Hood sent thousands of soldiers to their deaths in a reckless, failed frontal assault; two weeks later, he was defeated again by Thomas at the Battle of Nashville. Hood lost his command and the war ended, but his luck never improved: the "sad Quixote" died in 1879 in a yellow fever epidemic in New Orleans, where he had settled after the war.

RICHARD H. ANDERSON

Born in South Carolina in 1821 and an 1842 graduate of West Point, Anderson followed the path of so many Civil War leaders, winning praise for his deeds in the Mexican War and then serving along the Western frontier. He won Robert E. Lee's approval, and a promotion to major general, in the Peninsula Campaign early in 1862. He fought well at the Second Battle of Bull Run, and also at the deadliest front at Antietam, along Bloody Lane, where he was wounded in the leg. In May 1863, he engaged the Federal right flank at Chancellorsville, allowing Stonewall Jackson to execute his surprise attack on the Union left.

Anderson's divisions arrived late on July 1 at Gettysburg, and on July 2 he was at the center of the breakdown in Lee's planned echelon attack on Cemetery Ridge, when his units failed to follow up on the rebels' breach of the Union center. Chronicler Shelby Foote concluded, "The fault was primarily Anderson's." He salvaged his reputation with strong service in 1864, but his postwar career was far from illustrious. He died in 1879.

EDWARD ("ALLEGHENY") JOHNSON

For Johnson, a Virginia-born graduate of West Point and veteran of the Mexican War, the Civil War was a series of strange reverses and long periods on the sidelines. Leading six Georgia divisions at a battle on Allegheny Mountain late in 1861, he earned his nickname and the respect of Robert E. Lee. Serving under Stonewall Jackson, he took a bullet in his foot early in 1862 and spent long months recuperating in Richmond.

Johnson returned to active duty after Chancellorsville, taking command of Jackson's famed Stonewall Division. Serving under Richard S. Ewell at Gettysburg, he decided not to attack Culp's Hill late on July 1, even as Ewell chose not to vie for Cemetery Ridge. Johnson's units pressed hard against the hill on July 2 and 3, but the Federals' strong fortifications held them off. Taken prisoner at the Battle of Spotsylvania in 1864, Johnson was exchanged, but he was captured yet again at the Battle of Nashville late in 1864 and spent the last months of the war in the Old Capital Prison in Washington.

WILLIAM BARKSDALE

Unlike so many of the Confederate generals in the Civil War, the Tennessee-born Barksdale did not graduate from West Point. But he did enlist in the army in the Mexican War and served with distinction. Trained as a lawyer, he became the editor of a pro-slavery newspaper in Mississippi, then served in the U.S. House of Representatives, where he was among the rabid Southern "fire-eaters" who advocated secession.

Forty in 1861, Barksdale was given command of a regiment of Mississippians that fought well in the Peninsula Campaign of 1862, where he took part in an early version of Pickett's Charge, a failed Confederate attempt to assault a fortified, uphill Federal position. His units won praise for their fighting at Fredericksburg and Chancellorsville, but nothing became Barksdale so much as his death at Gettysburg on July 2. His headlong attack at the Peach Orchard was one of the most stirring moments in a battle filled with them: leading his troops on horseback, he was hit three times, and he asked an aide to tell his wife and children he had "died fighting at my post."

JOHN C. CALDWELL

Born in Vermont, Caldwell moved to Maine as a young man. Like another general from New England who fought at Gettysburg, Joshua Chamberlain, Caldwell was an academic, the principal of a boarding academy, who had no military experience before he enlisted in the Union Army at age 28 after the war broke out.

Yet Caldwell took to his new career: he was elected a colonel of his unit of Maine infantry volunteers and was promoted to brigadier general when his superior, Oliver O. Howard, was wounded in the Peninsula Campaign of 1862. But his troops were unable to withstand the onslaught of Confederate troops at the Bloody Lane at Antietam, and three months later they fled before advancing Confederates at the stone wall on Marye's Heights at the Battle of Fredericksburg.

Meanwhile, rumors circulated that Caldwell had cowered in the woods at Antietam—and when his units were routed in the Wheat Field at Gettysburg on July 2, his reputation was savaged. After the war he served as a U.S. diplomat in South America for decades.

WILLIAM J. COLVILL

There were many heroes wearing the Federal blue on July 2 at Gettysburg, but only one them was under military arrest on the morning of the battle. That man was Colonel Colvill, commander of the 1st Minnesota Infantry Division. By nightfall, Colvill had been freed, placed back in command of his troops, and led them in one of the most celebrated single charges of the war, when Winfield Scott Hancock asked him to perform a suicide mission at Cemetery Ridge: attack a rapidly advancing Confederate force five times larger than his, in order to gain five minutes for more Federals to arrive on the scene. Colvill was wounded twice, receiving injuries that would partially disable him for life. Then again, he was one of the lucky ones: of the 262 men he led racing downhill into battle, only 47 survived, most of them badly wounded.

If Colvill's downhill assault was larger than life, so was Colvill himself. At 6 ft. 5 in., he was an inch taller than President Lincoln (but two inches shorter than Solomon Meredith of the Iron Brigade). Perhaps it was his commanding size that led his fellow volunteers in Red Wing, Minn., to elect Colvill the captain of their group when war broke out. Colvill, who was born in New York State in 1830, was not a military man by trade: he was a lawyer and newspaper editor who supported the Union.

Colvill led the 1st Minnesota division when it was one of the few Union units to perform well at the First Battle of Bull Run (Manassas). He was wounded in the shoulder in the Peninsula Campaign, promoted to major, and again was noted for his bravery at Antietam—though a

few months later, his troops were among those that plundered Fredericksburg when Union troops took control of the town.

Colvill's men saw little action at Fredericksburg and Chancellorsville. As his unit shadowed Lee's movement north in June 1863, it tangled with Jeb Stuart's cavalry. That's when Colvill was arrested for allowing his men to cross a stream by walking across it on logs rather than wading, per their orders—the sort of bureaucratic nonsense that would never have happened in Lee's army. He was released just in time to become one of the Union's saviors.

Colvill returned to Minnesota after the war, where he lived until 1905, always refusing to play the hero. In one account, when a local woman demanded he tell the story of his famous charge, he demurred, prompting her to scold him: "Well, Colonel, I guess you wasn't in it at all; you just sat on a fence and watched it."

Joshua Lawrence Chamberlain

MAJOR GENERAL, ARMY OF THE POTOMAC

★

ONLY EIGHT WEEKS BEFORE THEY clashed at Gettysburg, the Confederacy's Army of Northern Virginia and the Union's Army of the Potomac locked horns at Chancellorsville, Va. In what has been called Robert E. Lee's perfect battle, the Confederate general defied military convention by dividing his army in the face of a numerically superior foe, sending Stonewall Jackson's corps of soldiers on a long, secret flanking march around the Union position, then dealing them a smashing surprise blow that once again demonstrated the superiority of Confederate generals in the war. It was one of Lee's greatest victories—among many—but the day's joy was tempered for the Confederates when General Jackson was hit by friendly fire on the night of his triumph and died eight days later.

The mourning for Jackson in the South was extravagant—so extravagant that it highlighted a glaring truth about the opposing sides in the war: thanks to its long string of battlefield successes, the South had a full complement of heroic warriors to admire, while the North was badly in need of a few American idols. Out west, far from the newspapers of the East Coast, General Ulysses S. Grant had emerged as a Union stalwart. But in the Virginia theater that commanded the bulk of attention during the conflict, the South boasted such heroes as Jackson, Jeb Stuart and A.P. Hill. In contrast, the Union leaders composed a succession of failures. George B. McClellan, loved by his troops and glorified in the press, turned out to be all swash and no buckle; John Pope, Ambrose Burnside and Joe Hooker each talked a good game but presided, in turn, over the disasters of Second Bull Run (Manassas), Fredericksburg and Chancellorsville.

A Union hero was needed—and Gettysburg at last gave the Federals authentic heroes, none more celebrated than the appealing young professor of rhetoric from Bowdoin College in Maine, Lieutenant Colonel Joshua Lawrence Chamberlain. Handsome, upright and demonstrably brave, Chamberlain was also intelligent, thoughtful and well spoken. In leading the stirring bayonet charge that rebuffed Confederate troops attacking Little Round Top on July 2, Chamberlain won a place for himself as one of the Union's foremost heroes in the war.

Utterly untrained in the military before the war, the erstwhile professor voluntarily enlisted in the Army in 1862 at age 33, over the strenuous objections of Bowdoin's leaders. Born and raised in Brewer, Me., Chamberlain had ancestors who served in the Revolutionary War; his middle name salutes Captain James Lawrence, the U.S. Navy commander who won fame in the War of 1812 by beseeching his men aboard the foundering U.S.S. *Chesapeake,* as he lay dying, "Don't give up the ship!"

Studious and bright, Chamberlain aimed for a career in education or as a missionary: he became fluent in nine foreign languages. After graduating from Bowdoin in 1852, he received a master's degree from the Bangor Theological Seminary and married Frances ("Fanny") Adams, then was offered a position at his alma mater.

After enlisting, Chamberlain studied furiously to become as fluent in military matters as he was in foreign

I am Kilrain of the 20th Maine
　and we fight for Chamberlain.
'Cause he stood right with us when the
　Johnnies came like a banshee on the wind.
When the smoke cleared out of Gettysburg
　many a mother wept.
For many a good boy died there, sure,
　and the air smelled just like death.

I am Kilrain of the 20th Maine
　and I'd march to hell and back again
For Colonel Joshua Chamberlain—
　we're all goin' down to Dixieland.

—Lyrics from Dixieland (1999),
by Steve Earle

tongues. But he gained little experience of battle prior to Gettysburg. He was present at Antietam but didn't serve on the front lines. His baptism by fire came in the Federals' rout at Fredericksburg, where he survived the carnage on Marye's Heights. His unit was sidelined by a smallpox outbreak during the Battle of Chancellorsville.

Chamberlain's pivotal role at Gettysburg was purely a matter of chance: his 20th Maine Regiment was simply in the right place at the right time to defend Little Round Top against the rebel assault on July 2. And his survival was just as much a matter of chance. Consider the fate of the other officers who rallied to defend the heights that evening. When General Gouverneur K. Warren, the engineer who first saw the need to rush troops to the undefended site, sought soldiers for the task, Colonel Strong Vincent, 26, responded immediately—and soon lay dead, shot through the heart in a Confederate volley. Colonel Patrick O'Rorke, 23, of New York, the No. 1 cadet in the West Point class of 1861, also fell early in the struggle. Brigadier General Stephen H. Weed, 29, diverted by Warren to Little Round Top from his assignment to reinforce General Daniel Sickles' position, was shot by a sniper. When Lieutenant Charles Hazlett, 24, commanding two artillery pieces atop the hill, bent to attend to Weed, he was in turn fatally shot in the head. Colonel William C. Oates, the leader of the Confederates at Little Round Top, later wrote, "The blood stood in puddles in some places on the rocks."

Chamberlain survived the battle, and he soon found himself dubbed "The Lion of Little Round Top." He was given command of a full brigade, and when he was shot through the hip and groin and the wound threatened his life at Petersburg in 1864, he was promoted to brigadier general by General Ulysses S. Grant. But Chamberlain survived that wound, as he did the five others he received in the conflict, and he served out the war with distinction as a top aide to Grant. At Appomattox, Grant honored Chamberlain by designating him to be the Union officer to accept the Confederate surrender. The erstwhile professor understood the rhetoric of military honor: he ordered the Union troops to doff their caps and stand at full attention to receive the Confederate arms. ∎

Honors *When Joshua Chamberlain was wounded for the sixth time in 1865, President Lincoln promoted him to major general. In 1893 he was awarded the Medal of Honor.*

After the war, the hero won four one-year terms as governor of Maine. He then returned to Bowdoin, serving as its president for 12 years. His home in Brunswick, Me., above, is now a museum

Medicine at Gettysburg: Battling the Bloodbath

By Jeffrey Kluger

I T DOESN'T TAKE LONG TO CUT OFF A LEG—maybe 15 minutes, if you know what you're doing. That's saying something, since cutting off a leg requires a lot more skill than merely being able to handle a saw. Muscle has to be cut away, veins and arteries have to be tied off, and when the only anesthetic you've got is chloroform, you need two more people to restrain the patient, and yet another to hold the limb steady as the doctor works. During the course of the Civil War, there were 29,990 amputations—of fingers, toes, arms, legs, even hip joints—and that was on the Union side alone. Roughly double it, and you

get the total of all the boys who survived the fighting but came out of it grievously incomplete. And amputations, of course, were only a small part of the toll.

The Civil War did not occur during the dark ages of medicine. Antonie van Leeuwenhoek first observed bacteria in 1676, a full 185 years before the hostilities between the North and South broke out. The smallpox vaccine was developed in 1796. The modern science of epidemiology was born in 1848, through the work of British physician John Snow, who later famously traced a London cholera outbreak to a single handle on a single water pump in one of the city's working-class wards.

But the Civil War was another kind of medical challenge entirely. Set 3.2 million men to murdering one another in the rain and muck and cold and the feverish heat of summer for more than four years, and you're going to lose a whole lot of them. About 620,000 men were killed in the course of the fighting: 206,000 from wounds and

416,000 from sicknesses that included typhus, typhoid, dysentery, pneumonia, measles, mumps, malaria, gangrene and surgical infections of all kinds.

The slaughter served a purpose, of course: it saved a nation and freed 4 million human beings from bondage. Less appreciated is how the lessons learned in the makeshift hospitals and surgical tents of the war forever changed—and improved—the practice of medicine, both on and off the battlefield. Never was that truer than during the Battle of Gettysburg.

Part of what made the Civil War the bloodbath it became was the advance of weapons technology. Canister shells stuffed with lead shot were designed to detonate

---

Kluger is the science editor of TIME *magazine and the co-author of* New Frontiers of Space (2013), *from* TIME Books. *With astronaut Jim Lovell, Kluger is the co-author of* Apollo 13, *the story of the aborted 1970 moon mission that was made into a 1995 film*

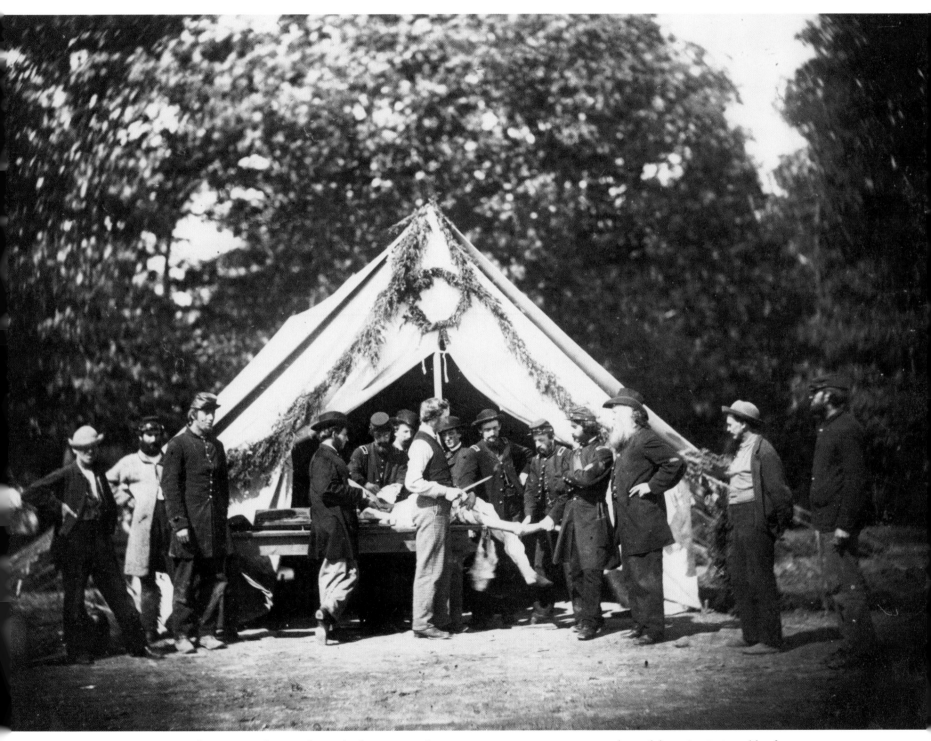

The operation *Spectators and assistants gather outside a medical tent at Gettysburg, as a surgeon prepares to amputate a leg, and the patient is given chloroform*

and scatter, shredding anything in their way. Massive cannonballs, some weighing up to 43 lbs., could be hurled with lethal ease by equally robust new cannons. There might have been nothing that did more damage to the men in the field, however, than the simple Minié ball, a 1-in. soft-lead, low-velocity bullet that was designed not just to penetrate the body but also to explode and expand there, ripping tissue and shattering bone. A Minié ball in the vitals would cause a man to bleed out the way an ordinary bullet wouldn't; a well-aimed hit in a limb would mean certain amputation.

Soldiers who were wounded and didn't die immediately faced additional dangers. During the 1862 Battle of Antietam, the bloodiest single day of the war, an estimated 17,300 men were wounded, yet there were no more than two functioning triage stations, or hospital tents, to tend to them. In the Second Battle of Bull Run (Manassas) in 1862, some of the wounded lay in the field for more than four days before they were found and carried off—assuming they survived the wait in the first place.

All that began to change with Gettysburg—thanks in no small part to Jonathan Letterman, a Union Army doc-

tor. Named medical director of the Army of the Potomac in 1862, he was given a free hand to fix what ailed the battlefield hospitals and ensure that while men might still die of their wounds, they would never again die due to the quality of care they were receiving. To that end, he set up a multitiered system of recovery and treatment.

Horse-drawn ambulances equipped with bandages, medicines, clean water and surgical tools would be arrayed at the edges of the battlefields before the fighting began and would be dispatched into the thick of things, often while the bullets were still flying. Receiving and

surgical stations would be set up in wooded or otherwise well-concealed areas as little as 50 yds. from the field, where immediately life-threatening injuries could be tended to. Farther away—perhaps a mile from the fighting—field hospitals would be established in any available building well in advance of the battle and would receive the solders who had been stabilized in the field.

Rail or long-distance horse-drawn transportation would be available within a reasonable ride from the field hospitals, so that soldiers could be transferred farther up the medical chain, to established hospitals

Racing against time
Above, medics in Zouave pants practice loading patients onto carriages for removal from the battlefield. The Letterman system, pioneered by Army of the Potomac medical chief Letterman, stressed speedy removal of the wounded for treatment at nearby triage centers

in cities like Philadelphia and Baltimore. This rolling processing of the injured would not only keep them well looked after but also ensure that there was always a bed or cot or surgical table available. And to help the medical teams handle the load, the ranks of surgeons and—critically—nurses would be dramatically increased.

The Letterman system was tried successfully on multiple battlefields in 1862 and 1863, but it was Gettysburg that gave it its sternest test. In the Union XI Corps alone, 100 ambulances, nine heavy medical wagons and 270 medics (with the help of 260 horses) carried wounded Federals to first-aid stations and tented field hospitals. More than 270 of these stations ringed the battlefield. A more permanent facility was built near a railroad station on the York Pike, filled with beds, clean linens and medical equipment and staffed with nurses. Thousands of men poured into the hospital—which was dubbed Camp Letterman—and up to 800 were successfully treated and shipped to the cities for further care every day. The fact that more than 3,000 Union soldiers and 4,700 Confederates died during the three days of fighting is a mark of how savage the clash was. But the fact that a high percentage of the more than 14,000 Federals who came under Letterman's care survived their wounds is equal testimony to how innovative—and just plain courageous—his methods were.

"Many a time did I see stretcher-carriers fired upon and wounded while bearing away the wounded," reported Lieutenant John S. Sullivan of the 14th Indiana regiment, after observing Letterman and his men at work. "But they did not desist from their humane work; and many a time did I watch anxiously, fearing every moment to see [a medic] fall. He coolly rode all over the field … not satisfied to see a single suffering man uncared for on the bloody field."

That legacy has endured. Civil War and medical historians agree that every field hospital off the beaches at Normandy, every MASH unit in Korea, every evac helicopter and fortified hospital in Afghanistan, has its roots in what is still known as the Letterman system. Modern drugs, high-tech equipment and state-of-the-art surgical techniques came much later, and can hardly be credited to a single Pennsylvania doctor born nearly 190 years ago. But if you can't get the soldiers off the battlefield and into the hands of the people who can care for them, you have no one to save in the first place. War is a grotesque business. Medical science—and medical people like Jonathan Letterman—bring it a bit of grace. ■

Surgeon's friend *The surgical saw above, tough enough to cut through bones and ligaments, was used to perform amputations during the war.*

At right is a recovery ward at the Armory Square Hospital, built in 1862 on the National Mall in Washington. The building stood until 1964, when it was torn down. Today the National Air and Space Museum occupies the hospital's former site

JULY 3, 1863

THE REGIMENT ASSISTED IN REPULSING THE
CHARGE OF THE ENEMY ON THIS LINE AT
THIS POINT AND IN CAPTURING MANY STANDARDS
AND PRISONERS

DURING THE CANNONADING PRECEDING THE CHARGE
THE REGIMENT WAS IN LINE 60 YARDS TO THE LEFT AND REAR
OF THIS MONUMENT WHEN THE REBELS FOUND THE TROOPS
FROM THEY LEFT LINES FOUGHT THEIR WAY TO THE FRONT
AND OCCUPIED THE WALL

PRESENT AT GETTYSBURG 452 KILLED AND DIED OF WOUNDS 46
WOUNDED 172 MISSING 3
TOTAL OF KILLED WOUNDED AND MISSING 192

72ND PENNA INFANTRY

July 3, 1863

Battlefield Guide: July 3, 1863

Artillery Guide

Civil War field artillery was organized into batteries of four to six guns. Regulations prescribed a captain as battery commander, while lieutenants commanded two-gun "sections." Manning each gun was a platoon, under a sergeant ("chief of the piece"), with eight crewmen and six drivers.

During transportation, each gun was attached to a limber, drawn by a six-horse team. The limber chest carried 30 to 50 rounds of ammunition. Each gun was assigned at least one caisson, also drawn by a six-horse team, which carried additional ammunition in its two chests, as well as a spare wheel and tools. A horse-drawn forge and a battery wagon with tools accompanied each battery.

A battery at full regulation strength might exceed 100 officers and men and 100 to 150 horses. A veteran unit could unlimber and fire an initial volley in about one minute.

Military Lexicon

caisson: A two-wheeled cart that carried two ammunition chests, tools and a spare wheel for artillery pieces. The caisson could be attached to a limber, which would allow both to be pulled by a team of horses.

double envelopment: A pincer movement on the battlefield, in which two units attack either side of an enemy force trapped between them.

double quick: A command to move faster, or "on the double."

grape: Technically called grapeshot, these are small metal balls packed in a case, then fired from a cannon to create a shotgun effect. Grape is like canister shot but with smaller balls packed into a metal case.

guide center: A command for marching or attacking soldiers to follow the lead of a person at the forward center of a unit.

Timeline

4:30 a.m. Struggle on Culp's Hill ①
Union artillery opens fire at Culp's Hill to prepare for infantry charge on Johnson's captured trenches. Rebels withdraw by 11 a.m.

9 a.m. Confederates move to attack position
Confederate infantry lines form up in woods northwest of the Peach Orchard and await order to charge Cemetery Ridge.

12 noon Stuart launches cavalry attack ②
Three miles east of Gettysburg, Stuart's and Hampton's 6,300 horsemen attack 4,500 Federals in a clash of cavalry. Federals under Custer and Gregg prevent Stuart from diverting Union forces from Cemetery Ridge.

1 p.m. A thunderous salvo ③
More than 150 Confederate guns begin bombarding the Federal center on Cemetery Ridge. Federals return fire.

2:30 p.m. Federal guns go silent
Federal artillery chief Hunt ceases fire in a ruse to draw the Confederate infantry attack.

3 p.m. Pickett consults Longstreet
Pickett asks for the order to launch the frontal assault. Longstreet bows his head to nod assent.

3:30 p.m. Pickett's Charge ④
12,000 Confederates weather resumed Union artillery fire to mount a major assault across Emmitsburg Road upon Hancock's II Corps on Cemetery Ridge. A small group breaks the Federal line at the Angle, but reinforcements plug the gap. The attack fails and last fighting in most areas ceases around 6 p.m.

5:30 p.m. A second cavalry charge ⑤
Southeast of Big Round Top, Federal cavalry troopers under Kilpatrick attack Confederate positions but are turned back, with great losses.

Faces in the Ranks

The Confederacy's famed Texas Brigade also included units from Georgia, South Carolina and other states at various times. The brigade was attached to James Longstreet's corps for much of the war, under the command of General Jerome B. Robertson. The brigade won acclaim at Gettysburg for taking Devil's Den on July 2.

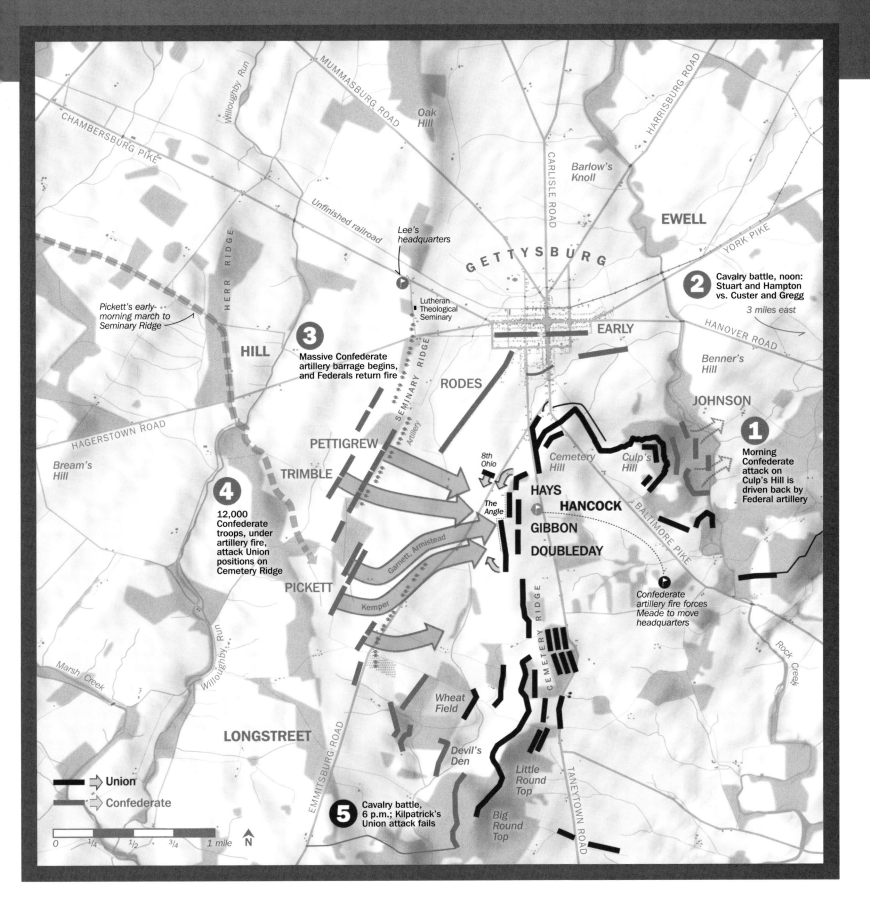

CHAMBERSBURG PIKE

Willoughby Run

MUMMASBURG ROAD

Oak Hill

HARRISBURG ROAD

Unfinished railroad

Lee's headquarters

G E T T Y S B U R G

CARLISLE ROAD

Barlow's Knoll

EWELL

YORK PIKE

Lutheran Theological Seminary

2 Cavalry battle, noon: Stuart and Hampton vs. Custer and Gregg

3 miles east

HILL

3 Massive Confederate artillery barrage begins, and Federals return fire

EARLY

HANOVER ROAD

Benner's Hill

HERR RIDGE

Pickett's early-morning march to Seminary Ridge

RODES

SEMINARY RIDGE

JOHNSON

HAGERSTOWN ROAD

PETTIGREW

Artillery

8th Ohio

Cemetery Hill

Culp's Hill

1 Morning Confederate attack on Culp's Hill is driven back by Federal artillery

Bream's Hill

TRIMBLE

The Angle

HAYS

HANCOCK

BALTIMORE PIKE

4 12,000 Confederate troops, under artillery fire, attack Union positions on Cemetery Ridge

Garnett, Armistead

GIBBON

DOUBLEDAY

Rock Creek

PICKETT

Kemper

Confederate artillery fire forces Meade to move headquarters

Willoughby Run

CEMETERY RIDGE

Marsh Creek

Wheat Field

LONGSTREET

EMMITSBURG ROAD

Devil's Den

Little Round Top

TANEYTOWN ROAD

➡ Union

➡ Confederate

5 Cavalry battle, 6 p.m.; Kilpatrick's Union attack fails

Big Round Top

0   1/4   1/2   3/4   1 mile

N

A Grand Assault Fails On a Bloody Third Day

The final day of combat begins with a gigantic artillery face-off and concludes with a failed infantry charge

E ACH DAY OF FIGHTING AT GETTYSBURG assumed its own distinctive character. The conflicts on July 1 were for the most part utterly impromptu, a series of alarms and excursions dictated not by a general and his staff meeting in grave council before a fray, but rather by officers on horseback, newly arrived at the scene of the fighting and struggling to discern large patterns amid the overwhelming chaos of the moment. The fighting became a battle for geography, as leaders of the two armies fought to gain control of the best positions in the elevated terrain around Gettysburg.

On July 2, with the topography decided and the battle lines drawn, the passage of time drove the story line: the two armies faced off with little action through much of the long, hot day, and the main fighting did not begin until late afternoon, when General James Longstreet at last completed a late-starting, lengthy march southward and attacked the left flank of the Federal line. But once the combat was launched in earnest, shortly after 4 p.m., it raged with a compressed ferocity across a patchwork of distinct fronts for six to seven hours, claiming thousands of lives before finally subsiding into silence.

On July 3, in the third act of this great martial drama, battles for space and time gave way to matters of mass. The rival armies engaged in a set piece of combat that carried echoes of the great Napoleonic Wars of 50 to 60 years before: after a huge artillery duel, one of the war's largest barrages, the Confederates launched a gigantic, old-school infantry assault that might have come straight from a West Point textbook. For once, Confederate commander Robert E. Lee, who had made his reputation by defying by-the-book battle plans, chose to execute a frontal infantry assault on an enemy commanding an elevated, entrenched position. Eyewitnesses remembered the orderly ranks of Confederate soldiers forming their line—almost a full mile in length—and marching across open fields and then uphill to meet the Federal guns as

Out of action *A dead horse and a broken-down artillery carriage offer mute testimony to the shattering violence of July 3 at Gettysburg, when the Confederates, at a huge cost in lives, failed to overwhelm the Federal positions along Cemetery Ridge*

105

one of the most stirring sights of their lives. With the failure of this grand attack, the battle ended, with both sides battered into exhaustion.

Lee Composes His Battle Plan

History has awarded the naming rights of the Confederate infantry assault to General George E. Pickett, but in truth the climax of the three-day battle might just as well be known today as Trimble's Charge or Pettigrew's Charge: with Pickett's divisions, those led by Major General Isaac Trimble and Brigadier General J. Johnston Pettigrew formed the spearhead of the attack. But Lee chose Pickett's divisions to hold the all-important right flank of the assault because they were fresh, having only arrived outside Gettysburg late on July 2. And perhaps fame found Pickett simply because he was a more memorable character than either Trimble or Pettigrew.

Though Pickett was 38 years old in 1863, there was something about him that smacked of the eternal sophomore. He had distinguished himself by his headlong bravery during the Mexican War and had been wounded while leading a charge at Gaines' Mill during the Union's Peninsula Campaign in June 1862. Yet the glory that he so greatly coveted had eluded him. In fact, there were those who thought he had achieved his rank by cozying up to General Longstreet, his corps commander. Longstreet did think the world of Pickett, and 35 years after the war he could still marvel at his favorite's "wondrous pulchritude and magnetic presence."

Longstreet's chief of staff, Lieutenant Colonel G. Moxley Sorrel, wrote later, "I could always see how he looked after Pickett." Like almost everyone else, Sorrel thought that Pickett was "a good fellow," despite the "long ringlets that flowed over his shoulders, trimmed and highly perfumed; his beard likewise was curling and giving out the scent of Araby."

Pickett had seen two wives die before the war, and in 1863 he was ecstatically in love with a teenage Virginia beauty named LaSalle Corbell; they married soon after Gettysburg. During his absences from her, Pickett all but drowned the young lady in a flood of Victorian blather. She was, he wrote her, "the sweetest, loveliest flower that ever blossomed." And on the march into Pennsylvania, he vowed that "every tramp-tramp-tramp is a thought-thought-thought of my darling." (In Pickett's defense: some scholars believe LaSalle Corbell may have fabricated some of the letters she claimed her swain sent her.)

Pickett's division, with fewer than 6,000 men in its 15 Virginia regiments, was one of the smallest in the Army of Northern Virginia. It also had little experience as a fighting unit. Formed in September 1862, the division had been held in reserve at Fredericksburg; it had been in southern Virginia during the Chancellorsville Campaign; and when the fighting started at Gettysburg, it had been guarding supply wagons at Chambersburg.

Relieved from that assignment on July 2, Pickett's division toiled across South Mountain and at about 6 p.m. halted four miles west of Gettysburg. Pickett sent word to Lee that the men were weary, but if necessary they could resume their march and pitch into the fight. "Tell General Pickett," Lee responded, "I shall not want him this evening; to let his men rest, and I will send him word when I want him."

Lee's plans evolved that night: Longstreet, supported by artillery and reinforced by Pickett's three brigades, would attack the Federal center the next day, while General Ewell would again assail the enemy's right. Both would launch their assaults from ground they had wrested from the Federals on July 2, with Longstreet driving from the Peach Orchard and the Devil's Den toward Cemetery Ridge and Ewell striking southward from the trenches that General Edward ("Allegheny") Johnson had seized late on the night of July 2 on Culp's Hill.

An Early Battle at Culp's Hill

The Confederates' plans were made, and the rebels were on the move before the sun was up. But at dawn, just as Pickett's troops approached their preattack position behind sheltering hills west of the Emmitsburg Road, Lee heard his plans disintegrate: a deep growl of gunfire from the direction of Culp's Hill informed him that Ewell and Johnson were already engaged.

The Federals had started the fight. Although General George Meade was determined to keep a defensive posture, he allowed one exception: during the night, the men of XII Corps, under Major General Henry W. Slocum, had been placed on high ground west of the Baltimore Pike so that their fire could enfilade the lines seized from the Federals by Johnson's troops late on July 2, in the last major fighting of that day. Thus, at about 4:30 a.m., as dawn broke through misty clouds, the artillery opened fire to prepare the way for an infantry charge.

Johnson, too, had been reinforced during the night— by General James A. Walker's redoubtable Stonewall Brigade and three other brigades under Generals Junius Daniel, William ("Extra Billy") Smith and Colonel Ed-

Edwin Forbes, illustrator
This book features a number of works by Edwin Forbes, who was born in New York City in 1839 and was one of the "special artists" for the popular magazine Frank Leslie's Illustrated Newspaper.

Printing technology was not sufficiently advanced in the 1860s to allow magazines to reproduce photographs, so Americans saw combat scenes during the war in the form of engravings based on sketches made in the heat of battle by Forbes and other artists, including Alfred Waud and Thomas Nast.

When time permitted, Forbes often converted his battlefield sketches into full-color paintings like the one at top right. After the war he chose to paint scenes of sheep and pastures, understandably exchanging visions of war for those of a serene, peaceful world

ward A. O'Neal. Under the savage bombardment, Johnson could not stay where he was. But he would not withdraw, and so, at 8 a.m., he attacked—the sort of gutsy choice that throughout the war so often distinguished Confederate officers from their cautious Federal foes.

For some three hours a vicious struggle raged at close quarters, amid what one Federal officer called "great rocks that lie there like a herd of sleeping elephants." From the cover of log breastworks, many Union soldiers fired more than 160 rounds into the advancing Confederates. The result was disastrous for the attackers. "The wonder is," wrote General Alpheus S. Williams of XII Corps later, "that the rebels persisted so long in an attempt that in the first half-hour must have seemed useless."

Yet persist they did. General John M. Jones was wounded at the head of his brigade, and his men fell back. O'Neal's brigade struggled up the hill but was pinned down before it could reach the Federal positions. Then the Stonewall Brigade tried and failed. Still unwilling to call it quits, Johnson at 10 a.m. ordered the brigades of Daniel and George H. Steuart to attack. Both were stopped before they reached the breastworks.

Time and again, the Confederates rallied and charged, their officers in the lead. Major Henry Kyd Douglas, Stonewall Jackson's longtime aide, was shot through the shoulder, pulled from his horse and captured. General Johnson's chief of staff, Major Benjamin W. Leigh, spurred to within feet of the Federal breastworks, where horse and rider fell, riddled with bullets. When the troops on Steuart's left wavered, he ran to the front of the 1st Maryland Battalion and led them forward.

"The little battalion never wavered nor hesitated," one officer recalled, "but kept on, closing up its ranks as great gaps were torn through them, and many of the brave fellows never stopped until they had passed through the enemy's first line or had fallen dead or wounded as they reached it." The Marylanders lost more than half of their 400 men; one soldier killed himself with a shot to the head rather than surrender. Finally, at about 11 a.m., a Federal countercharge swept down on Johnson's left,

Defending Culp's Hill

In this painting by Edwin Forbes, Federal troops behind breastworks atop Culp's Hill fend off a determined Confederate assault. Culp's Hill saw little action until late in the evening of July 2, when Confederates captured some Federal trenches, from which they launched an assault early on July 3

107

Do fence me in *After the battle, members of Mathew Brady's photographic corps take a break near the breastworks on Culp's Hill created by Federal troops under the direction of General George S. Greene, a West Point graduate who had resigned from the army before the war to become a professional civil engineer*

the Confederate line broke, and the soldiers were forced to withdraw east across Rock Creek at the foot of Culp's Hill. Johnson's division and, for that matter, Ewell's entire corps would do no more fighting at Gettysburg.

For decades after the conflict raged on Culp's Hill a ghostly forest would stand, its trees shorn of their limbs and stripped of their bark by flying metal—testimony to the savagery of the intense, seven-hour contest.

Lee Prepares to Strike

On hearing the Federal bombardment, Lee had ridden to Seminary Ridge to find Longstreet, whose words of greeting must have tested Lee's composure: "General, I have had my scouts out all night, and I find that you still have an excellent opportunity to move around to the right of Meade's army, and maneuver him into attacking us." That was, of course, the plan that Longstreet had been urging all along and that Lee had rejected several times. Grimly, the commanding general pointed to the Federal lines and reiterated his statement of July 1. "The enemy is there," the Confederate commander said, "and I am going to strike him."

Still Longstreet objected, especially to the use of John Bell Hood's and Lafayette McLaws' divisions in the assault. As he wrote later, "To have rushed forward my two divisions, then carrying bloody noses from their terrible conflict the day before, would have been madness." On this point Lee gave in, and he agreed to modify his plan.

The assault would be made by Pickett's fresh division, along with two others: Henry Heth's and a combination of four brigades from William Dorsey Pender's and Richard H. Anderson's divisions. At Lee's direction, the attackers would guide on a little, umbrella-shaped clump of oak trees on the otherwise bare crest of Cemetery Ridge, near the center of the Federal line.

The whole plan had a makeshift air about it. By this time, Heth's division had suffered casualties of at least 40% and was severely shaken. Among the wounded were Heth and all his brigade commanders except Pettigrew, who now led this second major unit in the assault. The third attack division was placed under the command of 61-year-old Trimble. Not only was Trimble a complete stranger to the brigades he was assigned to lead, but also he joined them after they were deployed—too late to correct what turned out to be fatal flaws in the plan.

With the strategy set, Longstreet asked how many men would participate in the attack. When Lee said about 15,000—a number that turned out to be over-estimated by 20%—a gravely concerned Longstreet made a final, impassioned plea: "General, I have been a soldier all my life. I have been with soldiers engaged in fights by couples, by squads, companies, regiments, divisions, and armies, and should know, as well as anyone, what soldiers can do. It is my opinion that no 15,000 men ever arrayed for battle can take that position." Lee refused to budge. By Longstreet's account, the commanding general "seemed a little impatient, so I said nothing more. Never was I so depressed as upon that day."

Lee had cast the die; he could not uncast it. By 9 a.m. the attacking forces were forming their lines of battle in the cover of the woods northwest of the Peach Orchard, with Pickett's division on the right, Pettigrew's on the left and Trimble's trailing in support on Pettigrew's right rear. There was a space of nearly a quarter-mile between Pickett's left and the right of Pettigrew, a gap that could not be effectively closed in the woods. Thus Pickett's line would have to shade to the left even while advancing across the field, a very tricky proposition indeed.

While supervising these arrangements, Lee apparently realized for the first time just how badly some of his brigades had been battered. Peering at the ranks of exhausted men, he said to Trimble, "Many of these poor boys should go the rear; they are not fit for duty." Yet there could be no turning back, and as Lee rode away he said, almost to himself, "The attack must succeed."

Meanwhile, Longstreet's artillerists prepared to blast a path for the infantrymen. The responsibility for the bombardment fell upon 27-year-old Colonel E. Porter Alexander. Although only a battalion commander, Alexander had performed brilliantly at Fredericksburg and Chancellorsville. Longstreet clearly had more faith in him than in the corps' senior artillery commander, Colonel J.B. Walton.

Alexander placed 75 guns along a front extending 1,300 yds. northward from the Peach Orchard; eight others were located to the south to cover the flank of the attacking infantry. Several hundred yards to the left and rear of Alexander's main line were 60 of A.P. Hill's cannons and, beyond them, 24 of Ewell's. All told, the Confederates deployed about 170 guns, each with 130 to 150 rounds of ammunition available. Everything was ready for the most colossal cannonade in the nation's history.

Just then, Alexander received a strange and disturbing note from Longstreet. In it, the corps commander seemed to place on Alexander the burden of assessing the results of the bombardment and deciding whether or not the infantry charge should be made. Appalled by his dilemma—to cancel Lee's assault was unthinkable yet so was open defiance of Longstreet—Alexander protested that the decisions should be made before the guns opened fire. Once again, Longstreet instructed the colonel to determine whether "the artillery has the desired effect of driving the enemy's [cannons] off."

It was a determination that the young officer felt he could not make; he could only follow the plan of battle. "When our fire is at its best," he wrote Longstreet, "I will advise General Pickett to advance." Reluctantly, Longstreet sent the order to begin the bombardment. At precisely 1 p.m., Alexander remembered, the roar of artillery "burst in on the silence, almost as suddenly as the full notes of an organ would fill a church."

The Federals Brace for a Charge

In 90-degree heat and smothering humidity, the Federals on Cemetery Ridge had passed much of the morning moving as if in slow motion; some had trouble staying awake. "We dozed in the heat," recalled one Federal officer, "and lolled upon the ground, with half-open eyes.

General, I have been a soldier all my life. I have been with soldiers engaged in fights by couples, by squads, companies, regiments, divisions, and armies, and should know, as well as anyone, what soldiers can do. It is my opinion that no 15,000 men ever arrayed for battle can take that position.

—*General Longstreet, to General Lee*

Our horses were hitched to the trees, munching some oats. Time was heavy."

At about 9 a.m., General Meade rode over to talk strategy with Major General Winfield Scott Hancock. For no apparent reason, Meade had decided that the Confederates probably would not attack the center of his line, as he had predicted the previous evening, but would instead hit his left in the vicinity of the Round Tops.

The Army was accordingly disposed. Massed on and near the two Round Tops on the Federal right were V Corps, the remnants of III Corps and most of VI Corps, now recovered from its arduous march. With XI and XII Corps and much of I Corps still occupying Cemetery and Culp's hills, that left the defense of the center, on Cemetery Ridge, to two divisions of Hancock's II Corps, along with part of Abner Doubleday's I Corps division. No more than 5,750 infantrymen were stretched along the half-mile front that would bear the brunt of a charge by 12,000 very determined Confederates.

At the northern part of the ridge, in front of Ziegler's Grove and an adjacent orchard, Alexander Hays' II Corps divisions were in position behind a stone wall that ran southward along the foot of the slope. At a point about 250 ft. north of the little clump of oaks that was the target for the Confederate attack, the wall turned to the west for 239 ft. Then it jogged back toward the south, forming a salient that would soon achieve sinister fame as the Angle.

Within the salient and north of the clump of trees was Battery A, 4th U.S. Artillery, composed of six 3-in. ordnance pieces under Lieutenant Alonzo H. Cushing. His artillerymen were supported by the 71st Pennsylvania of Brigadier General Alexander Webb's Philadelphia Brigade. Along the wall to the front of the trees was another of Webb's regiments, the largely Irish 69th Pennsylvania, which supported a Rhode Island battery of Napoleon cannons led by Lieutenant T. Fred Brown. Another of Webb's regiments, the 72nd Pennsylvania, was in reserve behind the stand of oaks. The other II Corps division, under Brigadier General John Gibbon, extended the line to the south. With no wall in front of

The Guns of Gettysburg
Mort Kunstler's painting shows artillerymen preparing to fire. At the time, most field artillery had a range of about one mile. But in fact, most guns were unable to fire accurately at any range beyond a half-mile

them, his men had created a slight barrier of earth that barely reached knee-high to the troops.

Meanwhile General Henry J. Hunt, the Federal artillery chief, had placed 77 guns along the crest of Cemetery Ridge, with well over half of the pieces on the southern end. Five batteries—25 guns—defended the crucial center. Another 50 cannons were posted on Cemetery Hill and Little Round Top, to support the Federal left flank.

Duel of the Artillery Batteries

About an hour before noon, as the fighting on Culp's Hill subsided, an oppressive silence fell over the field. "It became as still as the Sabbath day," wrote one Union soldier. Recalled another: "It was a queer sight to see men look at each other without speaking; the change was so great men seemed to go on tip-toe, not knowing how to act." Still another would remember that he could "distinctly hear the hum of the honeybees working."

For a favored few, there was even a good meal. A couple of Gibbon's foragers had scrounged what the general described as "an old and tough rooster," with which they made a stew. Gibbon invited Meade, Hancock and a few other generals and aides to share the repast. They sat in the shade of a tree near Meade's headquarters behind Cemetery Ridge, savoring their stew and, later, puffing on cigars. After a while, Meade and some of the others departed. But several were still taking their ease when the Confederate batteries opened. Suddenly, Gibbon recalled, "the air was all murderous iron." Among the first casualties was an orderly who had been serving butter to the commanders: he was cut in half by a flying shell.

The puffs of smoke and flashes of fire that traveled rapidly down the line of Confederate artillery reminded one Federal soldier on Cemetery Hill of "the 'powder snakes' we boys used to touch off on the 4th of July." Another would remember the sight of small birds fluttering about in confusion as the world around them was ripped apart. General Hunt, the coolly professional artilleryman, was enthralled by a spectacle that seemed to him "indescribably grand."

With a fine sense of theater, Hancock set out to show every soldier in II Corps that "his general was behind him in the storm." Sitting ramrod straight on his prancing horse, he rode down the line. More than 20 years later, Doubleday would write, "I can almost fancy I can see Hancock again, followed by a single orderly displaying his corps flag, while the missiles from a hundred pieces of artillery tore up the ground around him." Fi-

The big guns *This photograph from the Peninsula Campaign of 1862 shows Federal mobile artillery forces commanded by Captain Horatio Gibson. Each artillery battery generally consisted of six weapons, ammunition, supporting equipment and horses, and the men who tended and fired the guns.*

The unit in the foreground consists of a limber, a two-wheeled cart that lifted and carried the wooden trail of the artillery piece behind it, also mounted on two wheels. A caisson was a similar two-wheeled carriage that bore ammunition. To deploy for firing, the guns were "unlimbered" and stabilized to withstand the recoil of the discharge

★ The Bombs Bursting in Air

When Federal artillery chief General Henry Hunt stood at the center of the Union line on Cemetery Hill about 11 on the morning of July 3 and looked west, he saw a sight rare even in the Civil War. "A magnificent display greeted my eyes," he later wrote. "Our whole front for two miles was covered by [artillery] batteries already in line or going into position. They stretched—apparently in one unbroken mass—from opposite the town to the Peach Orchard, which bounded the view to the left, the ridges of which were planted thick with cannon. Never before had such a sight been witnessed on this continent, and rarely, if ever, abroad."

The artillery duel that followed was among the largest of the war: for some two hours Federal and Confederate cannons rained fire upon each other. Historian Stephen W. Sears calculates wthat Hunt's Federals massed 119 guns across their defensive line along the high ground of Cemetery Ridge and Little Round Top, while the Confederate artillery chief, Brigadier General William Nelson Pendleton, commanded even more firepower: he arranged 163 guns across a line that took the form of a semi-circular arc, stretching from the Peach Orchard along the heights of Seminary Ridge, behind the Emmitsburg Road, to Spangler's Woods, north of the town of Gettysburg.

Yet if the rebels boasted more weapons, Hunt was a much more accomplished artillery chief than Pendleton, an 1830 graduate of West Point who had left the U.S. Army in 1833 to become a university professor and later an Episcopal priest; he was called "Old Mother Pendleton" by his subordinates. Lee was counting on Pendleton's artillery to soften up the Federal forces for the great infantry attack on July 3, but the lengthy Confederate barrage failed to achieve that goal, and when the uphill assault began, Hunt's guns, firing grapeshot and canister, plowed great swaths of death across the advancing Confederate lines.

Artillery played an important role in Civil War battles, but it most often played an auxiliary role to the infantry and cavalry forces, seldom taking center stage. Two exceptions earlier in the war were remembered vividly by the soldiers at Gettysburg. In the Battle of Malvern Hill, during the Peninsula Campaign of 1862, General Lee, in an unusual misstep, sent his men marching uphill directly against Federal artillery batteries, losing more than 5,000 men while gaining no ground at all. That situation had been replayed at the Battle of Fredericksburg, in December 1862, with the roles reversed: Confederate artillery forces commanded lofty ground atop Marye's Heights west of the town, and sighted in their guns to cover every foot of the pastures leading up the hill. Federal officers, under orders from Army of the Potomac commander General Ambrose Burnside, obligingly dispatched 14 separate brigades across these open fields, sending, by most estimates, as many as 8,000 troops marching directly to their deaths in an exercise in slaughter.

Artillery weapons during the Civil War had either smoothbore or rifled barrels, the latter being more accurate, and they fired a variety of charges: cannonballs to batter away at buildings and fortifications; exploding shells to create maximum havoc upon impact; and grape and canister, aggregates of small projectiles used at close range against approaching infantry, transforming a cannon into a sort of giant shotgun. Once used primarily from fixed positions in fortifications, artillery had become highly mobile by the time of the Civil War, as shown in the picture above. But the great two-hour artillery duel that rang up the curtain on the final day of battle at Gettysburg was fought largely from stationary positions, in a scene that Napoleon Bonaparte would have recognized—and, most likely, thoroughly enjoyed.

The Brian House *Owned by African-American farmer Abraham Brian (also spelled Bryan), this small home and a nearby barn near Ziegler's Grove were on the front lines of Pickett's Charge. The house was used as a headquarters by Union General Alexander Hays during the fighting on both July 2 and 3 and was heavily damaged. It has been restored and still stands*

nally, a brigadier admonished him, "General the corps commander ought not to risk his life that way." Replied Hancock: "There are times when a corps commander's life does not count."

When Hancock saw that the Confederates were concentrating their fire around the little clump of trees, he sent word to Hunt to dispatch two more batteries there. Hunt complied, but in fact he and Hancock were at odds throughout much of the cannonade. Hunt, painfully aware of the need to conserve ammunition to meet the infantry charge he knew was coming, ordered his guns along Cemetery Ridge to hold their fire. Only the batteries on Cemetery Hill and Little Round Top replied to the enemy's guns.

Hancock, on the other hand, knew all too well how the morale of infantrymen can suffer in a bombardment when their own guns stay silent. After about 15 minutes, he overrode Hunt and ordered the II Corps's artillery commander, Captain John Hazard, to start firing. The five II Corps batteries complied with great gusto, but on the southern end of the ridge, 36 guns from the artillery reserve remained mute. They were commanded by Lieutenant Colonel Freeman McGilvery, who had the day before shown great courage against the enemy; now he showed that he was not afraid of the formidable Hancock either. Contending that he could take orders only from Hunt, McGilvery ignored Hancock's command.

Despite its volume, the Confederate cannonade was, in

the words of a Federal officer, "by no means as effective as it should have been, nine-tenths of their shot passing over our men." With their targets obscured by clouds of gun smoke billowing over the field, many of the Confederate cannoneers were shooting high—although not by much. "It seemed that nothing four feet from the ground could live," wrote one Union soldier. And another recalled, "All we had to do was flatten out a little thinner, and our empty stomachs did not prevent that."

But many of the shells that passed over the men on Cemetery Ridge found other targets, among them Meade's headquarters in the Leister House. Before long, 16 horses lay dead or maimed in the yard outside the home; one shell smashed through the roof, and another tore through the door, just missing Meade. Major General Daniel Butterfield was wounded by a shell fragment, and Meade and his staff were forced to move to a safer location. The reserve artillery and the army's ammunition train, massed on the far side of the ridge, were also threatened. Reluctantly, Brigadier General Robert O. Tyler, commander of the reserve artillery, ordered them moved half a mile farther south—thereby increasing the time required for reserve batteries and fresh supplies of ammunition to reach the front.

The Union batteries on Cemetery Ridge that had been ordered to fire away made easy marks for the Confederate gunners, even in the smoke; during the 90-minute cannonade, they were badly mauled. Captain James McKay Rorty's New York battery, on the southern end of Gibbon's line, was especially hard hit. "The scene was more than dramatic," an officer observed. "With guns dismounted, caissons blown up, and rapidly losing men and horses, the intrepid commander moved from gun to gun as coolly as if at a West Point review." Finally Rorty himself was killed.

Within the Angle, three of Cushing's ammunition chests were hit and exploded, wrecking the limbers. A gun in Brown's Rhode Island battery was struck on the muzzle while being loaded; the blast tore off a soldier's head and ripped away the left arm of Private Alfred Gardner, a devout man who died crying, "Glory to God! I am happy! Hallelujah!"

Shortly after 2:30 p.m., the Federals made a decision that would change the course of the battle. Artillery chief Hunt was approached on Cemetery Ridge by the commander of the XI Corps batteries, Major Thomas W. Osborn. It had occurred to Osborn that General Meade might actually be eager for Lee's infantry brigades to at-

tack. Hunt confirmed that he had heard Meade express just such an opinion.

"If this is so," said Osborn, "I would cease fire at once, and the enemy could reach but one conclusion, that of our being driven from the hill." The idea of luring the Confederates into an early assault was appealing to Hunt, who had been urging from the outset that ammunition be conserved. Soon the order to cease fire was passed down the line, and one by one, the Federal batteries fell silent.

At the same time it became apparent that Brown's shattered battery—with all its officers killed or wounded, its ammunition nearly exhausted and scarcely enough men left to work its remaining guns—could not survive the ordeal. Ordered to withdraw, the battery did so, to be replaced by a fresh battery under Captain Andrew Cowan, a Scot who immigrated to the U.S. as a boy.

Into the Valley of Death

On Seminary Ridge, Confederate artillery commander Alexander spotted Brown's withdrawal, saw some of Cushing's damaged guns in the Angle being pushed to the rear and noted that the spew of flame and smoke from the Federal guns was diminishing. Until then, Alexander had been convinced (and rightly so) that the Confederates were losing the artillery duel. Federal shells were devastating the infantry waiting in the woods behind the Confederate artillery line for the attack to begin. "There were to be seen at almost every moment of time," wrote one Confederate, "guns, swords, haversacks, human flesh flying above the earth, which now trembled beneath us as shaken by an earthquake." As many as 500 men were killed or wounded in Pickett's divisions alone by the Federal artillery barrage.

But once Colonel Alexander saw to his vast delight that the fire from the ridge was fading and that some of the guns were withdrawing, he reached a fateful conclusion: the time was ripe for an assault. Hastily, Alexander scribbled a message to Pickett: "The 18 guns have been driven off. For God's sake, come quick, or we cannot support you. Ammunition nearly out." He had fallen for the Union gambit; as seemed to happen so often at Gettysburg, Federal officers were now employing the risk-taking and capable deception that had allowed their enemies to gain the upper hand in so many previous battles.

On receiving Alexander's note at about 3 p.m., Pickett rode to see Longstreet. "General," Pickett asked, "shall I advance?" Overwhelmed by an emotion that rendered

Porter Alexander
The 1857 West Point graduate who directed the Confederate artilley batteries at Gettysburg was a pioneer in the use of banners to send long-distance signals in battle. His use of signal flags at the First Battle of Bull Run (Manassas) was the first time this form of messaging was employed in the midst of conflict

A little further we take temporary position in the hollow of a field. Before us is a rising slope which hides the Yankee position from view ... Around us are some trees with very small green apples; and while we are resting here we amuse ourselves by pelting each other with green apples. So frivolous men can be even in the hour of death ...

—Captain John E. Dooley,
1st Virginia Infantry

him unable—or unwilling—to reply, Longstreet merely bowed his head. Taking this to be affirmation, Pickett declared, "I shall lead my division forward, sir."

As Pickett departed, General Cadmus M. Wilcox rode up to him, offering the contents of a flask. "Pickett, take a drink with me," he said. "In an hour you'll be in hell or glory." Pickett declined, saying he had pledged abstinence to his LaSalle. Taking his place in front of the division, Pickett addressed the men in a loud, clear voice,

"Charge the enemy, and remember old Virginia!" And then, "Forward! Guide center! March!"

Under orders neither to fire nor to emit their fearsome rebel yell, the three divisions of Confederates advanced through the woods in eerie silence at a steady pace of about 100 yds. per minute, blue flags flying over Pickett's regiments and red colors over Pettigrew's and Trimble's. Longstreet, seated on a rail fence, watched them go.

Brigadier General James L. Kemper, a 40-year-old for-

mer Virginia legislator who had been fighting since First Bull Run, led Pickett's right-front brigade. To Kemper's left, on a black horse, rode Brigadier General Richard B. Garnett. Though severely injured by a kick from his horse and barely able to walk, the 45-year-old Garnett was more than willing to risk his life: he had made it his mission to refute the unjust charges of cowardice that Stonewall Jackson had brought against him after the Battle of Kernstown in the Shenandoah Valley in 1862.

Behind Garnett's brigade was that of 46-year-old Brigadier General Lewis A. Armistead of North Carolina. Waving his black slouch hat from the tip of his sword, Armistead advanced on foot against the line commanded by one of his dearest friends from the Regular Army, General Hancock. Pickett rode about 20 yds. to the rear, the proper place for a division commander; the fond Longstreet would remember him advancing "gracefully, with his jaunty cap raked well over his right ear."

Pickett's Charge
In this painting by eye-witness Edwin Forbes, Confederates form a line as they prepare to assault Union soldiers entrenched on Cemetery Ridge, in the distance, where Ziegler's Grove is on the left and the "clump of trees" is on the right

To a Federal officer near the clump of trees, the oncoming tide of men in gray had "the appearance of being fearfully irresistible." Instructing his troops to hold their fire until the last possible moment, Colonel Dennis O'Kane of the 69th Pennsylvania cried out, "Let your work this day be for victory or death!" Farther north on the line, General Hays formed his men behind the stone wall and put them through a brisk drill to keep them from growing skittish while waiting for the rebel blow to fall.

Once clear of the woods, Pickett's division at an order faced 45 degrees left and headed northeast to close with Pettigrew's division; the watching Federals marveled at the brilliance with which the Confederate infantry executed this complex left-oblique maneuver. In so doing, Pickett exposed his right flank to raking fire from six Parrotts (rifled cannons) on Little Round Top and McGilvery's guns on the southern end of Cemetery Ridge. When the guns opened up, "we could not help hitting them at every shot," said one of McGilvery's officers. According to Major Charles Peyton, with the 19th Virginia in Garnett's brigade, the Federal cannons fired "with fearful effect, sometimes as many as 10 men being killed and wounded by the bursting of a single shell."

Nearing the Emmitsburg Road, the division came to a shallow swale that provided partial cover. But men were still falling as the Confederate regiments halted and, with a parade-ground aplomb that once again awed the Federal troops on the ridge, closed the gaps that had been blasted in their ranks and re-dressed their lines.

On the Confederate left, Colonel Robert Mayo's brigade of General Pettigrew's division had for unknown reasons been slow to emerge from the woods and was just catching up when it came under fire from the XI Corps batteries on Cemetery Hill. Almost immediately, men began to trickle toward the rear—and then disaster struck the brigade.

The Assault Breaks Down

On the afternoon before, the 8th Ohio, part of Colonel Samuel S. Carroll's brigade, had been sent west of the Emmitsburg Road to form a skirmish line. Unlike most skirmishers, who are expected to withdraw before a strong infantry advance, the 8th Ohio, under Lieutenant Colonel Franklin Sawyer, had been instructed by the bellicose Carroll to hold its ground. That evening Carroll had gone to help defend Culp's Hill, leaving his order in effect—and so it remained.

If the 8th Ohio's men had stayed where they were,

the Confederate line of advance would have swept past them to the south. But Sawyer, a man who took orders seriously, clearly believed that he had been sent forward to get into a fight, not to stay out of one. And so, while onlookers on Cemetery Ridge speculated that he must be drunk, Sawyer faced his men south, waited until the enemy was passing about 100 yds. from his little line and then opened fire on a Confederate brigade that outnumbered his understrength regiment by about 5 to 1.

Sawyer's quixotic effort had an immediate, astonishing effect: Mayo's brigade, already severely shaken by Federal artillery fire, broke and ran for the safety of Seminary Ridge. The Ohioans charged forward, capturing 200 prisoners. The rout exposed the left of Joseph R. Davis' Mississippi brigade. Those troops, now caught in a heavy crossfire from left and front, began to crumble.

The units on Pettigrew's right continued to advance in good order, however, and just before reaching the Emmitsburg Road, Pickett's left linked up with them. Maintaining its deliberate pace, and still, with immense bravery, withholding its fire, the united Confederate force approached the long, gentle slope that led to the crest of Cemetery Ridge. As the gray lines started up the rise, a sword-waving lieutenant expressed the heart's desire of them all: "Home, boys, home!" he cried. "Remember, home is over beyond those hills!"

But thousands of them would never get home. Especially on the left, the advancing brigades were now taking terrible punishment from the Federal guns on Cemetery Hill and Lieutenant George Woodruff's battery at Ziegler's Grove—the guns their officers believed had been knocked out of commission. And now the Confederates were approaching the stone wall, behind which General Hays and his men waited.

Hays, who enjoyed mortal combat, was having the time of his life. As the Confederate forces neared, he enjoined his troops, "Now, boys, look out; you will see some fun!" Hays waited until the enemy brigade under Colonel Birkett D. Fry got tangled up with a pair of stout rail fences about 200 yds. to his front. Then Hays bellowed "Fire!" and from his line there blazed the concentrated fury of 1,700 muskets and 11 cannons. A Federal officer wrote later that the Confederate lines "underwent an instantaneous transformation. They were at once enveloped in a dense cloud of dust. Arms, heads, blankets, guns and knapsacks were tossed into the clear air. A moan went up from the field distinctly to be heard amid the storm of battle."

Franklin Sawyer
When the musketeers of the 8th Ohio Infantry Regiment, under Lieutenant Colonel Sawyer, unexpectedly opened fire on Virginia troops under Colonel John M. Brockenbrough, the Confederates, already shaken by Federal artillery fire, broke and ran.

Sawyer was born in Auburn, Ohio, in 1825. He was wounded on July 1 at Gettysburg but continued to lead his troops for the following two days

First Person

Captain Henry T. Owen
18th Virginia Infantry

Owen was a railway agent who enlisted in the Army of Northern Virginia at age 31 and watched the preparations for Pickett's Charge.

On Friday morning, July 3, Pickett's Division left its bivouac at dawn of day and moving around to the right reached the position assigned it in the ravine behind Seminary Ridge soon after 6 o'clock. Long dark lines of infantry were massed along the bottoms, concealed from the enemy's view, and orders were given "to lie down and keep still …"

About 8 o'clock Generals Lee, Longstreet and Pickett, in company, rode slowly along up and down in front of the long lines of prostrate infantry, viewing them closely and critically as they rode along. They were not greeted with the usual cheers, as orders had preceded them forbidding this, but the men voluntarily rose up and stood in line with uncovered heads and hats held aloft while their chieftains rode by.

Owen continues his narrative, recounting his experiences in the afternoon's historic assault.

We were now 400 yards … from Cemetery Hill, when away off to the right, nearly half a mile, there appeared in the open field a line of men at right angles with our own, a long, dark mass, dressed in blue, and coming down at a "double quick" upon the unprotected right flank of Pickett's men, with their muskets "upon the right shoulder shift," their battle flags dancing and fluttering in the breeze created by their own rapid motion, and their burnished bayonets glistening above their heads like forest twigs covered with sheets of sparkling ice when shaken by a blast.

Garnett galloped along the line saying "Fast, men! Faster!" and the front line broke forward into a double quick, when Garnett called out: "Steady, men, Steady! Don't double quick. Save your wind and your ammunition for the final charge!" and then went down among the dead, and his clarion voice was no more heard above the roar of the battle.

Captain Edward R. Bowen
114th Pennsylvania Infantry

Bowen was among the Federal troops who were aligned to defend against the infantry attack.

At a double quick we moved to the position assigned to us in the second line … Here we waited the coming assault of Pickett's brave men. For a brief space there was an ominous pause of the artillery fire of both sides, General Hunt, chief of the artillery of the Army of the Potomac, having ordered it to cease on our side in order that the guns might have an opportunity to cool and the ammunition be economized for the assault he knew was about to be made. The enemy, supposing from our artillery ceasing to fire that they had silenced our batteries, caused their firing to cease also.

The silence was, however, of but short duration. The enemy rapidly crossed the intervening space. Our batteries, loaded with grape and cannister, were trained upon them at point-blank range and opened again upon them with deadly effect. Still they closed up the gaps and pressed on. Our men reserved their fire and allowed them to come so far as in their judgment was far enough and then blazed upon them such a withering musketry fire as literally mowed them down.

Lieutenant George G. Benedict
12th Vermont Infantry

Benedict, a staff officer to Brigadier General George J. Stannard, was present when Union General Winfield Scott Hancock was hit by enemy fire during Pickett's Charge.

Hooker [a fellow officer] and I with a common impulse sprang toward him [Hancock], and caught him as he toppled from his horse into our out-stretched arms. General Stannard bent over him as we laid him upon the ground, and opened his clothing where he … was hurt, a ragged hole, an inch or more in diameter, from which the blood was pouring profusely, was disclosed in the upper part and on the side of his thigh. He was naturally in some alarm for his life …

"Don't let me bleed to death," he said. "Get something around it quick." Stannard had whipped out his handkerchief, and as I helped to pass it around General Hancock's legs, I saw that the blood, being of dark color and not coming in jets, could not be from an artery, and I said to him: "This is not arterial blood, General; you will not bleed to death." From my use of the surgical term he took me for a surgeon, and replied, with a sigh of relief: "That's good; thank you for that, Doctor." We tightened the ligature by twisting it with the barrel of a pistol and soon stopped the flow of blood.

Colonel James K. Marshall, leading Pettigrew's only intact brigade, was shot dead from his horse. Pettigrew himself took an ugly wound in his right hand. The doughty old Colonel Fry crossed the stone wall just north of the Angle, flag in hand. There he went down with a thigh wound, still shouting encouragement, "Go on! It will not last five minutes longer!"

The excitable Hays had a keen tactical eye, and he presently spotted a splendid opportunity. The flight of Mayo's brigade and the drastic shrinking of Davis' had contracted the left of the oncoming Confederate line until it was overlapped by Hays' troops. Immediately Hays ordered his northernmost regiment, the 126th New York, along with a section of Woodruff's battery, to wheel left so that they faced south. Woodruff fell with a mortal wound as this maneuver was being executed, but within minutes his two brass Napoleons and 400 of the New Yorkers' muskets were pouring a lethal flanking fire into Pettigrew's remaining troops.

Up to the Angle—But no Further

On spotting Hays' move, Hancock was struck by the possibility of a double envelopment—the dream of every infantry commander. To see if a maneuver similar to Hays' could be executed at the other end of the Federal line, Hancock galloped southward—where, as it turned out, just such an envelopment was already being tried.

The men of Brigadier General George J. Stannard's Vermont brigade had been feeling edgy about their assigned position on the far left of Meade's Cemetery Ridge line. The ground was low there, but about 100 yds. to their front was a little knoll that looked much more secure. Though Hancock had expressed fears that they would be dangerously exposing themselves, two of Stannard's regiments, the 13th and 14th Vermont, had gone out in front of the rest of the army and had begun piling up dirt and brush to fortify the hillock. Later, they were joined there by the 16th Vermont, which had fallen back from the Federal skirmish line.

Initially, Pickett's Confederates had been heading straight toward Stannard's brigade. A Vermont private recalled spotting them "as they reached the crest of Seminary Ridge a full half-mile away, at first a horse and rider, then glistening bayonets and flags and banners waving and fluttering in the sultry air." But after changing direction to join Pettigrew's line, Pickett's troops moved at an angle across Stannard's front, and the Vermonters were able to pour damaging fire into their ranks. It became

apparent that the Confederates meant to bypass Stannard's men and strike Cemetery Ridge farther north.

Whether it was Hancock or Stannard who was responsible for what happened next was never determined; both would claim credit. In any case, just as Pickett's brigades were starting up Cemetery Ridge, the Vermonters wheeled toward the north, halted within easy range and fired a volley into the 24th Virginia on Kemper's right flank. From his position higher on the slope, Doubleday saw Stannard's attack, waved his hat wildly and shouted, "Glory to God, glory to God! See the Vermonters go it!"

Shying away from the unexpected fire on its right, Kemper's brigade began crowding to its left, pushing into the brigades of Garnett and Armistead. Desperate to get his men back on track, Kemper sought to urge them toward the main enemy line to the east. "There are the guns, boys," he cried. "Go for them!" But in the wild confusion, he inadvertently pointed his sword to the north, thereby accelerating the stampede in that direction. In the next moment he fell from his horse as a bullet struck him near his spine and left him partially paralyzed.

The attacking Confederates, still shrinking from the lethal flanking fire on both right and left, continued to herd toward the center. Soon the better part of five brigades became, in the words of one Confederate officer, "a mingled mass, from 15 to 30 deep." Garnett was striving to restore order, riding up and down exhorting the troops, when he disappeared into the inferno. Private James Clay of the 18th Virginia later wrote, "The last I saw of General Garnett he was astride his big black charger in the forefront of the charge and near the stone wall, gallantly waving his hat and cheering the men on." Moments later, Garnett's frenzied, riderless horse came dashing back, horribly wounded and covered with blood. The general was never seen again.

The jostling mob of Pickett's division was now directly in front of the Angle and the clump of trees. In the Angle, 250 soldiers of the 69th Pennsylvania, supported by the five guns of Cowan's 1st New York battery, fired volley after volley into the Confederate ranks.

The guns of Cushing and Cowan were cutting wagon-wide swaths in the roiling mass of Confederates. Federal artillery chief Hunt was with Cowan's battery, shouting "See 'em! See 'em!" as he fired his revolver into the Virginians swarming over the wall. Then Hunt's horse fell, pinning him to the ground, and the Confederates, led by Colonel James G. Hodges of the 14th Virginia, surged to within 10 paces of Cowan's guns. At that moment Cow-

George J. Stannard
The infantry leader from Vermont marched his men 18 miles a day for a week west from Washington to reach Gettysburg late on July 1. They saw little action on July 2, but on July 3 the Vermonters were among those most instrumental in stopping Pickett's Charge.

Stannard lost his right arm in battle late in the war and later served as doorkeeper in the U.S. House of Representatives

an yelled "Fire!" With a roar, the five guns spewed out double-shotted canister, and when the smoke cleared not a Confederate in front of the battery remained standing. In places, their mutilated bodies lay three deep.

During the Confederate bombardment, Cushing had suffered a shoulder wound but remained in action. Then a shell fragment tore into his groin. He ordered his one serviceable gun wheeled down to the wall and was shouting orders to his gunners when a bullet entered through his open mouth. As he crumpled dead to the ground,

his gun fired its last load of canister. The Confederates swarmed over the wall, and Cushing's gunners hastily abandoned their position.

The disorganized Confederates were thus offered a priceless opportunity, but to seize it, they needed a leader—and now, pushing through the mob came General Armistead, his hat still atop his sword. "Come on, boys," he cried. "Give them the cold steel! Who will follow me?"

Armistead leaped over the wall, followed by a mob of officers and men, and the spine-tingling rebel yell

Awaiting their last journey
The bodies of Confederate dead lie ready for burial on July 5, 1863. This photo was originally thought to show McPherson's Ridge, scene of combat on July 1. It is now believed to have been taken near the Rose Woods at the base of Little Round Top, scene of fighting on July 2 and very late on July 3

Armistead's valor

In this somewhat over-wrought 19th century engraving, General Armistead, his hat perched upon his sword, exhorts his men to follow as he penetrates the Union position at the Angle

shrilled across the field. Faced with this onslaught, the 71st Pennsylvania broke. In his instant of greatest glory, Armistead reached for the barrel of one of Cushing's guns—and fell, mortally wounded by a rifle ball. His men pressed on, some of them overrunning part of the 69th Pennsylvania and reaching the copse of trees before their cries of triumph were cut short by a Federal volley.

It came from the 72nd Pennsylvania, brought forward by General Webb just as the 71st collapsed. The first volley from the 72nd stopped the Confederate rush, though many stayed within the Angle while others took cover on the west side of the stone wall and continued to fire. Webb then ordered the 72nd to charge. No one moved. Waving his sword, Webb repeated the command. Again, the men refused to budge. Wild with frustration, Webb

tried to seize the regimental flag; its bearer would not yield it. The two men wrestled ignominiously for it until Webb, in utter disgust, went down to the clump of trees to spur on the 69th Pennsylvania.

Other Federals were now pushing into the fight. On his way to Stannard's line, General Hancock was stopped by Colonel Arthur Devereux of the 19th Massachusetts. That regiment, along with the 42nd New York, had been posted southeast of the clump of trees. "See, General," said Devereux, "they have broken through; the colors are coming over the stone wall; let me go in there!" Snapped Hancock: "Go in there pretty God-damned quick!"

Following Colonel Devereux, the 19th Massachusetts and the 42nd New York crashed into the Confederates within the Angle. A Massachusetts soldier remembered the collision: "The two lines come together with a shock which stops them both and causes a slight rebound. Foot to foot, body to body and man to man they struggled, pushed and strived and killed. The mass of wounded and heaps of dead entangled the feet of the contestants, and underneath the trampling mass, wounded men who could no longer stand, struggled, fought, shouted and killed—hatless, coatless, drowned in sweat, black with powder, red with blood, with fiendish yells and strange oaths they blindly plied the work of slaughter."

Within minutes every Confederate who had crossed the wall was killed or captured. Then at last, one by one, by twos and by threes, and finally by the hundreds, men in gray began ebbing back down the slope of Cemetery Ridge. Federal officers tried fruitlessly to get their shaken troops to pursue the withdrawing enemy; attempting to lead his 19th Maine beyond the wall, General Gibbon was shot through the shoulder and was led from the field.

Farther south, Hancock too was grievously wounded. A Minié ball tore through the pommel of Hancock's saddle and into his thigh, carrying with it several splinters and a bent tenpenny nail. Lowered to the ground by two of Stannard's staff officers, Hancock extracted the nail, which he evidently thought had been fired at him by the enemy. "They must be hard up for ammunition," he gasped, "when they throw such shot as that." Only the application of a tourniquet saved Hancock's life; a little later, he was carried away on a stretcher.

General Pickett had watched the valiant, failed charge from the Codori Farm just east of the Emmitsburg Road. With all his aides away on errands, he was alone as his men came trudging back from the little clump of trees. After a final, forlorn attempt by Trimble's division to break Hays' line to the north—an attack that cost Trimble his left leg—Pickett wheeled his horse and rode away. Later he met Lee, and the commander instructed him to prepare his division to repel a possible counterattack. "General Lee," said Pickett, "I have no division now."

Pickett's words were close to the truth. He had lost nearly 3,000 men—or more than half of his complement—in the charge, and the division's officer corps had been virtually annihilated. Every one of the 15 regimental commanders had fallen, as had 16 of 17 field officers under them. Two brigadier generals and six colonels were among the division's dead.

For the rest of his life, Pickett would grieve for his men lost that day and would blame Lee for the disaster. Thus, five years after the war, when Pickett and the Confeder-

★ High Tides and Lost Causes

When the 72nd Pennsylvania Infantry turned back the courageous Confederates led by General Lewis A. Armistead at the Angle during Pickett's Charge—and particularly after the general himself fell in action, mortally wounded—the flow of the battle seemed to turn. Armistead's advance was the deepest penetration of the Federal lines on that day, and this moment is often called "The High-Water Mark of the Confederacy" or "The Confederate High Tide." Above is a modern-day photograph of this historic location.

That title may help us recall a critical moment in the battle, but it is more a memorable coinage than an astute historical judgment. The term is correct in so far as it notes the furthest advance of Confederate troops during Pickett's Charge. But the grandiosity of the term seems to invite the notion that, had Armistead's valiant effort only prevailed, the Confederates might have triumphed at Gettysburg and gone on to win not only this battle but the entire war. And that's placing a very large hypothetical burden upon a very delicate straw.

In a wider view, Lee's invasion of the North constituted his attempt to change the terms of the conflict with a single, brilliant blow. Failing to achieve that, he was forced to retreat and was once again bottled up, defending Richmond. What is certainly true is that the Confederacy's prospects for victory in the war receded sharply after the two defeats at Gettysburg and Vicksburg early in July 1863.

In the long decades after the war was lost, some former Confederates sought out scapegoats for blame, in order to assuage the bitterness of their defeat. Champions of the "Lost Cause" movement, which included General Jubal Early and other officers, ascribed the South's failure to a number of errant officers, including a few of Robert E. Lee's top lieutenants. The first manifestation of this impulse came early, in 1866, when historian Edward A. Pollard published *The Lost Cause: A New Southern History of the War of the Confederates*. Early's writings in the 1870s further pursued the theme, tarnishing the reputations of James Longstreet, Richard Ewell and others, including George Pickett and Jeb Stuart, who was faulted for his long absence from the main army before the battle at Gettysburg. In the curious mathematics of such matters, every virtue subtracted from the characters of these scapegoats seemed to be added to those of Lee and Stonewall Jackson, who were transformed into infallible idols, incapable of error.

ate guerrilla leader John S. Mosby paid a courtesy call on Lee in Richmond, the atmosphere was less than cordial. On departing, Pickett launched into a bitter diatribe. "That old man," he said, "had my division slaughtered at Gettysburg."

For an instant of memory, men in gray marched beneath fluttering flags up a long, grassy slope. Then Mosby broke the silence. "Well," he said to Pickett, "it made you immortal."

To the South, a Cavalry Battle

As Pickett's Charge unfolded along Cemetery Ridge, cavalry forces clashed three miles east of Gettysburg in a bitter contest that could have changed the course of the battle had it gone the Confederates' way.

Around noon, Confederate cavalry commander Stuart deployed his four brigades—6,300 men—in the woods on Cress Ridge, bent on pushing westward across an open plain and into the rear of the Federal army. Across this plain, along Hanover Road, were arrayed 4,500 Federal troopers—two brigades of Brigadier General David M. Gregg's division and newly promoted Brigadier General George Armstrong Custer's brigade of Brigadier General Judson Kilpatrick's division.

After dismounted horsemen fought in the plain, Stuart sent the 1st Virginia on a headlong charge down the ridge. Gregg answered with a countercharge by the 7th Michigan that stopped the Confederates. Not to be denied, Stuart committed most of Lieutenant General Wade Hampton's and Brigadier General Fitzhugh Lee's brigades in a narrow column of squadrons. (The capable Lee was Robert E. Lee's nephew.) The polish of the advancing Confederate horsemen drew a murmur of admiration from the Federals. "They marched with well-aligned fronts and steady reins," an appreciative Federal wrote later. "Their polished saber-blades dazzled in the sun." But for all its precision, Stuart's long column proved dangerously vulnerable. Federal shells and shrapnel tore holes along its length.

Then Gregg ordered the 1st Michigan to charge the head of Stuart's column. Custer took the lead, brandishing his saber and shouting, "Come on, you Wolverines!" The Michiganders rushed forward with a fierce yell, and the enemy horsemen raced into their foes with a crash one participant likened to "falling timber. So violent was the collision that many horses were turned end over end and crushed their riders beneath them."

As fierce hand-to-hand fighting ensued, Union forces closed in from the flanks and ripped through Stuart's column from both sides. Captain William E. Miller's squadron of the 3rd Pennsylvania Cavalry, attacking from the east, severed the rear of the column from the main body and drove it back.

The Confederates soon gave way under the furious frontal and flank attacks and punishing artillery. They retreated to Cress Ridge, and the battle subsided. In three hours of fighting, at least 181 Confederates (one brigade failed to report losses) and 254 Federals were killed, wounded or captured. Neither side lost ground, and both would claim victory. But Gregg's brilliant parry prevented Stuart from breaking through and diverting Federal forces from the main battle along Cemetery Ridge. A proud Federal cavalryman would subsequently boast, "We saved the day at the most critical moment of the Battle of Gettysburg."

Or not. Many Federal officers and men helped save the day at Gettysburg—and their actions helped build a new sense of confidence for the Army of the Potomac that would carry it to victory in April 1865. On the night of July 3, the Confederates knew they had been beaten; there would be no renewal of the fighting for a fourth day.

Across the battlefield, thousands of young men lay badly wounded or dead. By universal testimony of witnesses to Civil War battles, these grievously wounded young men, many of them still teens, often lay untended in the fields, calling out for their mothers, while scavengers stole their shoes, weapons and possessions. After this third day of battle, the Confederate dead, wounded and missing in action for the entire three days added up to more than 28,000. The Federals, on the defensive, suffered fewer losses: 23,000 casualties and missing in action.

In his acclaimed one-volume account of the Civil War, *Battle Cry of Freedom* (1988), historian James McPherson notes that Pickett's Charge recapitulated in microcosm the Confederacy's experience in the entire war: "matchless valor, apparent initial success, and ultimate disaster." In fact, the three days of the Battle of Gettysburg carry the same trajectory of decline: from the triumphs of July 1 to the brutal stalemate of July 2 to the catastrophe of July 3.

As John Mosby told George Pickett in 1870, the battle had made the general immortal. But it was a thorny sort of immortality: for the rest of his life, Pickett would be asked, over and over, why his valiant charge had failed. To one such questioner, he confided: "I always thought the Yankees had something to do with it." ∎

Wade Hampton
A scion of one of South Carolina's great landed families, Hampton was one of the single largest slave-holders in the South. The brilliant cavalry leader was wounded on both July 2 and 3 at Gettysburg. After the war he became a prominent foe of Reconstruction. He was elected Governor of South Carolina in 1876, then served two terms in the U.S. Senate, from 1879-91

Come On, You Wolverines!
Don Troiani's painting takes its title from Custer's rallying cry to his Michigan cavalrymen as they charged into battle against the forces of Jeb Stuart and Wade Hampton some 3 miles southeast of Gettysburg

★ Bound for Glory—and Infamy

When Federal cavalry commander Alfred Pleasonton promoted George Armstrong Custer from captain to brigadier general two days before the Battle of Gettysburg began, Custer, then only 23, became the youngest to hold that rank in the Union Army. In the July 3 cavalry action at Cress Ridge, Custer demonstrated the courage and leadership that had led to his promotion. Teaming up with David Gregg, Custer helped dash the plans of Robert E. Lee and Jeb Stuart to draw attention and troops away from the Confederates' gigantic infantry assault on Cemetery Ridge and perhaps even break through the Federal lines with a devastating strike to their rear.

Pleasonton had directed Custer's cavalry brigade to support Gregg by holding a position at the intersection of the Hanover and Low Dutch roads, but on the morning of July 3 he sent an order for Custer to withdraw. But both Gregg and Custer were aware of Stuart's movements and knew Pleasonton was not; the two decided to override Pleasonton's order and keep Custer's division on the scene. Like the day's larger battle, the action there began with an artillery duel that was won by the Federals. When a frustrated Stuart unleashed a direct assault on the Union position, Gregg ordered Custer to advance, and the cavalry divisions clashed in a scene of roiling battle that devolved into desperate hand-to-hand combat before the Confederates withdrew.

Custer, of course, is recalled by history not so much for his Civil War heroism but for his vainglorious behavior 13 years after Gettysburg, when he led U.S. Army forces into a debacle at the Battle of Little Bighorn, where an alliance of Indian tribes overwhelmed Custer's troops, killing the general and some 266 others. But the young Custer, who helped withstand Stuart's legendary cavalry fighters at Gettysburg, was respected by his men for his courage and his leadership and was known for always leading from the front. Even then he liked the limelight and dressed to thrill: at Gettysburg he led his Michiganders into battle wearing a hussar's jacket with gold trim; a flowing, bright red neckerchief; and a wide-brimmed hat. He lost several horses in the wild battle, but he found new mounts and continued to fight.

Though Custer placed last in his class of 34 upon graduating from West Point in 1861, his star ascended rapidly during the war, thanks to his bravery, his dispatch and his cultivation of older mentors. He was taken up first by General George B. McClellan and then by Pleasonton, and he experienced the full arc of the war: he fought in the First Battle of Bull Run, and he helped pressure Robert E. Lee to surrender at Appomattox Court House in 1865. Indeed, Custer's contributions in the Overland Campaign, the Shenandoah Valley Campaign of 1864 and the Siege of Petersburg led Union General Philip Sheridan—yet another older mentor—to present Flora Custer with a gift: the table upon which Lee signed the surrender.

The Commanders

LEWIS A. ARMISTEAD

Like so many of the generals who served the Confederacy well during the war, Armistead hailed from a proud military family. His uncle was the commander of Fort McHenry in Baltimore Harbor during the War of 1812, when Francis Scott Key wrote *The Star-Spangled Banner* about the British bombardment of the U.S. post. Young Lewis attended West Point but left before graduation; according to cadet lore, he got into an argument with fellow plebe Jubal Early and broke a plate upon Early's pate.

Family connections secured Armistead a post as a second lieutenant in the U.S. Army, and he served with distinction in that advanced tutorial for future Civil War leaders, the Mexican War. Long years in the wars against Indians and Mormons in the West followed. As the war approached, Armistead was posted in San Diego, while Winfield Scott Hancock was serv-ing at a U.S. post in Los Angeles; both were small settlements at the time. The future foes became good friends, a relationship that is a memorable central element in both Michael Shaara's 1974 novel of Gettysburg, *The Killer Angels*, and Jeff Shaara's 1996 prequel to that book, *Gods and Generals*.

When the war broke out, Armistead returned home, where he rose rapidly under Lee in the Army of Northern Virginia. During the Peninsula Campaign, Lee tasked him with leading the fruitless uphill Confederate charge at Malvern Hill, where he was lucky to survive. He gained further command experience at Fredericksburg, but he did not fight at Chancellorsville.

Armistead was serving under General George Pickett during the Gettysburg campaign. Pickett's divisions arrived at the battlefield late on July 2 and were set aside by Lee to lead the next day's assault. Armistead's troops, with their leader famously waving his hat upon his sword, penetrated the deepest of all the rebel troops into the Federal line at the Angle, the moment sometimes called "the high-water mark of the Confederacy." There, Armistead was hit three times and fell, flashing a Masonic sign as he did so. Union officer Captain Henry Bingham came to his aid, and upon asking Armistead's name, advised him that his old friend Hancock had been in command of the Federal line and had also fallen, wounded, nearby.

Armistead was taken from the battlefield and placed in a Union field hospital, where he died two days later. Doctors declared his wounds were not mortal; rather, he died from an infection.

ISAAC R. TRIMBLE

Trimble, 61 in 1863, was a West Point graduate. But he was not a career military man; instead, he left the U.S. Army in 1832, when he was 30 years old, to become one of the nation's most respected railroad engineers. Born in Virginia, Trimble settled in Maryland, and when that state did not secede, he enlisted with a Virginia unit of engineers.

Trimble's leadership skills distinguished him, and he became a brigadier general in August 1861. Initially tasked with building fortifications, he emerged as a strong field commander during the Peninsula Campaign and in Stonewall Jackson's storied Shenandoah Valley Campaign of 1862. His attack on a Federal supply train helped lead to a rebel victory at the Second Battle of Bull Run (Manassas), where he was shot in the leg.

A slow recuperation kept Trimble on the sidelines for months; when Lee invaded the North, he followed the army, eager to serve. On July 3 he was named to step in for the wounded William Dorsey Pender and found himself in a historic action, as one of the three leaders of Pickett's Charge—a charge he barely survived.

J. JOHNSTON PETTIGREW

Born to North Carolina gentry, Pettigrew was an intellectual whose academic career carried him from the University of North Carolina to a teaching position at the U.S. Naval Observatory. But he became interested in the law and spent two years traveling in Europe, eventually writing a book about his journeys in Spain.

Returning to the U.S., Pettigrew served in the South Carolina legislature in 1856-58 and enlisted in the Confederate army in 1861, where he quickly rose to a general's rank. Badly wounded during the Peninsula Campaign, he was taken prisoner, then released in an exchange. At Gettysburg his troops tangled with the Iron Brigade on July 1, suffering large losses, but helped take McPherson's Ridge. His divisions were in no condition to fight in Pickett's Charge on July 3, but Lee sent them into action. They were repelled, with huge losses, and Pettigrew was wounded. Eleven days later, he was shot and killed during the retreat to Virginia.

GEORGE E. PICKETT

The man whose name became attached to the great, failed Confederate assault on July 3 is one of the most controversial characters in the Gettysburg cast. Like George Armstrong Custer, he graduated last in his class at West Point—which included George B. McClellan and Thomas (later "Stonewall") Jackson. He befriended James Longstreet in the Mexican War, then served in the Pacific Northwest.

Pickett served honorably early in the war and was wounded at Gaines' Mill in 1862. He saw no more major action until Gettysburg, where he directed the center of the July 3 assault on Cemetery Hill, a bloody failure. His fortunes never improved: during the Siege of Petersburg in 1865, he was in command when a Confederate outpost was over-run at the Battle of Five Forks on April 1, which led directly to Lee's surrender days later. But Pickett missed the battle: he was enjoying a leisurely lunch with other officers during the fray. He died in 1875, at only 50, but his young wife, LaSalle Corbell Pickett, helped restore his reputation after his death by writing exaggerated accounts of his heroism.

ALFRED PLEASONTON

Despite his genial surname, the Union cavalry commander was far from pleasant. Scheming and a braggart, he rose in the Union Army by politicking in the barracks rather than excelling on the battlefield. The 1844 West Point graduate fought in Mexico, served in the West and was named a brigadier general in July 1862. At Antietam, he seems to have taken credit for far more than he achieved—as he did later at Chancellorsville, so convincingly that he was chosen to lead the cavalry corps of the Army of the Potomac just before Lee moved north in 1863.

Pleasonton battled Jeb Stuart's cavalry at Brandy Station, where the Union troops fought well, at last feeling themselves equal to Jeb Stuart's men. Yet their leader's flaws were now clear: George Meade kept him reined in at Gettysburg, and eventually sent him to serve in Siberia—a.k.a. Missouri—until war's end.

HENRY HUNT

He was born on the Western frontier—that is, in Detroit—in 1819. After graduating from West Point in 1839, Hunt returned to the wide-open spaces, fighting in the Mexican War and then pulling duty in "Bloody Kansas" and in a U.S. war with Mormons in Utah in 1857.

In the Army of the Potomac, where so many leaders were indecisive or ill-suited to command, Hunt was a pillar of good sense and strategic thinking. When it came to artillery, he wrote the book: with two others, he created a new version of the U.S. Army's *Instruction for Field Artillery* that was published in 1861. Strategically, he favored centralizing control of artillery batteries to ensure coordination. And he preached a slow, steady pace of firing to ensure more accurate targeting. He proved his methods at the Battle of Malvern Hill in the Peninsula Campaign in 1862, when he controlled scores of cannons that methodically mowed down waves of Confederates advancing upon an uphill, entrenched Federal position.

After General Joseph Hooker was appointed to lead the Army of the Potomac in 1863, he removed Hunt from active command of the artillery just before Chancellorsville. The move proved disastrous: Union artillery units failed to coordinate their efforts, contributing to their rout by Lee. In the weeks before Gettysburg, Hunt was once again directing artillery affairs.

On July 2, Hunt's artillery placements atop Cemetery Ridge proved pivotal in the Union victories that day. Never a glory hog, in his official report after the battle, he stated, "At about 3:30 p.m. the enemy established a battery of 10 guns … in a wheat field to the north and a little to the east of the Cemetery Hill … and opened a remarkably accurate fire upon our batteries. We soon gained a decided advantage over them, and at the end of an hour or more compelled them to withdraw." On July 3, it was Hunt's clever ruse—silencing his guns to invite a Confederate charge—that helped ensure the Federals' triumph.

James Longstreet

LIEUTENANT GENERAL, CONFEDERATE STATES ARMY

★

ROBERT E. LEE CALLED HIS ABLE AND trusted lieutenant his "Old War Horse," yet for 150 years now James Longstreet has been one of the Civil War's designated whipping boys, his reputation flogged with gusto by assorted critics, colleagues, conspiracy-mongers and custodians of Confederate charisma. The title of a sympathetic 1994 biography, Jeffry D. Wert's *General James Longstreet: The Confederacy's Most Controversial Soldier,* sums up his plight.

What is indisputable is that Longstreet was at once a plodding commander who made haste slowly—and a genius of military strategy and tactics. He was a trusted subordinate of Lee's but also a barracks politician who conspired against his fellow officers. He was a pioneer of defensive tactics in battle who spent the decades after the war defending his career, yet seldom attacked his critics. He not only allowed his vocal detractors—many of them his former colleagues—to savage his character but also seemed to seek new ways to keep the smoke of partisan controversy billowing around his reputation.

Born in South Carolina and brought up in Georgia, Longstreet was near the bottom of his class at West Point, and he graduated in 1842 not much higher than his good friend Ulysses S. Grant. He served well in the Mexican War, but by the time the Civil War started he was toiling in the paymaster department. His experience and self-confidence started him off in the Confederate army as a brigadier general. "Six feet tall, broad as a door, hairy as a goat," by one colleague's account, Longstreet was ambitious and stubborn. The summer campaign of 1861 showed that he was a first-rate defensive fighter but unaggressive and slow on the attack.

Lee understood Longstreet, but Longstreet did not understand Lee and often found himself at odds with his superior. After Antietam, where he disagreed with Lee's strategy, Longstreet became outspokenly critical of his commander. He also thought little of Stonewall Jackson. Itching for an independent command, Longstreet seized the opportunity when he was given the Department of Southern Virginia and North Carolina, to augment his army at the expense of Lee's. Ordered to rejoin Lee before the Battle of Chancellorsville, he moved so slowly that he missed the fighting by days.

At Gettysburg, Longstreet again disagreed with Lee's plan: arriving on the scene late on July 1, he advised against attacking the entrenched Federals and urged Lee to outflank General George G. Meade's army to the south and east, so as to get between the Army of the Potomac and Washington, forcing Meade off Cemetery Ridge and making him attack the Confederates. Overruled, Longstreet seemed to turn sulky and defeatist. On July 2, he took his time in preparing the attack Lee requested for 11 a.m., then got his directions all fouled up as he marched his troops to the Federals' left flank. By 4 p.m., when he finally attacked, the Federals had been reinforced, and the assault failed.

The next day, when Lee again resisted his pitch to attempt to outflank the Union Army, Longstreet was so stricken by Lee's decision to mount a massive frontal

The original Chicago version of the work is now in the hands of private investors, awaiting restoration. According to the National Park Service, one of the two no longer extant versions of the painting was exhibited for a time in Denver, and sections of that iteration of the work were eventually cut up and used to create tents on a Shoshone res- ervation early in the 20th century. The fate of the fourth version of Philippoteaux's spectacular work is unknown. Readers wishing to learn more about the Gettysburg Cyclorama will find an informative discussion of the work at *nps.gov/gettysburg*. Information on the cyclorama can be found in the Photos & Multimedia area.

The Gettysburg Cyclorama

Among the most memorable depictions of a Civil War conflict is *The Battle of Gettysburg*, French artist Paul Philippoteaux's magnificent panorama of Pickett's Charge on July 3. This massive artwork was created as a cyclorama, a popular entertainment format in the 19th century, in which immense paintings of historic events were hung along the walls of a cylindrical gallery to create a 360°-surround effect. Although the chief glory of Philippoteaux's work—its expanse—cannot be shown here, the painting remains powerful even at diminished size.

Philippoteaux was commissioned by a group of Chicago investors to create the painting. He visited the battlefield in 1882 and hired local photographer William Tipton to take pictures from a wooden tower to capture the lay of the land. The painter also consulted with veterans of the battle, including Winfield Scott Hancock and others, in his research for the work. The painting took some 18 months to complete, with the chief artist employing a number of assistants. Though Philippoteaux took pains to achieve a sense of realism, his European assistants included a number of inaccurate details of uniforms and weaponry.

Today, only two of the original four versions of Philippoteaux's work have survived. The most fully restored version, first exhibited in Boston, is now owned by the National Park Service. It was restored between 2003-2008 and is now displayed at the Museum and Visitor Center at Gettysburg National Military Park. From 1962 to 2005, the painting was shown at Gettysburg in a cylindrical building designed by modernist architect Richard Neutra. That structure has both admirers and critics; amid controversy, it is slated to be torn down in 2013.

Cycloramas were the IMAX theaters of their time, immense spectacles that wowed viewers with scenic grandeur. In many cases, exhibitors gave the 360° installation a 3-D quality by placing life-sized objects in front of it, blurring the boundary between reality and illusion. When *The Battle of* *Gettysburg* was first shown in a purpose-built cylindrical theater in Chicago in 1883, fences, stone walls and shattered trees were placed in front of it. The Chicago exhibit was so successful that three more versions were commissioned for display in other cities.

The original cyclorama, exhibited in Chicago, is estimated to have been 22 ft. high and 276 ft. in circumference. The version now displayed at Gettysburg was first shown in Boston in 1884, and it is an even larger work than the original. At 42 ft. high and 377 ft. in circumference, it is the equivalent of a 4-story building that is 25 yards longer than a football field. Created in sections, the entire work weighs four tons. It was displayed in the Cyclorama Building on Boston's Tremont Street, where lectures on Gettysburg were also held. The other two versions of the painting were first shown in Brooklyn, N.Y., and Philadelphia.

I ... learned that you intended commencing business in New Orleans. If you become as good a merchant as you were a soldier, I shall be content. No one will then excel you, and no one can wish you more success and more happiness than I. My interest and affection for you will never cease, and my prayers are always offered for your prosperity.

—Robert E. Lee, to Longstreet,
Jan. 19, 1866

assault against the Federals that he sought to make his artillery chief, E. Porter Alexander, give the command for Pickett's Charge. When that failed, he could not bring himself to say the words, but simply nodded his head when General George Pickett asked for the order.

After Gettysburg, Longstreet was detached from Lee's army for service in Tennessee. A master of logistics, he carried off a brilliant coup in September 1863, transporting 12,000 of his troops 800 miles by rail for 12 days to arrive at the battlefield on the second day of the Battle of Chickamauga and sweep the field with a surprise assault. But he got along badly with his new chief, the dyspeptic Braxton Bragg, and, with others, openly called for his dismissal. When the proposed coup failed, he was not sorry to be ordered back to Lee again.

At the 1864 Battle of the Wilderness he was late as usual, but when his tardy veterans did arrive, they saved the day. There he almost met Stonewall Jackson's fate, when in the fog of battle he was wounded by friendly fire. He recovered in time to fight in the last hopeless battles around Richmond, and was still covering the rear

of Lee's ragged army when the end came at Appomattox. Longstreet's critics should note that he enjoyed Lee's firm support through all four years of the conflict.

After the war, the embittered Longstreet seemed to relish whipping up controversy. Living in New Orleans, he was alone among Confederate veterans in turning Republican, the party of Lincoln. In 1867 a newspaper published his signed letter counseling submission to the North. By the 1870s, he was the foremost target of Jubal Early and other proponents of the Lost Cause school of thought. As adjutant general of the Louisiana State Militia in 1874, he led troops that included African Americans against a group of white supremacists in what amounted to a small race war. Small wonder that he was scorned in the South well into the 20th century.

Only in recent years have scholars like Wert and the general public begun to take a more rounded view of his legacy—aided, in part, by a sympathetic treatment of him in Michael Shaara's 1974 novel *The Killer Angels*. The South may not rise again, but its favorite whipping boy might just do so. ■

Helen Dortch Longstreet
After his wife of 41 years died in 1889, Longstreet married Helen Dortch, above, in 1897, when he was 76 and she was 34. After his death in 1904, Helen fought to restore his reputation until her death in 1962, 99 years after Gettysburg. Straddling worlds, she worked as a riveter in a factory in World War II.

At Gettysburg, Death And Transformation

By Drew Gilpin Faust and Ric Burns

THE LAST GUNS FELL SILENT sometime around 6 on the evening of July 3, 1863. For three days, the massive, Armageddon-like conflict had raged south of the little crossroads town in southeast Pennsylvania, involving 75,000 Confederate and 83,000 Federal soldiers in all. The battle had left more than 50,000 casualties: almost four times more dead and wounded men than the total number of killed and wounded in the entire eight-year-long Revolutionary War. More casualties, in fact, than had been tallied in all previous American wars combined.

It was a Union victory, to be sure, but an immensely costly one. As Robert E. Lee and the badly battered Army of Northern Virginia retreated southward from Pennsylvania, ending the second and final Confederate invasion of the North, 7,000 slain men and 3,000 dead horses—an estimated 6 million lbs. of human and animal carcasses—lay strewn across the field in the summer heat. With 23,000 Union casualties alone, the town of Gettysburg, with a population of 2,400, now had some 10 times that number of dead and wounded men to care for.

One hundred fifty years on, it is hard to imagine an America at war producing dead and dying soldiers, in any number—let alone such enormous ones—with no federal relief organizations; no adequate federal hospitals; no dog tags or other formal provisions for identifying the dead; no procedures for notifying next of kin or for providing aid to the suffering families of dead veterans; no formal system for interring the dead; and no national cemeteries to bury them in.

Americans North and South had embarked on civil war little anticipating the scale of destruction it would inflict and little prepared to meet its imperatives. In important ways the almost unimaginable carnage of Gettysburg would mark a turning point, transforming forever the relation of citizen and state in America as the nation came to recognize and embrace the sacred obligation it owes to those who fight and die in its service.

"Sometimes," the historian Bernard DeVoto once observed, "there are exceedingly brief periods which determine a long future." It is commonplace to acknowledge that the four-year-long American Civil War was such a time. But the three-day battle of Gettysburg itself—along

Faust is president of Harvard University and the author of the acclaimed study of death in the Civil War, This Republic of Suffering *(2008).*

Burns is a noted filmmaker whose PBS documentary Death and the Civil War *(2012) was made in collaboration with Faust*

The slain *After the battle concluded, bodies of the dead still lay unburied on the battlefield. The wagon at rear was used as a darkroom by photographer Alexander Gardner*

with the moral, political, cultural and rhetorical forces propelled into being by the enormous tide of death left in its wake—can be said to be one of the great founding moments in American life: an exceedingly brief point in time during which some key aspects of the American Republic we know today began to take a recognizable shape.

The Battle's Toll

In the immediate aftermath of the Battle of Gettysburg, the work of burying thousands upon thousands of dead fell to the Union forces who held the devastated battleground—and to the stunned citizens of the town itself, who were implored to help the beleaguered Union soldiers, overwhelmed by the magnitude of the task before them. And many of the residents found themselves all but overwhelmed as well. John S. Forney faced the task of burying the 79 North Carolinians who had fallen in a perfect line on his farm; Lydia Leister, a widow, confronted 15 dead horses in her front yard on July 4.

Mass burials of enemy soldiers proceeded in the summer heat. Details of Union soldiers interred dead Confederates in trenches containing as many as 150 or more men, the decomposing bodies often hurled rather than laid to rest. Soldiers stomped on top of the dead, according to an Iowa soldier who observed such duty in the wake of the 1862 Battle of Shiloh, "straightening out their legs and arms and tramping them down so as to make the hole contain as many as possible."

Sometimes the rotting bodies ruptured, compelling burial parties to work elsewhere until the stench had dissipated. So many bodies lay unburied after three days of battle that a surgeon described the atmosphere as almost intolerable. One young boy who lived in town recalled that everyone "went about with a bottle of pennyroyal or peppermint oil" to counteract the smell. Gettysburg residents complained of a stench that persisted until October, when at last the frost came.

Slain Union comrades were accorded more respect and, if possible, an individual grave. Soldiers, perhaps imagining how they would wish to be treated in similar circumstances, improvised ways of providing dignified treatment for the soldiers who had fought alongside them. It was a matter of affirming the humanity of both the living and the dead. Often soldiers sought out friends of the missing, in hopes they could provide aid, help identify bodies and graves, or assist in gathering information for loved ones at home, who otherwise might never know the fate of their absent kin. One soldier from Michigan

was relieved to find that a burial party had already interred his friend along with dozens of his fellow soldiers. "All pains possible was taken in their burial," he wrote. "In some cases their bloody garments were removed and washed and dried on limbs of trees, then replaced."

Two soldiers from Maine received permission to return to the part of the field where they had last seen a close friend on the third day of battle, and search for any sign of him. "We found him," one of them wrote, "face down, and with many others the flesh eaten (in that hot climate) by maggots, but not so bad but that we could recognize him. When we went to bury him, all we could find to dig a grave was an old hoe in a small building.

The bottom of the grave was covered with empty knapsacks; we laid in our beloved brother and covered him with another knapsack, and over all put as much earth as we could find. The grave was dug at the foot of a large tree. We found a piece of a hard wood box cover and cut his name on it with a jackknife and nailed it to the tree at the head of his grave."

The Comrades Left Behind

As news of the enormous battle spread to Washington, Philadelphia and beyond, families and volunteers began to descend on the little Pennsylvania town, stretching its capacities to the limit but also offering help in caring for the wounded and dead. Agents of the U.S. Sanitary Commission—a federally authorized, privately-funded relief organization established early in the war to provide aid for sick and wounded Union soldiers—were well aware that their work made them an important and often unique resource for anxious families desperate for information of any kind about their sons, fathers and brothers. They began systematically surveying field hospitals and burial sites, creating ledgers of casualties and directories of patients in order to be able to respond to inquiries from worried and often frantic relatives. The agency was soon inundated with letters and requests.

During the battle, Confederate units had established

Works of mercy

Representatives of the U.S. Sanitary Commission, a private agency founded in 1861 to care for casualties, are shown outside their headquarters tent at Gettysburg after the battle.

Frederick Law Olmsted, the celebrated landscape architect who helped design New York City's Central Park, was executive director of the group

Lincoln knew that he was in a place of death. But his work was to give this intolerable sacrifice meaning, and in so doing explain the purposes of the war and, indeed, of the American nation.

nearly 40 makeshift field hospitals close to the battle-ground to care for an eventual 15,000 wounded and 5,000 sick officers and men. But when Lee's defeated army moved south in retreat, hurrying to cross the Potomac to safety, thousands of suffering Confederate soldiers who could not safely be moved were left behind to die or to be taken as prisoners of war. Others were hastily loaded onto carts and wagons or instructed to walk alongside the ragtag procession of retreating men that represented the remains of the Confederate army.

Soon all the men were drenched by an unrelenting summer rain—a downpour so heavy, one witness said, it was as if "the very windows of heaven seemed to have opened." For the suffering, it seemed perhaps more like the windows of hell. Many of them died en route, and hastily dug shallow graves dotted the roadside along Lee's route of retreat. For some of the more privileged among the rebel dead, personal slaves who had accompanied their masters north carried their bodies south for burial at home.

The repatriation of the Confederate slain would continue long after both the battle and the war were over, as would the pain and anguish and dislocation those deaths caused. In the early 1870s, memorial associations of white Southern women would arrange for several thousand more Confederate dead from Gettysburg to be disinterred and transported to cemeteries in Richmond and Charleston, where they were reburied with solemn pageantry and celebrations of the South's Lost Cause.

From the Dead, a Nation Reborn

And yet for all the horror, heartache and dismay, something new in the American experience would begin to arise from the fields of Gettysburg in the days, weeks and months following the battle. For nine months—since the Battle of Antietam, in September 1862, the bloodiest single day in American history—the inexorably rising death tolls of the war, the cumulative experience of mass death in America, had been exerting a powerfully transforming impact on American culture, at least in the North: on military strategy, on public policy, on the very definition of the war's meaning and purpose; as if death itself, under certain circumstances, could take on an enormous generative power and creativity.

No formal policy or appropriation for burying the dead would emerge during the war itself. However, in 1862, as the death tolls soared, the U.S. Congress had passed measures granting the President and the War

Department the power to purchase grounds near battle-fields—on an emergency basis, as circumstance and public health concerns dictated.

But the burial ground that now began to take shape south of Gettysburg would go far beyond the practical needs of disposing of dead bodies. Soldiers and citizens; businessmen and military officers; and local, state and federal officials came together in an unprecedented collective action, one that would foreshadow and for the first time begin to embody a new sense of obligation and responsibility to the dead and a new sense of national purpose in the North—and would begin to suggest how a restored U.S. might eventually bind itself together again into a new American Republic, one with a past and a future, consecrated both to memory and to hope, a Republic of the living and the dead.

Not long after the battle—with financial help from every Northern state that had lost men in the engagement—a local lawyer named David Wills oversaw the purchase of 17 acres in the town, adjoining the existing private cemetery, which was soon taken over by the Federal Government. In October, contracts were let for the reburial of Union soldiers on the new ground, at the rate of $1.59 for each body.

On Nov. 19, 1863, a host of dignitaries from Boston, Philadelphia and Washington, including President Abraham Lincoln himself, journeyed to Pennsylvania to dedicate Gettysburg's new Soldiers' National Cemetery. Just a few months before, 7,000 corpses had lain strewn across the surrounding fields; even now still unburied coffins stood stacked nearby. Lincoln knew he was in a place of death. But his work was to give this intolerable sacrifice meaning, and in so doing explain the purposes of the war and, indeed, of the American nation.

Lincoln's brief but soaring remarks—like the new burial ground itself at Gettysburg, with its rows of identical graves radiating symmetrically, and democratically, around the cemetery's central focus—marked a seismic shift in governmental attitude and policy toward the dead. The President's words affirmed that the dead were no longer simply the responsibility of their families, but rather that the deceased, and their loss, and their meaning, belonged to the entire nation.

The address—what the historian Garry Wills called "the words that remade America"—was nothing less than a prescription for civic rebirth, a call for a kind of collective transubstantiation of the American body politic, one that urgently stressed the steps the nation and its

citizens must take so that the deaths on the battlefield might not have been in vain but have meaning and purpose; such that death, in short, might be transformed into life, not in a religious sense but in a political sense: deaths incurred that a nation might live; a redefining of the nation's future as being tied to the deaths that had secured it.

"These honored dead" had died "that a nation might live." In their honor, this nation must now ensure "a new birth of freedom" and the survival of that form of government Lincoln had elsewhere described as "the last, best hope of earth": a government "of the people, by the people, for the people." The President's words transformed the loss of death into the immortality of a redeemer nation. The price paid by the Gettysburg dead required not just that the unfinished work of the war be completed but also that it be dedicated to the cause of equality and freedom, which would consecrate their sacrifice by ensuring its transcendent purpose.

Gettysburg presented the nation with a roll of death and a landscape of carnage unlike any it had either experienced or imagined. But it also redefined the meaning of death in the nation's service and the purposes of the nation itself. We still live in the world those who died at Gettysburg created for us, with the work of freedom and equality to which they gave their lives still unfinished. ∎

The final passage
Timothy O'Sullivan took this photograph of the bodies of Confederate soldiers lying in makeshift graves. The boards served as tombstones identifying the dead, suggesting the temporary graves were dug by fellow Confederates

Lee Escapes to Fight Again

The Union's victory at Gettysburg has the Army of Northern Virginia on the ropes—but while General Meade and his minions dither, Lee slips away

W HILE GENERAL GEORGE E. PICK-ett's shattered divisions were still straggling back to Seminary Ridge in the lengthening shadows of late afternoon on July 3, Alfred Pleasonton, the cocky cavalry chief of the Army of the Potomac, rode up to General George E. Meade. "I will give you half an hour to show yourself a great general," Pleasonton said. "Order the army to advance, while I take the cavalry and get in Lee's rear, and we will finish the campaign in a week."

For once restraining his notorious temper at this gratuitous advice from a subordinate, Meade answered mildly, "How do you know Lee will not attack me again?" Complacently, he added, "We have done well enough."

In command of the army for only six days, Meade had spent three of them fighting one of history's most ferocious battles, and he had held his ground. To move now from the defensive to the offensive would be a task of awesome difficulty, especially with a long line of Confederate cannons still glaring at him from the west.

Moreover, Meade had the condition of his own army to consider. An early-morning head count on July 4 showed only 51,414 officers and men reporting for duty. This seemed to indicate that more than 38,000 men had been lost in battle. In fact, almost 15,000 of those soldiers had merely been separated from their outfits during the fighting and would soon return. But Meade could hardly be expected to know that.

Most of the losses—23,409 by later count—had been suffered by four of Meade's seven corps (in fact, two of them, I and III Corps, would eventually pass from existence, the men being dispersed to other commands). Any

A long trudge south *Magazine illustrator Edwin Forbes painted this scene, based on his eyewitness view of Lee's army as the retreating Confederate troops marched towards Emmitsburg, Md., on July 7, 1863, four days after the fighting ceased at Gettysburg. The town lies about 12 miles south of the battlefields*

assault, then, would have to rely on three corps attacking a Confederate army that, however badly hurt, had never in the war been dislodged from a defensive position. The prospect was daunting—and Meade decided against it.

Thus while the opposing armies glowered at each other from ridges scarcely a mile apart, Meade contented himself with occupying Gettysburg and sending out patrols and burial parties. At about 1 p.m. on July 4, sullen clouds rolled across the region, thunder roared, lightning cracked, and there began a deluge that, as one man put it, "washed the blood from the grass."

Against that apocalyptic backdrop, General Meade composed his congratulations to the Army of the Potomac, concluding with a flourish he would later regret: "Our task is not yet accomplished, and the commanding general looks to the army for greater efforts to drive from our soil every vestige of the presence of the invader."

Since the beginning of the war, Abraham Lincoln had been trying to convince his successive commanders that their objective should not be the possession of real estate but rather the complete destruction of Lee's army. Upon reading Meade's message, Lincoln's face darkened; he slapped his knee in frustration and groaned, "Drive the invader from our soil? My God! Is that all?"

Lee Faces His Defeat

As Confederate commanders mustered their troops on the morning of July 4, the degree of the Confederate disaster became apparent. Official records would place the army's losses at 20,448, but the actual figure was probably closer to 28,000—or nearly 40% of those engaged, compared with the Federal casualty rate of 25%.

Robert E. Lee knew what he must do. His casualties were too high, his ammunition and supplies too low, to remain in enemy territory. He told one subordinate after the sound of the guns had faded, "We must now return to Virginia." But getting there was another matter, and it would call on all Lee's capabilities for active leadership. Late into the night of July 3 he labored, studying maps in the flickering candlelight of his tent and issuing a stream of orders.

Among the first to get instructions was Brigadier General John D. Imboden, whose cavalry brigade had not arrived at Gettysburg until noon on July 3. Summoned that night to army headquarters, Imboden reported to Lee around 1 a.m., when, Imboden recalled, "he came riding alone, at a slow walk, and evidently wrapped in profound thought." When Lee attempted to dismount,

he seemed so exhausted that Imboden stepped forward to assist his chief. But Lee waved him aside and stood leaning against Traveller, supporting himself with his arm across the saddle.

"The moon shone full upon his massive features," Imboden wrote, "and revealed an expression of sadness I had never seen before upon his face." Embarrassed, Imboden broke the awkward silence. "General," he said, "this has been a hard day for you." "Yes," replied Lee, "it has been a sad, sad day to us." And then, after a pause of more than a minute, he sighed with infinite regret: "Too bad. Oh! Too bad."

Recovering himself, Lee gave Imboden a grim task—to escort the Confederate wounded and most of the army's supply wagons back to Virginia. First he was to head northwest across South Mountain to Chambersburg, then turn south to Hagerstown and thence to Williamsport on the Potomac, where both a ford and pontoon bridge awaited him. Imboden would have about 2,100 troopers and 23 guns. Fitzhugh Lee's cavalry brigade and part of Wade Hampton's would guard his rear and flank.

At 4 p.m. Imboden's wagon train departed on its dismal journey. "The rain fell in blinding sheets," Imboden wrote later. "Canvas was no protection against its fury, and the wounded men lying upon the naked boards of the wagon-bodies were drenched. Horse and mules were blinded and maddened by the wind and water."

Throughout that terrible night the 17-mile-long train lumbered on; by dawn the head of the column was nearing Chambersburg. In Greencastle, 30 or 40 ax-wielding citizens, Union loyalists, hacked out spokes from the wheels of the passing wagons, toppling a dozen vehicles before Imboden's men could stop them.

At last, late on the afternoon of July 5, Imboden's lead elements reached Williamsport—only to find that the pontoon bridge had been destroyed by a Federal cavalry detachment and that heavy rain had raised the river and made fording it impossible.

Worse, early the next morning Imboden was informed of the approach of Federal cavalry in strength—as it turned out, the 3,000 men of John Buford's division, the unit that had set the giant battle at Gettysburg in motion only five days before. Wearily, Imboden deployed his somewhat smaller force, including about 700 wagoners commanded by wounded officers, to meet the threat. Imboden gamely held on, diverting Buford's main attack to an area he had already reinforced, and the Federals withdrew later in the day when fresh rebel cavalry arrived.

John D. Imboden
A lawyer and Virginia state legislator before the war, Imboden was named a captain when he enlisted and served under Stonewall Jackson during the Shenandoah Valley Campaign. In April and May 1863, he and General William E. Jones led a famed, successful cavalry raid against Federal train lines and other resources in northwestern Virginia, a Union stronghold

A city under siege
The hillside beneath the elegant Shirley House in Vicksburg, at left, was carved into caves by Union soldiers who occupied the home during the siege and sought shelter from Confederate shelling. Similar caves were carved into many of the hills within the city, where residents weathered Union artillery fire during the six weeks of the siege

★ In the West, Another Major Victory for the Union

Even as the Army of the Potomac and the Army of Northern Virginia were battling in the hills of eastern Pennsylvania, another major turning point in the war was edging closer to conclusion. The scene was Vicksburg, Miss., a grand old river town perched on bluffs along the Mississippi River and now one of the last preserves of Confederate power along the vital waterway. Its big artillery batteries loomed over the Big Muddy's course, preventing Union vessels from passing either up or down the river. Confederate President Jefferson Davis called Vicksburg, "the nailhead that held the South's two halves together," while Abraham Lincoln described the city as the key to the West. "The war can never be brought to a close until that key is in our pocket," he declared. "I am acquainted with that region and know what I am talking about."

Lincoln knew of Vicksburg's importance; and in General Ulysses S. Grant, he had just the man to wrest the city from the rebels' grasp. Earlier in the war, Grant had risen to renown by taking two key Confederate positions along the Tennessee River, Fort Henry and Fort Donelson. Now, beginning in the fall of 1862, Grant set his sights on winning control of the "Gibraltar of the West."

In October, Grant launched a tentative campaign against Vicksburg, only to be repelled by Confederate cavalry. But as the year ended, the Union won a slim victory at Stones River in Tennessee, allowing Grant to again focus on Vicksburg. The primary challenge was geographical: the city was protected to the north by impenetrable swamps, bogs and marshes, while its big guns forbade attack from the river on its west; Union Flag Officer David Farragut had tried on several occasions to storm the city from the Mississippi, without success.

Grant, a man who liked to keep his troops actively engaged, launched four "experiments" designed to see if he could engineer a path to reach Vicksburg from the north; all failed. Finally, he was forced to choose the option of attacking from the south—which meant he would have to slip his troops past Vicksburg's lofty guns and approach the city from the south and east.

On the moonless night of April 16, 1863, Admiral David Dixon Porter, working with Grant, managed to slip eight gunboats and three transports past Vicksburg to the south, landing them in Bruinsburg, Miss. By April 30, Grant linked up with 23,000 Federal troops who had been marching south on the west side of the river in Louisiana. In the next weeks, he kept up the pressure. First he attacked and won Port Gibson, Miss., a city 10 miles east of the river. Then, in a surprise, he moved northeast and captured Jackson, Miss., securing his eastern flank. Turning west, Grant won the campaign's largest battle, on May 16 at Champion Hill, midway between Jackson and Vicksburg, sending Confederate troops reeling back to Vicksburg. On May 23, after two direct attacks against the river city's massive fortifications failed, Grant settled down to conduct one of warfare's oldest maneuvers: a siege.

The weeks that followed saw Vicksburg's citizens and the 30,000 troops defending the town gradually being starved into submission. As Federal guns shelled the city, residents took shelter in crude caves carved into hillsides, and prices for food soared. Morale among Confederate troops, led by Lieutenant General John C. Pemberton, plummeted (Pemberton, a Pennsylvania-born Northerner, never won their trust).

After weeks of misery and starvation, Pemberton surrendered the city to Grant on the morning of July 4, 1863, only hours after Pickett's Charge ended at Gettysburg. When the news from Vicksburg reached the East Coast, it triggered enormous celebrations: the twin triumphs were a one-two punch that tilted the odds in the war firmly in the Union's favor. Yet victory would elude the North until April 1865.

Safe for the moment, Imboden settled down to wait for Lee's infantry, which had begun its march immediately after the wagons departed. Rather than following Imboden's easier, roundabout route, the foot soldiers marched on a shorter path to Hagerstown through the rugged high gaps and passes of South Mountain.

General Richard S. Ewell's corps, bringing up the rear, was constantly harassed by enemy cavalry. At Monterey Pass a wildly confused little fight flared in darkness illuminated only by bolts of lightning; Ewell lost many of his wagons, but the strategic results were negligible.

On the morning of July 7, General James Longstreet's corps led the army into Williamsport. The Potomac was still too high to be crossed on foot. Lee set his rough-and-ready quartermaster, Major John A. Harman, to work on a new pontoon bridge and ordered his engineers to lay out a defensive line. The army redeployed, facing generally eastward in an arc along the north-south stretch of the river at Williamsport; Lee's left was anchored just north of the town, and his right near Falling Waters, six miles south. Digging furiously, the Confederates soon built a strong parapet, 6 ft. wide at the top, with abundant gun emplacements. By the time they were done, many men were actually looking forward to the arrival of the Army of the Potomac. One soldier wrote, "We hope soon to get up another fight."

But General Meade was in no hurry to comply. Not until midday on July 5 did he begin to move his troops out of Gettysburg. Even then, Meade sent only Major General John Sedgwick's VI Corps to follow Lee's infantry. At 8:30 the following morning, Sedgwick reported, mistakenly, that Monterey Pass was strongly defended and that he would not care "to dash my corps against it."

That prospect did not please Meade either. Instead of continuing to follow Lee's path, he sent his army south along three separate routes into Maryland, then westward across Catoctin Mountain to a rendezvous at Middletown, where they would still have to cross South Mountain to get at Lee's forces.

On the afternoon of July 6, still at Gettysburg, Meade wired the War Department, complaining about the difficulty of closing with Lee's army. The message sounded timid to President Lincoln, who that night wrote an annoyed note to his military chief, Henry Halleck. The President said that Meade's actions seemed calculated "to get the enemy across the river again without a further collision, and they do not appear connected with a purpose to prevent his crossing and to destroy him."

By July 9, a large part of Meade's army had crossed South Mountain to Boonsboro, eight miles southeast of Williamsport. Meade reported to Halleck, "I think the decisive battle of the war will be fought in a few days." Yet he was still taking no chances: "I desire to adopt such measures as in my judgment will tend to insure success, even though these may be deemed tardy."

The army crept forward, and it was the afternoon of the 12th before Meade announced in a message to Halleck, "It is my intention to attack them tomorrow unless something intervenes to prevent it." Something did intervene: a council of war called by Meade at which he asked his corps commanders to vote on his plan of attack. Two approved, but the other five voted against it, and at 5 p.m. on July 13 Meade informed Washington of the council's results. The attack was off, but he promised to continue with his reconnaissances. After the vote, Meade was handed a furious message from Halleck, demanding that Meade order the assault rather than have his lieutenants vote upon the subject. But by then it was too late. The final escape was under way.

Lee Slips Back into Virginia

By the morning of July 13, General Lee's quartermaster had torn down some warehouses for wood, built some makeshift boats and strung across the Potomac at Falling Waters what Colonel Moxley Sorrel described as a "crazy affair." But Lee pronounced it a "good bridge" and ordered the corps of Longstreet and A.P. Hill to start across the river at nightfall. To speed the process, Ewell's corps would use the ford at Williamsport, where the river had at last subsided sufficiently to permit passage.

That afternoon, however, disaster threatened. Heavy rain began to fall, the river started to rise again, and the rough dirt road between Williamsport and Falling Waters quickly became a quagmire. Nonetheless, in the pitch-black, eerie night, the movement began. As a dismal dawn approached, Lee received word that nearly all of Ewell's corps had reached the sodden soil of Virginia. But at Falling Waters, where Lee was keeping an anxious watch, Longstreet's corps had just started across the pontoon bridge, while Hill's was still some distance

Pontoon boat

Both the Union and Confederate armies relied heavily on pontoon bridges to serve as river crossings during the war, particularly in northern Virginia and southern Maryland, where many standing bridges were deliberately destroyed to prevent crossings.

Above is an 1864 photograph of a Federal pontoon boat loaded on a carriage. The boats were placed parallel to the flow of the river, then lashed together to form a solid unit upon which a wooden surface was built to create a roadway

Heading for home
Edwin Forbes sketched Confederate troops as they fought heavy rains on July 10 in their retreat to Virginia. As Forbes' notes on the sketch show, the guns on the move were big ones: 30-lb. cannons. Within the next few days, Lee's entire army would reach Virginia, almost unchallenged by Federal troops

away. A Federal attack now could very likely have destroyed the Army of Northern Virginia.

Yet even though Federal cavalry had discovered as early as 3 a.m. on July 14 that the Confederates were on the move, no attack came. Longstreet's corps crossed the river, followed by most of Hill's. General Henry Heth's division, bringing up the rear, was approaching the bridge shortly after 11 a.m., when firing erupted close by. Buford's and General Hugh Kilpatrick's Federal cavalry were now hot on Lee's trail. "There!" Lee exclaimed. "I was expecting it—the beginning of the attack!"

The most determined assault was led by a regiment in George A. Custer's brigade—the 6th Michigan Cavalry, under Major Peter A. Weber, who charged General Heth's division. Within three or four minutes, many of the Michigan troopers, including Weber, lay dead. Soon more Federals entered the fray, driving the Confederates back toward the river. In the process, General J. Johnston Pettigrew, commander of Heth's rear guard and one of Lee's most promising officers, was mortally wounded, and nearly 1,500 rebel infantrymen were taken prisoner.

But those defendants had bought time for Lee's escape.

Before long, Lee was watching the last of his troops cross the Potomac. "As the bulk of the rear guard of the army safely passed over the shaky bridge," one Confederate wrote, "as it swayed to and fro, lashed by the current, Lee uttered a sigh of relief, and a great weight seemed taken from his shoulders." As Buford's pursuing horsemen started down the bluff to the river, Lee ordered the bridge cut loose.

In Washington, President Lincoln could not contain his despair. "We had them within our grasp," he told his secretary, John Hay. "We only had to stretch forth our hands and they were ours. And nothing I could say or do could make the army move."

On July 3, Alfred Pleasonton had offered George Meade 30 minutes to prove he was a great general by attacking Lee. As it turned out, Meade had been given 10 days more to answer Pleasonton's challenge, and he still had failed to take advantage of the enemy's plight. Lee had escaped to fight again—and the war would grind on for another 21 months. ■

Gettysburg
In Memory

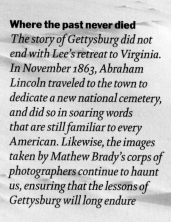

Where the past never died
The story of Gettysburg did not end with Lee's retreat to Virginia. In November 1863, Abraham Lincoln traveled to the town to dedicate a new national cemetery, and did so in soaring words that are still familiar to every American. Likewise, the images taken by Mathew Brady's corps of photographers continue to haunt us, ensuring that the lessons of Gettysburg will long endure

The New Face of War

By Richard Lacayo

AFTER THE BATTLE OF ANTIETAM, in September 1862, Oliver Wendell Holmes, the American physician and man of letters, had the grim experience of searching the battlefield for his wounded son. To his great relief, he would learn that Oliver Jr., a lieutenant in the Union Army—and a future Supreme Court Justice—had survived. But the painful feelings of that day returned to the elder Holmes only a month later, when he visited photographer Mathew Brady's historic exhibition in New York City, "The Dead of Antietam." Recalling his experience in an 1863 article for the

Atlantic Monthly magazine, the senior Holmes wrote: "It was so nearly like visiting the battlefield to look over these views, that all of the emotions excited by the actual sight of the stained and sordid scene, strewed with rags and wrecks, came back to us, and we buried them in the recesses of our cabinet as we would have buried the mutilated remains of the dead they too vividly represented."

The Civil War wasn't the first armed conflict to be documented by photographers. As early as the 1840s, a handful had worked around the edges of the Mexican War. And in the next decade the British lawyer turned photographer Roger Fenton had made scenes of the Crimean War. But no previous war had been recorded as thoroughly, as powerfully or with such shocking immediacy. Photography was for the Civil War what television was to the War in Vietnam, a relatively new medium that brought the war home with bracing, revealing clarity.

And it was a new medium, dating back only to 1839, the year that the French artist Louis-Jacques-Mandé Da-

guerre patented his daguerreotype process, which produced highly detailed, one-of-a-kind-images on glass, and the English gentleman scientist Henry Fox Talbot separately announced a method for producing images on paper that were more soft-edged but could be printed in multiple copies. Within just a few years, hundreds of commercial photographers had set themselves up in business on both sides of the Atlantic. By the time the Civil War erupted in 1861, a small industry was in place and ready to record war in a compelling new way.

One of the most successful of those commercial practitioners was Mathew Brady, a would-be artist who had been diverted into becoming a kind of impresario of photography. In 1844, when he was in his early 20s, Brady opened the first in his ever grander series of photo gal-

Lacayo is the art and architecture critic for TIME *magazine. He has written and edited several volumes for* TIME Books, *including* Man-Made Wonders *(2012)*

The early days of photography

Above, photographers from Mathew Brady's corps enjoy an al fresco lunch. Behind them is one of the special wagons fitted out as rolling darkrooms, with which Brady's cadre of camera-men documented the battlefields.

At bottom left is Brady's photo gallery in New York City; another was in Washington. Both were tourist attractions that showed celebrity portraits.

At bottom right is a carte de visite showing Lola Montez, the famed dancer, actress and courtesan of the time

leries in New York City to exhibit the portraits of illustrious Americans taken under his supervision. (Due to poor eyesight, "Brady of Broadway" rarely handled the camera himself.) By the 1850s he was operating a second thriving gallery in Washington, where Congressmen and even Presidents came to have their portraits produced and displayed in a rich setting of mirrored walls and chandeliers. Brady was, in effect, a court artist to the nation's capital.

The Washington operation positioned Brady and his team to rush to the scene at one of the first engagements of the war, the First Battle of Bull Run (Manassas), fought on July 21, 1861, just a few miles outside the capital. Through his close connections with the President and his top military officers, he had already secured permission for his photographers to accompany the Union forces. Bull Run, which ended in a chaotic Union retreat in which Brady himself was lost for days in thick woods, was the first battlefield at which "Brady wagons" made an appearance. Horse-drawn vans, they served as mobile darkrooms where Brady's men developed and printed their pictures on the spot.

Brady's Corps Takes to the Roads
The war had transformed the capital's favorite photographer into a new sort of war correspondent, one we now call a photojournalist. The 20 or so members of Brady's corps of photographers—their numbers would fluctuate throughout the war—were trained in an awkward camera technology called the wet-plate process. Developed in the 1850s, it required coating a sheet of glass in the wagon's darkroom with collodion, a fluid made from gun cotton dissolved in alcohol and ether with other chemicals. When the compound had dried to the proper gummy consistency, the plate was bathed in silver nitrate, then enclosed in a lightproof holding frame before being taken outside to be slotted into a wooden box camera on a tripod. The camera had no shutter, just a lens cap that was removed by hand for 10 sec. or so, then fitted back on. The glass plate was then whisked back into the wagon for developing. With luck, it wouldn't shatter on the rough roads back to the city, where prints of the image it held would be made.

Fewer than 100 photographers covered the Crimean War. More than 3,000 documented the Civil War in some way, though perhaps no more than 300 from battlefield positions. Many more operated on the outskirts of army camps, where soldiers liked to have their portrait

A Harvest of Death
*Perhaps the best known
of the photographs of the
aftermath of Gettysburg
is this image by Brady
cameraman Timothy
O'Sullivan. Colleague
Alexander Gardner gave
the photo its memorable
title in* Gardner's Photographic Sketch Book of
the War, *published in 1865.
Since technology was
not advanced enough to
permit printing photos
in books, the images in
these volumes were actual
prints, pasted in place*

made, a new kind of affordable keepsake for families and sweethearts. The war also added to the store of subjects for the already brisk trade in portraits of the famous (and infamous), which were sold in shops in a cheap format called the carte de visite, after the French term for "visitor's calling card." Measuring about 3½ by 2½ in., they featured photos of popular pubic figures. In an age before YouTube and People magazine, the soprano Jenny Lind and the femme fatale Lola Montez owed much of their public visibility to their widely circulated carte portraits. Once the war got under way, noteworthy officers made a natural subject. In the aftermath of the Confederate fir-

ing on Fort Sumter, portraits of Major Robert Anderson, a Union hero of the attack, sold at a rate of 1,000 a day.

But the pictures that have inscribed themselves most deeply in the national memory are the ones made in the field. Brady's team was just one of several squads of private photographers who would document the war. Much of what they recorded was the day-to-day detail of life at camp, the drills and pickets and downtime. But they also captured the devastation. George N. Barnard, one of Brady's men, accompanied General William T. Sherman on his campaign through Georgia and the Carolinas and took picture after picture of shattered cities, streetscapes

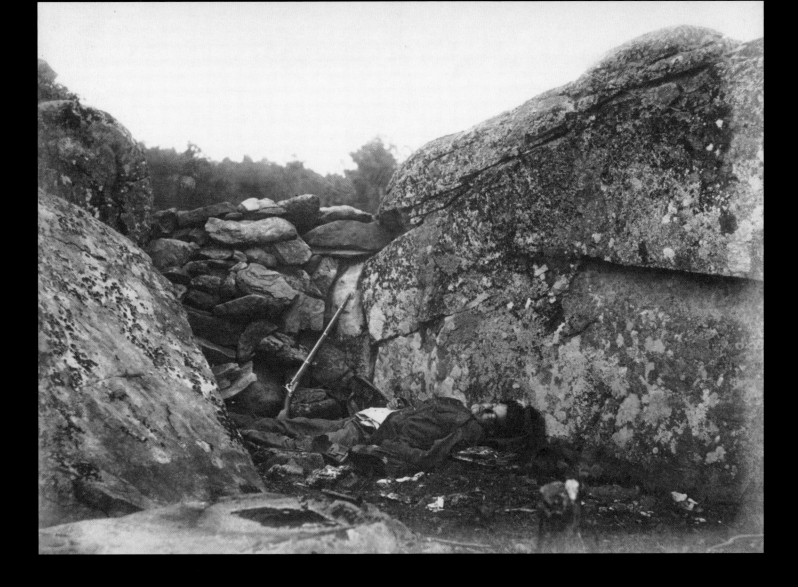

that were no more than jagged silhouettes of rubble.

Yet no pictures that emerged from the Civil War were as shocking as the many images of battlefield dead. These were not the first of their kind. The Italian-British photographer Felice Beato had displayed dead and even partially decomposed bodies in his pictures of the Sepoy Mutiny of 1857-58 and the Second Opium War in China (1856-60). But Beato made photos of foreign casualties for a viewership back home. In the Civil War there were no foreigners, at least not for the American audience. So much the worse that in photographs, battlefield death wasn't glorified, as it had been for centuries in painting.

No one died in noble poses borrowed from antiquity. They died in postures of cold decrepitude, stiff and bloated facts on the ground.

Photographing the dead became standard practice during the war. The military made no rules forbidding it—a position that would change in later wars, at least with respect to photos of American casualties. Not only were these images irresistibly powerful, but they were also perfectly suited to the limitations of mid-19th century photographic equipment. The long exposure time required by the glass plate negatives meant that any movement registered merely as a blur. Subjects before the camera were required to remain still for many seconds. The dead could be counted on to cooperate.

After the War, Photography Heads West

As they still do today, wartime images of death had both a grisly, voyeuristic appeal and a potential moral value. This was the lesson Gardner was reaching for in the caption for the most famous picture in his 1866 *Gardner's Sketch Book of the War,* the first published collection of Civil War photographs. *A Harvest of Death* is a view of a field strewn with corpses at Gettysburg, shot by his colleague Timothy O'Sullivan. Gardner's caption reads in part, "It shows the blank horror and reality of war, in opposition to its pageantry. Here are the dreadful details! Let them aid in preventing such another calamity falling upon the nation!"

It would be wrong to think of these images as news photographs. It wasn't yet possible in the 1860s to print photos in the pages of newspapers and magazines. The halftone process that uses tiny dots to create gray shades wouldn't be perfected for another two decades. So most people encountered photographs of the conflict indirectly, through renderings based on the photos, which appeared in the illustrated press. Publications like *Frank Leslie's Illustrated* and *Harper's Weekly* bought reproduction rights to photos, then handed them to illustrators who might copy them closely, embellish them for dramatic effect or combine elements from several into a composite image. Even well-regarded periodicals didn't always let scruples about journalistic accuracy get in the way of a good picture.

Nor did the photographers, who weren't above rearranging battlefield scenes to suit their purposes. The most famous instance involves two pictures from the aftermath of Gettysburg that appear in Gardner's *Sketch Book* and have been variously attributed to either him or O'Sullivan, though both seem to have been involved. One, called *A Sharpshooter's Last Sleep,* purports to show the body of a Union soldier. The other, called *The Home of a Rebel Sharpshooter,* depicts what Gardner's caption tells us is a dead Confederate. But 20th century researchers have concluded that both pictures show the same deceased man, already stiff with rigor mortis, who was

dragged by the photographers about 40 yds. from one location to another and recast in a rebel uniform to create a moral symmetry of death.

During and after the war, photographs were also circulated as albums or mounted prints produced by Brady and others. Brady's practice of attaching his own name to all the pictures he sold or published, despite the fact that he took almost none of them, alienated some of his most talented staffers, like Gardner and O'Sullivan, who struck out on their own. When Gardner published his *Sketch Book*, he scrupulously credited each picture to the man who made it, even giving a second credit if someone other than the photographer made the print.

Brady, c. 1875

After the fighting ended, the Civil War photographers went on to new lives. Gardner documented the trial and execution of the conspirators involved in Lincoln's assassination, then became official photographer of the Kansas Pacific Railroad. In that position he would make some of the first and still most famous photographs of the American West. Likewise, O'Sullivan served as photographer for several government expeditions surveying the new territories in the West, a landscape that many Easterners would see for the first time through his pictures.

As for Brady, when the war ended he had a collection of 7,000 negatives and prints. But the public had grown weary of the fighting and wanted no reminders. Unable to sell prints any longer, he went bankrupt. In 1875 Congress agreed to purchase his collection for $25,000 and pass it to the Library of Congress. But when Brady died in 1896, he was penniless again, though he had lived long enough to see a revival of interest in Civil War photography that led to several new published collections.

We know now that the pictures circulated by Brady and others changed our collective vision of war, and not just the Civil War. It's not that combat could never again be glorified. It could be, and it would be. But now there would always be a counterargument made by photography. There would always be blunt pictures of ruined cities and refugee columns, and always the melancholy images of the dead, with their mute confirmation of Lincoln's words in his message to Congress on Dec. 1, 1862: "Fellow-citizens, we cannot escape history." ∎

The last months of the war

George N. Barnard was a member of Brady's corps who documented the war in Virginia, then went to the Western Theater, where he accompanied General William T. Sherman and his Federal troops as they marched south from Chattanooga, captured Atlanta, then took Savannah and Charleston, S.C. Barnard's photos constitute a valuable photographic history of Sherman's campaigns. The scene above shows the Roman arches of the train depot in Charleston, devastated by artillery fire. After capturing the city where the war began with the Confederate siege of Fort Sumter, Sherman marched on to occupy Columbia, the capital of South Carolina. The city was burned to the ground on Feb. 17, 1865, as Federal forces were withdrawing, with each side blaming the other for the conflagration.

A New Birth of Freedom

President Abraham Lincoln dedicates a national cemetery at Gettysburg
with a speech that remains a touchstone of the ideals of democracy

THE BATTLE OF GETTYSBURG MAINtains its grip on the American imagination not only because it was a major turning point in the military history of the Civil War, but also because it was on this hallowed ground, more than four months after the war, that Abraham Lincoln delivered his celebrated Gettysburg Address at the dedication of the new Soldiers' National Cemetery (now the Gettysburg National Cemetery). The President had high hopes for this speech: he aimed to use it to help Americans look beyond the war's daily strife and loss of life and place the conflict in a wider historical perspective. He intended his remarks to justify the horrendous loss of life suffered by both sides in the war, to honor the soldiers who had perished there, to rededicate the nation to its founding principles of democracy and human equality and to redefine the nature of the Union and its constituent states.

It was a tall order—and perhaps only Lincoln could achieve those ambitious goals in a mere 272 words. Yet achieve them he did, in phrases of such power that the address has become one of the central documents of American democracy, the equal of the Declaration of Independence and the U.S. Constitution.

Popular lore has it that Lincoln wrote his remarks at the last minute, scrawling them on the back of an envelope as his train rolled toward Gettysburg on Nov. 18, 1863, the day before the ceremony. It's a fine story, but the truth is, Lincoln seldom spoke without giving careful thought to the occasion, his audience and his message. In fact, he often begged off when asked to give spontaneous

remarks—as he did on the night of the 18th, after he arrived in Gettysburg, when a crowd of admirers gathered outside the home of David Wills, a prominent local attorney who had spearheaded the creation of the national cemetery. The President was spending the night there, and the crowd asked him to say a few words after the 5th New York Artillery Band had offered a serenade.

Lincoln refused to take the bait, declaring that he had "several substantial reasons" for not making a speech—primarily that he had prepared no speech to make. He added, "In my position, it is somewhat important that I should not say any foolish things." A wag in the crowd cried out, "If you can help it!" Amused, the President agreed, saying, "It very often happens that the only way to help it is to say nothing at all."

Lincoln, of course, had a magnificent speech to make, but he was saving it for the next day's ceremony. As historian David Herbert Donald relates in his authoritative 1996 biography, *Lincoln,* the President had been reflecting on the key themes of his remarks for months. Oddly enough, he had articulated some of them in rudimentary form on a similar occasion in Washington only a few days after the twin victories at Gettysburg and Vicksburg, when a celebrating crowd had gathered outside the White House and asked the President to say a few words.

In response, Lincoln reminded the crowd that Vicks-

Red-letter day *The special train carrying President Lincoln's party to Gettysburg stopped for fewer than 10 minutes in Hanover Junction, Pa., on Nov. 18. Local citizens and members of the President's group posed for pictures to recall the occasion*

Edward Everett

It's commonplace for admirers of Lincoln's address to slight the effort of the day's principal speaker, Edward Everett. But the Massachusetts politician's remarks were not overly florid; rather, they offered an accurate summary of the battle, informed by accounts provided by General George Meade and other eyewitnesses

DEDICATION OF THE SOLDIERS' NATIONAL
CEMETERY AT GETTYSBURG
NOV. 19, 1863

PROGRAM
MUSIC, BY BIRGFIELD'S BAND
PRAYER, BY THE REV. T.H. STOCKTON, D.D.
MUSIC, BY THE MARINE BAND
ORATION, BY THE HON. EDWARD EVERETT
MUSIC, HYMN COMPOSED BY B.B. FRENCH, ESQ.
DEDICATORY REMARKS,
BY THE PRESIDENT OF THE UNITED STATES
DIRGE, SUNG BY CHOIR SELECTED FOR THE OCCASION
BENEDICTION, BY THE REV. H.L. BAUGHER, D.D.

launched the current war in "an effort to overthrow the principle that all men were created equal"—by upholding slavery, he meant. The fortuitous timing of the great victories, he was suggesting, was a powerful reminder that the war was being waged not over territory or wealth or even over slavery, but over the preservation and advancement of the most basic ideals of democracy.

Restoring Jefferson's Vision

Lincoln was not the featured speaker at the dedication; that role was taken by a celebrated orator, Edward Everett, an educator and politician from Massachusetts. To modern readers, this may seem a slight to the President, but at a time when oratory was considered a primary medium for entertainment and enlightenment—and was a physically demanding exercise that asked its practitioners to speak loud enough to reach crowds of thousands for long periods—a professional speaker was called for, and Everett filled the bill. His speech was the day's main event; the President's appearance and brief remarks were intended to be the icing on the cake.

Lincoln's remarks were so short that the crowd was just tuning in when he concluded. As one Gettysburg resident later recalled, "There was one disappointing feature about [the speech]—its marked brevity. The speaker had, as we thought, but barely commenced when he stopped. That clear, ringing voice ceased before we were ready for it." Yet Lincoln compressed a world of meaning into his few words. His message, richly evoking images of birth and creation, envisioned the war as a means of bringing about a new understanding of the nation's founding principles—those best expressed in the Declaration of Independence. Lincoln and many Republicans chose to view the Union as predating the U.S. Constitution, the 1789 document that outlined a new form for the U.S. government. The Constitution, they believed, was a flawed product of compromise that never mentioned the issue of slavery, in compliance with Southern demands. Thus the essential American promise resided not in the Constitution but in Thomas Jefferson's clarion call in the Declaration: that all men are created equal and endowed by their creator with certain unalienable rights.

Moreover, Lincoln stressed his view that the United States was not a loose confederation of states but rather a nation, in which the foremost power resided in the central government and not the states. Indeed, Lincoln used the word *nation* five times in his brief remarks. Yet, with an eye to future reconciliation, Lincoln chose not to

burg had fallen on July 4, the day when news reached Washington of the Union victory at Gettysburg, and remarked on the historical aptness of the date. He asked the crowd, "How long ago is it?—80-odd years—since on the Fourth of July for the first time in the history of the world a nation by its representatives, assembled and declared as a self-evident truth that 'all men are created equal.'" The seceding states, he told his listeners, had

★ Lincoln at Gettysburg: The Visual Record

As Lincoln biographer David Herbert Donald tells it, many listeners near the front of the crowd of some 15,000 people who attended the dedication of the Soldiers' National Cemetery at Gettysburg were distracted during the first moments of the President's speech by a cameraman who was trying to get his equipment set up to photograph Lincoln during his remarks. But Lincoln's speech was so short that the photographer never got his shot. Alexander Gardner and others did take photos of the crowd that day, but it was not until almost 90 years after the ceremony that someone thought to scrutinize the old photos of the event to see if Lincoln could be discerned when the images were enlarged using modern technology.

That someone was Josephine Cobb, then the chief of the Still Photo section of the National Archives. Searching in the background of a photo of the crowd taken by professional cameraman David Bachrach (right), and looking where a slight elevation in the image suggested the speakers' platform was located, Cobb successfully identified the President, who is not wearing his trademark stovepipe hat. Scholars agreed with Cobb's conclusion, and for many decades the photograph was renowned as the only image of Lincoln at the cemetery.

On Nov. 16, 2007, John Richter, a member of the board of the Center for Civil War Photography, an online organization, announced that he believed he had located two more images of Lincoln at the ceremony, using modern 3-D technology to enhance Gardner's stereographic photos. Richter believes the enlarged images show Lincoln on horseback, wearing his top hat and, in the one at below right, waving to the crowd with a white glove on his left hand. Unfortunately, the angle of the photograph does not allow us a clear view of the man's face, although the profile certainly resembles the familiar visage of the President.

Many observers agree with Richter's conclusion, but one prominent dissenter is William A. Frassanito, the dean of Gettysburg photography scholars, who revised our views of many early photos of the battleground in his 1975 book *Gettysburg: A Journey in Time*. Frassanito argues that the beard of the man in the photos does not resemble the way Lincoln wore his beard in 1863. And he finds several context clues involving the location of the speakers' stand that he believes argue against the Lincoln identification. The debate, a healthy one, is likely to continue.

A face in the crowd *Using modern-day technology to enlarge details that are very small in the original photograph at left, taken before the program began at Gettysburg on Nov. 19, historical photo sleuth John Richter believes he found Lincoln, in top hat, at right, facing away from the camera and raising his left hand in response to the crowd. But other experts believe the figure in the top hat is not Lincoln*

portray the war as a quest to end slavery or destroy the heritage of the South but rather as an opportunity for all Americans to take part in "a new birth of freedom."

History's Verdict

After delivering the speech, Lincoln was dissatisfied with it, and he wasn't alone. The nearby Harrisburg (Pa.) *Patriot and Union* proclaimed, "We pass over the silly remarks of the President: for the credit of the nation we are willing that the veil of oblivion shall be dropped over them ..." The London *Times* agreed, stating, "The ceremony was rendered ludicrous by some of the sallies of that poor President Lincoln. Anything more dull and commonplace it would not be easy to produce."

Yet Lincoln had his defenders as well. The Springfield (Mass.) *Republican* cheered, "His little speech is a perfect gem, deep in feeling, compact in thought and expression, and tasteful and elegant in every word and comma." A gracious Everett wrote Lincoln a note, stating, "I should be glad if I could flatter myself that I came as near to the central idea of the occasion, in two hours, as you did in two minutes." Senator Charles Sumner of Massachusetts was even more fulsome. "The battle itself was less important than the speech," he declared.

Sumner may have been right: the address has outgrown its historical context and taken on a life of its own, transcending time and geography. Winston Churchill, perhaps Lincoln's equal as an orator, called it "the ultimate expression of the majesty of Shakespeare's language." Generations of American children, forced to memorize it, might not agree. One surprising admirer was China's former leader Jiang Zemin, who enjoyed citing the address when meeting with U.S. leaders.

On Aug. 28, 1963, Martin Luther King Jr. stood on the steps of the Lincoln Memorial in Washington and referred to the address in the opening phrases of his "I Have a Dream" speech. "Five score years ago, a great American, in whose symbolic shadow we stand today, signed the Emancipation Proclamation," King declared. The substance of his remarks was that Lincoln's promise of equality for all Americans had yet to be fully realized: it was a "promissory note" that had not yet been cashed.

King, like Lincoln, was a master wordsmith. On another occasion, King famously observed, "The arc of the moral universe is long, but it bends toward justice." Both Lincoln and King understood that when eloquent speakers articulate old ideals in shining new language, that moral arc seems to bend a little more easily. ■

Strolling the grounds
Spectators attending the dedication of the Soldiers' National Cemetery stretch their legs in this photo taken on Nov. 19, 1863. The photographer is unknown, but among those present to record the ceremony that day were cameramen Alexander Gardner, David Bachrach and local brothers Charles and Isaac Tyson and their apprentice, William H. Tipton

The Last Full Measure

By Douglas L. Wilson

NO AMERICAN WRITER'S WORDS are more admired than those of Abraham Lincoln. By the time of his assassination in 1865, he had written passages by which everything that followed would be measured. But such an ability was the last thing the American public expected from the obscure prairie lawyer who took office just four years earlier. "We have a President without brains," wrote the country's leading historian, George Bancroft. Bancroft was, admittedly, a Democrat, but many self-respecting Republicans were also concerned about the implications of having an untried, self-educated "rail splitter" as a leader in time of grave national crisis. Charles Francis Adams, a leading Republican and the son and grandson of Presidents, wrote of the new President-elect in his diary, "Good natured, kindly, honest, but frivolous and uncertain." The doubts and fears of many Americans were expressed by a newspaper editor who asked, "Who will write this ignorant man's state papers?"

The Northern intelligentsia was initially blind to Lincoln's writing ability for at least two reasons. First, there was the strong impression, reinforced by his unkempt appearance and awkward demeanor, that he was a rube. His obvious discomfort in formal clothes on ceremonial occasions and his constant fidgeting with his ill-fitting kid gloves did little to dispel those misgivings. Moreover, he insisted on entertaining sophisticated visitors by telling country stories in a broad Hoosier accent. Wall Street lawyer George Templeton Strong wrote in his diary after their first meeting that the President was a "barbarian," a "yahoo." And Strong liked him.

Another reason Lincoln's writing ability was underrated was that his typically plain diction and straightforward expression were at odds with the public's expectations. The recognized standard for a statesmanlike address in mid-19th century America called for considerably more formality and pretension. The prose of acknowledged masters of that kind of writing—such as Lincoln's fellow orator at Gettysburg, Edward Everett, and Massachusetts Senator Charles Sumner—generally featured elevated diction, self-consciously artful expression and a certain moral unction. Lincoln's insistence on direct and forthright language, by contrast, seemed "odd" or "peculiar," as in this passage from a public letter he sent to Horace Greeley, founder and editor of the New York *Tribune,* an antislavery paper: "My paramount object in this struggle is to save the Union, and is not either to save or to destroy slavery. If I could save the Union without freeing any slave I would do it; and if I could save it by freeing all the slaves I would do it; and if I could save it by freeing some and leaving others alone I would also do that."

When discerning observers noticed that his words had power, they often assumed that someone else must have written them. His Secretary of State, William H. Seward, was a noted orator and wordsmith who was thought to have had a hand in Lincoln's first Inaugural. That was in

Douglas L. Wilson is a co-director of the Lincoln Studies Center at Knox College in Galesburg, Ill., and the author of Lincoln's Sword: The Presidency and the Power of Words *(2006)*

fact true, but few of Seward's suggested changes were stylistic improvements, and we know from the manuscript that his chief contribution, a more conciliatory ending, was brilliantly rewritten by Lincoln. The Secretary of the Treasury, Salmon P. Chase, was sometimes thought to be responsible for Lincoln's best work, and occasionally it was credited to the Secretary of War, Edwin M. Stanton. But when approached with such a suggestion by a friend, Stanton told him bluntly, "Lincoln wrote it—every word of it. And he is capable of more than that."

In the hindsight of history, we can see that Stanton knew what he was talking about. But how was it that Lincoln turned out to be so exceptional a writer and that it was so little apparent to his contemporaries? Studying Lincoln's writing over the years has convinced me that most of the factors that contributed to Lincoln's extraordinary literary achievement were invisible to his public and were even contrary to its general sense of who he was.

As a child, Lincoln was fascinated with words and meanings and obsessed with clarity, both in understanding and in being understood. He wrote all his life for local newspapers, although mostly anonymously, and harbored a lifelong tendency to meet provocation with a written response. By the 1850s, when he came to political prominence, he had already formed the habit of making notes on scraps of paper of ideas and phrases as they occurred to him, which he then used in composing speeches. And perhaps his most valuable and most unsuspected trait as a writer was his devotion to revision.

We know, of course, how it all turned out. Nowhere is that more evident than in the contrast between two speeches given on Nov. 19, 1863. Everett, who had been a president of Harvard, a Congressman, a Senator and a Governor of Massachusetts as well as a Secretary of State and a minister to England, was chosen to deliver the principal address at the dedication of the new national cemetery on the battlefield at Gettysburg. Lincoln was invited almost as an afterthought. One man spoke for two hours, the other for two minutes. One speech was printed and distributed in advance and has rarely been read since. The other is one of the most famous compositions in the American language. ■

Long remembered
This copy of the address, written in Lincoln's hand, with corrections, is one of five manuscript copies of the text, each of them slightly different. This copy—known as the "Hay copy," because Lincoln gave it to his secretary John Hay—is believed to be a slightly revised version of the remarks delivered by Lincoln at the cemetery dedication

157

A Long Road to Peace

Union victories at Gettysburg and Vicksburg change the war's course, but the conflict rages for 21 more months before the war ends with Lee's surrender — and the death of Lincoln

As of the end of July 1863, citizens of both the Union and the Confederacy had every reason to believe that the conclusion of the war was in sight. At Gettysburg, in the war's Eastern Theater, Robert E. Lee's grand gamble had been firmly checked, and the tattered remnants of the Army of Northern Virginia had barely escaped back to their homeland, saved once again from utter destruction by the inability of Federal generals to capitalize on their successes. In the Western Theater, the surrender of Vicksburg had firmly placed control of the vital Mississippi River in Union hands.

The Confederacy was reeling from the twin blows, but there was to be no early end to the conflict. The seceding states once again demonstrated their grit and resourcefulness, fending off the Federal armies for 21 more months before—rapidly running short of men, guns and supplies—they finally ran short of time. Yet even as the Confederates began facing up to their defeat, their foes were also plunged into sadness. In a final paroxysm of violence that rang down the curtain on the era, President Abraham Lincoln was assassinated only days after Lee surrendered to General Ulysses S. Grant on April 9, 1865.

In the East there was little combat for the remainder of 1863, as both the Federal and Confederate armies recovered their bearings after the shattering bloodbath in Pennsylvania. Lee, thoroughly beaten, now found himself in precisely the position that had forced him to turn his sights to the North after the Battle of Chancellors-ville: he was once again bottled up in northern Virginia, charged with defending Richmond and doomed to reacting to his opponents' maneuvers rather than seizing control of events on his own. As for General George G. Meade, he had won glory at Gettysburg, only to squander it with his inept behavior after the battle, allowing Lee to escape. Meade had lost the confidence of Lincoln and his top military chief, General Henry Halleck, and the leader of the Army of the Potomac knew it.

In November and December of 1863, Meade mounted two invasions of Virginia, but after losing battles in both the Bristoe Campaign and the Mine Run Campaign, his army went into winter quarters. The next breakthroughs in the war would not come in Virginia and Maryland; they would come from the Western Theater, where the resourceful Grant would win a complex battle for control of eastern Tennessee, opening a gateway into the heart of the Deep South that would allow Grant's longtime subordinate, General William T. Sherman, to capture Atlanta by the fall of 1864. Grant would be summoned to Washington by Lincoln in March, 1864, and handed control of the Union armies. For the first time, Lee would find himself up against a foe who—though utterly different in character and outlook—was his match on the

Wasteland *Workers collect cannonballs in the ruins of the arsenal in Richmond, Va., after Confederate leaders and troops fled the city on April 2, 1865, and put the Confederate capital to the torch*

battlefield. Thirteen months after the Union's hero of the West first came to the East, Grant faced Lee in the parlor of a farmhouse in Appomattox Court House, Va., and accepted the Confederate general's surrender.

The Union Wins Control of Chattanooga

Before Grant could come to Washington, he had a shorter journey to make: to eastern Tennessee. Once Vicksburg had fallen, the focus of the two sides in the Western Theater turned to Chattanooga, the great riverport city in eastern Tennessee that was a railroad hub and supply center for the entire mid-South. Here, soldiers under Union Major General William Rosecrans and Confederate General Braxton Bragg had conducted a long, deadly duel that found both sides exhausted by the summer of 1863. But urged on by Lincoln, the diffident Rosecrans finally roused himself to action. Marching on Chattanooga in September and outflanking Bragg severely, he occupied commanding artillery positions in the mountains surrounding the town and managed to drive Bragg's army into a retreat from the city.

Bragg's withdrawal was part of a grand Confederate plan: unknown to Rosecrans, General James Longstreet and his army were en route to the scene via railway, in one of the war's single most audacious exercises in logistics. When Rosecrans followed the retreating Bragg down the Chickamauga River southeast of Chattanooga, in the shadow of Lookout Mountain, the two sides clashed in a bloody, two-day battle. Longstreet's timely arrival at the scene tipped the balance, and the Confederates won a significant victory in which General George Henry Thomas emerged as a hero for the Union side, saving the Federals from utter destruction.

The battle's toll was formidable: 18,000 casualties on the Confederate side and 16,000 for the Federals. In one of the war's oddest turn of events, the Union troops now retreated back to Chattanooga, where they found themselves in the position the Confederates had occupied earlier: trapped and running out of food and supplies in the low-lying city, with rebel guns firing at them from the surrounding hills.

It was Vicksburg in reverse, and President Lincoln had just the man to halt the receding tide of Federal fortunes: he dispatched Grant to take command in Chattanooga. Rosecrans, the President remarked, was "confused and stunned, like a duck hit on the head." Now Grant performed one of his most impressive feats of the war. Arriving in the besieged city on Oct. 23, 1863, he rallied his subordinates and managed to open a supply line into it within five days of his arrival. On Nov. 23, one month after arriving at the city, he led the Federal troops to a major victory in a two-day battle at Missionary Ridge and Lookout Mountain. When Union General Ambrose Burnside defeated Longstreet's army at Knoxville, Tenn., the Federals had won effective control of the important border state.

Grant Takes Charge; Sherman Takes Atlanta

Grant's commanding successes at Vicksburg and Chattanooga had finally given the Federals a general whom Union sympathizers could rally behind. So few people were surprised when President Lincoln summoned Grant to Washington in the spring of 1864 and invited him to become the general in chief of all the Union armies, replacing General Henry W. Halleck, who would now become Grant's chief of staff. General George G. Meade would remain nominally in command of the Army of the Potomac, but everyone understood that Grant would be giving the orders in the Eastern Theater: his top priority was to crush Lee's Army of Northern Virginia and capture the Confederate capital at Richmond.

Lincoln and Grant had not yet met in the course of the war. On the night of March 8, 1864, Grant appeared at a White House reception, galvanizing the crowd and creating such a ruckus that the President asked the stubby general to stand on a sofa so that the entire crowd could get a look at him. The next day, the President and his new top commander began crafting a strategy that would, for the first time, coordinate Union activities on both the war's fronts. In the West, Grant's highly capable subordinate, General Sherman, would drive south from Chattanooga in hopes of capturing the major city of Atlanta. In the East, Grant, Meade, and Grant's longtime cavalry commander, the tough General Philip Sheridan, would launch an invasion of Virginia, designed to subdue Lee and capture Richmond.

Sherman achieved his goal by summer's end, defeating Confederate armies led by General Joseph Johnston, who had failed to hold Vicksburg against Grant, and General John Bell Hood, the veteran warrior who had lost the use of his left arm at Gettysburg and now fought with an increased, strident intensity. The two sides battled down the length of Georgia, with the Federals suffering large losses but always moving closer to Atlanta, a major manufacturing center for the Confederate armies. Along the way, Hood replaced Johnston, but he could not

William T. Sherman
General Sherman's middle name was Tecumseh, after the great Native American warrior who challenged the white newcomers who were displacing Indians from their homelands. Tecumseh's efforts failed, but his namesake waged a successful campaign of what we now call "total war" against the citizens, resources and infrastructure of secessionist states

Acting under orders from Sherman, Union soldiers tear up railroad lines in Atlanta, aiming to make the city no longer an important transit line for Confederate arms and troops.

On his march through Georgia, Sherman's goal was to destroy the Confederacy's ability to wage war. He also wrote that the Union "must make old and young, rich and poor, feel the hard hand of war." He ordered the city burned to the ground when he evacuated it on Nov. 15, 1864, heading for Savannah

prevent the city's fall. Hood withdrew on Sept. 1, ordering the destruction of all supplies and arms in the city, and leaving a blazing conflagration behind him.

Grant Advances on Richmond

On May 4, the Army of the Potomac crossed the Rapidan River and entered Virginia. Lee was ready for Grant, and the two armies quickly did battle amid the thorns and briars of the area called the Wilderness, where they had tangled before. Once again the Confederates were victorious, thanks to General Longstreet, who replayed his timely arrival at Chickamauga in Tennessee—and who almost endured the fate of his old colleague Stonewall Jackson: he was hit by friendly fire in the first blush of victory but survived.

Now Grant demonstrated his mettle: despite taking 17,500 casualties in two days of fighting at the Wilderness, he continued the Overland Campaign—becoming the first Union general to continue operations after suffering an initial loss while invading Virginia. "If you see the President, tell him from me that whatever happens, there will be no turning back," he told a newspaper reporter. In the next weeks, the two sides intensified their conflicts around Spotsylvania Court House, east of the Wilderness. The losses were staggering: some 18,000 casualties for the Federals, an estimated 13,000 for the Confederates. Yet Grant was unfazed. "I propose to fight it out on this line if it takes all summer," he declared.

And he did, with losses that Grant could afford to suffer but Lee could not. What followed devolved into a bloody war of attrition: after another Union defeat at the Battle of Cold Harbor, the two armies went to ground outside the town of Petersburg, 25 miles outside Richmond, where the Confederates guarded the last railroad line into the capital. The foes now entered upon a new phase of the conflict, one that strongly foreshadowed World War I, as soldiers huddled in trenches behind strong barricades, facing off across a blasted no-man's-land. Here they would stay through the winter of 1864.

While Grant was plaguing Lee in northern Virginia, Sherman occupied Atlanta until Nov. 15, when he ordered the remnants of the shattered city burned and he

Surrender at Appomattox

Tom Lovell (1909-97) was best known as an illustrator of scenes from the West. His painting of Lee's surrender brings the occasion to life with a hushed, muted palette

began his destructive March to the Sea. In the 36 days that followed, he and his 62,000 soldiers, trailed by a shadow army of some 10,000 liberated slaves, marched from Atlanta to Savannah, leaving a wasteland behind them. On Dec. 22, Sherman sent a telegram to President Lincoln, declaring, "I beg to present you, as a Christmas gift, the city of Savannah, with 150 heavy guns and plen-

ty of ammunition, and also about 25,000 bales of cotton." The endgame of the war had begun.

Lincoln Is Re-Elected as the War Winds Down

With Sherman plowing his way across the South, almost unopposed by Confederate armies, the weakness of the secessionists' position was becoming ever more appar-

Major Battles After Gettysburg

Sept. 18 - 20, 1863 • BATTLE OF CHICKAMAUGA
Western Theater; Confederate victory. Bragg defeats Rosecrans, thanks to Longstreet's timely arrival. General George H. Thomas stands tall for Federals.

Nov. 23 - 25, 1863 • BATTLE OF CHATTANOOGA
Western Theater; Federal victory. At Lookout Mountain and Missionary Ridge, Grant and Thomas defeat Bragg and relieve Conderate siege of Chattanooga.

May 5 - 7, 1864 • BATTLE OF THE WILDERNESS
Eastern Theater; inconclusive. Lee holds off Grant's initial foray into Virginia at the beginning of the Overland Campaign. The body count is very high on both sides, but Grant pledges to Lincoln that he will continue to fight.

May 8 - 21, 1864 • BATTLE OF SPOTSYLVANIA COURT HOUSE
Eastern Theater; inconclusive. Grant absorbs huge losses but continues to reduce Lee's forces in a war of attrition. Grant vows to continue his campaign.

May 31 – June 12, 1864 • BATTLE OF COLD HARBOR
Eastern Theater; Confederate victory. The Overland Campaign continues, with Grant sending 5,000 men to almost certain death in a frontal assault on Lee's position. Some Northern newspapers attack Grant as a "butcher."

Aug. 2 - 23, 1864 • MOBILE BAY CAMPAIGN
Gulf Coast Theater; Federal victory. Farragut commands, "Damn the torpedoes!" and captures one of the last Confederate ports on the Gulf of Mexico.

May 7 – Sept. 1, 1864 • ATLANTA CAMPAIGN
Western Theater; Federal victory. Driving south from Chattanooga, Sherman conquers the major transit hub on Sept. 1, 1864. Following his March to the Sea, he captures Savannah, Ga., on Dec. 21.

June 15, 1864 – April 2, 1865 • SIEGE OF PETERSBURG
Eastern Theater; Union victory. After Lee defeats Grant in June 1864 at the "back door" to Richmond, Grant launches a siege of the city. In early April 1865, Union attacks on Confederate lines succeed and Richmond falls.

ent. In tandem with Sherman's successes, the Union also won other significant victories in the summer of 1864. In August, Admiral David Farragut—crying "Damn the torpedoes! Full speed ahead!"—eluded floating Confederate mines to capture Mobile Bay, the major Alabama port on the Gulf of Mexico. And in the Shenandoah, the longtime breadbasket and refuge of Jackson, Federal cav-

alry leader General Sheridan, Grant's colleague from the Western Theater, handily defeated the armies of Gettysburg veteran General Jubal Early. In the fall of 1864, it no longer seemed a question as to whether the Confederate cause would prevail: the issue now was how long the Confederacy could survive.

The sense that victory was at hand helped Lincoln win the presidential election on Nov. 8, 1864. Only months earlier, Lincoln had feared he would be handily defeated at the polls, for in the summer Grant's Overland Campaign had bogged down outside Petersburg, and Sherman's Atlanta Campaign had also been briefly thrown off-stride. Peace-seeking Democrats in the North were gaining adherents, and they had found a commanding figure to represent them: General George B. McClellan, Lincoln's old nemesis from the first years of the war, was the Democrats' candidate.

Yet by the fall, Sherman had taken Atlanta, Farragut had taken Mobile, Sheridan had prevailed in the Shenandoah Valley, the Union cause was prospering—and Lincoln won a decisive victory over McClellan, the vainglorious boaster who had often referred to his Commander in Chief as "the Gorilla" in letters to his wife when he was leading the Army of the Potomac. For the first time in U.S. history, soldiers in uniform were allowed to vote in this election via absentee ballots, and the men in blue uniforms preferred Lincoln over McClellan by a landslide, 78% to 22%.

With the end of the war in sight, Lincoln now turned his thoughts to healing the wounds of secession and division. Through the winter of 1864-65, Lincoln fought to see the 13th Amendment to the U.S. Constitution passed; the measure made human slavery illegal in the U.S. And he began laying the groundwork for the admission of the former Confederate states back into the Union.

In his Second Inaugural Address, delivered on March 4, 1865, the President expressed his vision for the future. The seceding states, he insisted, must be welcomed back into the Union, with no punishment or vengeance expressed for their failed attempt at independence. The President declared, in timeless words, "With malice

Lying in state *This seldom-seen image is the only photo that shows Lincoln in death, lying in state in New York City. The original photo plates were long thought to have been destroyed, but a print was located in 1952 at the Illinois State Historic Library by a 14-year-old boy who is now a history professor*

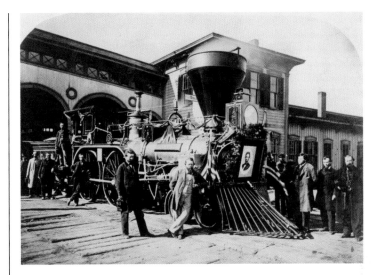

★ Lincoln Passes from the Scene

The assassination of President Abraham Lincoln by a Southern-sympathizing actor, John Wilkes Booth, seemed to put history's final stamp on the ordeal of the Civil War. In many ways, it prefigured the death 80 years later of four-term President Franklin D. Roosevelt, who died in April 1945, only weeks before the U.S. and its allies won final victory over Adolf Hitler's Germany in the European Theater of World War II. Lincoln's murder shocked and stunned the nation, bringing the long, harrowing story of the war to an abrupt and unsatisfactory conclusion and plunging Americans into a new, threatening age they were unprepared to address.

After firing a single bullet into Lincoln's brain as the President and his wife Mary were enjoying a comedy at Ford's Theatre in Washington, Booth led authorities on a long manhunt, eluding capture with the help of accomplices. He was not located until April 26, 13 days after the murder, when he was trapped in a barn and shot by U.S. soldiers who had set the building on fire. The assassination of Lincoln was part of a larger, ill-conceived and poorly executed plan by Booth and others to slay the entire upper echelon of the Lincoln Administration. Only Booth succeeded in his plan; four of his co-conspirators were arrested, tried, found guilty and hanged in July 1865. Four other defendants were also tried and given hefty jail sentences.

Murdered on Good Friday of Easter week, Lincoln—who had for so long been a controversial figure, scorned and admired in equal measure—now became canonized as a kind of secular saint. His death, coming on the heels of the more than 600,000 other deaths in the war, seemed to tap into a common wellspring of deep sorrow. His body was carried across the states of the Union on a funeral train, above, that stopped in a host of major cities on its two-week journey from Washington to Lincoln's burial site in Springfield, Ill.

Sadly, Lincoln's vision of an America once again united and healed died with him. When the weak Vice President, Andrew Johnson of Tennessee, succeeded him, radical elements of the Republican Party, whose fanaticism Lincoln had long held in check, took power in Washington. Under their guidance, the Reconstruction of the former Confederate states devolved into a program of revenge and Federal occupation that ensured the wounds of the war would long endure.

toward none; with charity for all; with firmness in the right as God gives us to see the right, let us strive on to finish the work we are in; to bind up the nation's wounds; to care for him who shall have borne the battle, and for his widow, and his orphan—to do all which may achieve and cherish a just, and a lasting peace among ourselves, and with all nations."

Lincoln's soaring phrases were not for show; they were intended as the guiding light of his second term. And the chance to put them into action came soon. On March 24, 1865, Lee attempted to break through the Federal lines around Petersburg, only to be repelled by a strong counterattack. A week later, General Sheridan's cavalry broke down the Confederate defenses southwest of Petersburg. By Sunday, April 2, Lee was forced to evacuate his troops from their defensive positions—and Confederate President Jefferson Davis and the members of his Cabinet fled Richmond, putting the city to the torch rather than allowing it to fall into the hands of the hated Yankees.

Lee's soldiers withdrew west of the city, and desertion plagued the army. Defeat was in the air, and on April 9, Lee finally signaled to Grant that he was ready to surrender. Meeting at a farmhouse in the small county seat of Appomattox Court House, the two men met for the first time, Lee resplendent in his formal uniform, the grittier Grant mud-spattered and slightly disheveled.

Following Lincoln's vision of reconciliation rather than revenge, Grant allowed Lee's soldiers to retain their horses, so they could return to their homes and plow their fields for spring planting. All Confederate soldiers were given paroles, meaning they would never be charged with treason for their wartime deeds. Confederate officers were allowed to keep their weapons. Grant charged Joshua Chamberlain, the hero of Little Round Top, with accepting the surrender of the remaining Confederate arms, and Chamberlain ordered his Federal soldiers to stand at attention and offer a salute to their former adversaries as they surrendered their weapons.

The war had ended, but the nation's great internal struggle would claim one more victim. On April 14, Lincoln was struck down by an assassin's bullet. His successor, Andrew Johnson of Tennessee, possessed few of the qualities that had made Lincoln such a towering figure. In the years to come, his promise of malice toward none and charity for all would be betrayed. In killing Lincoln, his assassin had also killed his vision of the future. The "new birth of freedom" the President had called for at Gettysburg would be long, long, in the delivery. ∎

Heritage *From left, Confederate President Jefferson Davis and Generals Robert E. Lee and Stonewall Jackson are carved in bas-relief on the north face of Stone Mountain in Georgia. The sculpture takes up three acres of space and towers 400 ft. above the ground. Work on the monument began in 1916 and proceeded in fits and starts for decades until it was concluded in 1972*

In the Footsteps
Of Mathew Brady

Photographs by Todd Harrington

ONE OF THE MOST POPULAR BOOKS on the Civil War of recent years is *Confederates in the Attic: Dispatches from the Unfinished Civil War,* Tony Horwitz's 1998 exploration of the conflict's legacy. The book introduced many readers to the concept of historical re-enactment, as Horwitz explores—and often skewers—those who choose to investigate the lives of our forefathers by attempting to emulate them. Indeed, there's rich soil for humor in the notion of grown men arguing over the thread count in the uniforms worn by soldiers of the Union's Iron Brigade. But in a larger

perspective, the re-enacting movement has created an enthralling new way for students of history to learn from a very close encounter with the past. Thanks in part to the ranks of the nation's re-enactors, interest in Civil War history appears to be not only strong but growing—and that's something that Robert E. Lee, Joshua Chamberlain and all the other veterans of Gettysburg deserve.

As this movement has grown, its aperture of interests has widened, and the art of re-enacting has moved beyond soldiering. Visit a sutler's camp at a battle re-enactment today, and you're liable to find coopers, cobblers, farriers and pharmacists all plying their trade, 1860s-style. You also might find Todd Harrington, 52, one of the growing number of photographers who have mastered the wet-plate collodion process used by Mathew Brady and his corps of cameramen. Harrington's customers are generally re-enactors who want a glass-plate portrait of themselves in uniform. But in the fall of 2012, as this book took shape, TIME asked Harrington to take on a different assignment, inviting him to visit Gettysburg with his wet-plate camera, find the sites made

famous in Brady's photographs and shoot them again, from exactly the same angles, using the original processes of 1860s photographers.

The assignment promised to answer a number of questions. In terms of simply documenting the state of today's battlefield, the photos would show the extent to which modernity has—or has not—imposed itself between today's viewers and the battlefields captured by the Brady team's cameras. But the larger interest was to explore the nature of the power that is compressed into Brady's frames. Of course the bodies of the dead in the original photos will always draw our attention. Yet even the Brady photos that show only hilltops, boulders and fields of wheat are charged with a haunting intensity. Is that power imparted by the antique technology of the process that produced them? Or is it added to the photo by the viewer's knowledge of the riveting events that took place in these locations? By juxtaposing recent visions of Gettysburg created by Brady's process against his originals, we hoped to explore those questions. The answers, of course, lie in the eye of the beholder. ∎

Harrington, 2012: The gatehouse of Evergreen Cemetery

Timothy O'Sullivan (print by Alexander Gardner), 1863: The gatehouse of Evergreen Cemetery

Eternity's portal

The gatehouse of Evergreen Cemetery, a private facility that gave Cemetery Ridge its name, is one of the most striking original buildings still standing on the battlefield. It was near this spot that General Winfield Scott Hancock began to rally the Union troops who were retreating through the town of Gettysburg on July 1, and where the Union "fishhook" line began to form. The photo of the gateway at left was taken by Brady photographer Timothy O'Sullivan on July 7, 1863.

More than the other pictures in Harrington's portfolio, the photo above captures clear marks of modernity: a caretaker's house added in 1885 now mars the view of the 1855 gateway building, while a paved road and the telltale signatures of the 20th century—telephone and power lines—bisect the view

Brady corps, 1863: Little Round Top, left, and Big Round Top

Sentinels of the Union left

This vision of the heights held by the Federal left flank against relentless Confederate assaults throughout the battle shows the extent to which much of the natural land-scape of the battlefields endures, well preserved. That's a tribute to the decades-long struggle to maintain the integrity of the park in the face of those who view this hal-lowed ground as a venue for moneymaking schemes and tourist attractions. When a land-use issue over a proposed tourist railway reached the U.S. Supreme Court in the 1890s, the Attorney General wrote in a brief: "The ground whereon great conflicts have taken place, especially those where great interests or principles were at stake, becomes at once of so much public interest that its preservation is essentially a matter of public concern." The Court unanimously ruled against the railway company

Harrington, 2012: Woods near the Rose Farm

A question of location

The cleft rock at right and the boulder poking into the frame on bottom left are clear indicators that Harrington's modern-day photograph shows the same site where the Brady team photographed dead Confederate soldiers in the first days after the battle ceased. Photo historian William A. Frassanito was among the first to point out that the Brady team, not familiar with the lay of the land and relying on information gleaned from remaining soldiers at the site, often gave incorrect locations for the scenes they were photographing. This location was said to be near "the center of the battlefield." Based on the cleft rock and other indicators, scholars now believe the photo was taken by the Rose Woods, near the Wheat Field, the scene of intense fighting on July 2.

Alexander Gardner, 1863: Slain soldiers by woods near the Rose Farm

Harrington, 2012: Eastern edge of McPherson's Woods, looking toward Seminary Ridge

Brady corps, 1863: Eastern edge of McPherson's Woods, looking toward Seminary Ridge

The Seminary spire

The protruding spire of the Lutheran Theological Seminary atop Seminary Ridge is the guidepost that reveals Harrington is shooting from the same location as was Brady's cameraman. (That's Brady, in hat on the right, in the 1863 photo at left). But the topography has changed over the course of 150 years.

In his 2003 book, Hallowed Ground, A Walk at Gettysburg, *historian James M. McPherson notes that Gettysburg was a great orchard town in 1863, but many of those orchards no longer exist. Furthermore, some 150 acres of battlefield land, previously forested, has now been cleared, while another 600 acres of woods now covers ground that was open fields 150 years ago, making it difficult for modern visitors to trace the movements of troops across the battlefield*

Bringing a Lost Art to Life

THE WET-PLATE COLLODION PROCESS USED by Mathew Brady, Alexander Gardner, Timothy O'Sullivan and the majority of other photographers in the 1860s was the logical outgrowth of the two pioneering forms of picture-taking that arose in the period from the late 1820s to the '50s. The first, the daguerreotype, was a one-off process that developed an exposure as a positive image on a metal plate. The more sophisticated calotype process, introduced by William Henry Fox Talbot, produced a paper negative, which could be used to create multiple positive images.

The wet-plate process employed a glass plate coated with collodion, a light-sensitive mixture of chemicals, to create a negative image, which could be printed out to produce multiple paper copies of an image. The process could also produce a variety of one-off positive images on glass (ambrotypes) or blackened metal plates (melainotypes, ferrotypes or tintypes). The prints produced by Todd Harrington on the preceding pages are contact printed on paper hand-coated with albumen (egg white) and toned with gold to create an image with rich, velvety character.

The shingle Harrington hangs out by his photo booth at re-enactments declares him to be a "collodion artist," and as the photographer describes his craft, the artistry required becomes apparent. The secret to creating a good image, he says, involves properly pouring the chemicals upon the glass plate, then managing the time the plate is exposed to light—a judgment call by the photographer, since it involves knowing when to place a cap over the lens to stop the process. On a sunny day, a good exposure might require only 3 sec.; on a cloudy day, it might require 30 sec. or even more than a minute.

The development process also calls for a high degree of skill involving the choice of the chemicals to use and the medium upon which the image is printed. The timing of the development is in the hands of the photographer, who can vary contrast and tone. As Harrington puts it, "It's one thing to learn how to do the process, another to learn to do it well." Considering he has been following in the footsteps of Brady only since 2008, Harrington seems to be well along on his journey.

Inside the wet-plate process

Tools of the trade *The wooden rack at right is slotted in order to hold a series of fragile glass plates; ghostly negative images can be seen on these exposed plates. The glass trays on the left are used to develop and process the glass plate after taking the exposure.*

The inside story *To take a photo, the camera operator opens the back of the camera and inserts the plate holder at left, a light-tight carrier for the sensitized glass plate. To make the exposure, the operator pulls the dark slide, exposing the glass plate to the back of the lens, and removes the lens cap, which acts as the shutter. Exposure times range from a few seconds to minutes depending on available natural light and the speed of the lens.*

All-seeing eyes *The camera can accommodate a variety of lenses, chosen to offer different size plate coverage and focal length. Exposure on the sensitized plate begins when the lens cap is opened and ceases when it is replaced.*

A box to trap light *The complete camera is a Victorian-era artifact that combines a highly advanced technology for the time with the fine wood craftsmanship that is a hallmark of the age*

Where Are All the Gettysburg Movies?

By Richard Corliss

D.W. GRIFFITH'S *THE BIRTH OF A NATION*, by far the biggest hit of the silent-film period, saw the Union Army as transgressors on a hallowed land, the Reconstruction Era as an act of obscene punishment, blacks as barbarians turned useful fools by Northern politicians and the Ku Klux Klan as a heroic vigilante force—knights in white bedsheets. Buster Keaton's *The General,* surely the funniest and perhaps the most specifically accurate of classic Civil War movies, is also solidly on the rebel side. *Gone With the Wind,* which remains the all-time top movie in terms of

tickets sold (*Star Wars* is second), may paint a knowing panorama of the antebellum and postwar South, but it skirts the sad fact that the source of the region's wealth was its cheap slave labor, a 200-year traffic in souls.

Part of the bias in these films may be attributed to the antique times in which they were made. *The Birth of a Nation* premiered in 1915, the 50th anniversary of Robert E. Lee's surrender at Appomattox, when the Civil War still stirred and roiled the memories of many its survivors, as the Vietnam conflict does today. *The General* came out in 1927; and *Gone With the Wind* opened in 1939, exactly as distant from today (74 years) as it was from 1865.

When those films first played in theaters, racial attitudes had only incrementally evolved from Civil War days; African Americans were counted as citizens but not always as equals. Further, the Old South, as dewily portrayed in these movies and many others, radiated the romance of some mythical kingdom, where drawling

gents sipped mint juleps and kissed the hands of belles in crinoline. This courtly society was seen as more precious because it had forever vanished. Thus did the lingering fantasy of a Cotton Camelot allow history to be written by the losers.

In this rosy miasma, any serious depiction of the Battle of Gettysburg would carry the rude shock of a face slap back to reality. Some of the military strategies utilized on that Pennsylvania field in early July 1863 were bold and successful, others rash and nearly suicidal. But in essence it was mutually assured destruction: a three-day slaughter that ended with more than 50,000 soldiers killed, wounded or missing—compared to some 30,000 casualties in the entire eight-year span of the Revolutionary War. What heart-warming lessons could be taken

Corliss has written for TIME *Magazine on movies and other entertainment subjects since 1980*

Celluloid hero *An artillery soldier loads a cannon in D.W. Griffith's 1915 epic, one-sided story of the South during and after the war,* The Birth of a Nation

from America's largest single bloodbath? Only those enunciated in Nov. 1863 by Abraham Lincoln—which is why the Gettysburg Address is cherished in popular culture, and the Battle of Gettysburg all but ignored, until an anniversary year invites us to recall its importance. Eloquence trumps atrocity.

The 16th President has been the subject of more than 300 movies since the beginning of cinema, portrayed by Ralph Ince in the 1911 *Battle Hymn of the Republic*, by Benjamin Walker in 2012's *Abraham Lincoln: Vampire Hunter* and by Daniel Day-Lewis, the 2013 Oscar winner for Best Actor, in Steven Spielberg's *Lincoln*. Walter Huston played Honest Abe in Griffith's first talking picture, *Abraham Lincoln* (1930), which the director may have intended as an atonement of sorts for *The Birth of a Nation*. Henry Fonda, Raymond Massey, Gregory Peck, Charlton Heston, Tom Hanks, Sam Waterston, Jason Robards and Hal Holbrook have all lent their faces and voices to extend the legend of the Great Emancipator. Lincoln, of course, was Commander in Chief, not a General, and the films that put him at their center rarely stray for long onto the Civil War battlefield.

In 1913, a few one- or two-reel shorts marked Gettysburg's golden anniversary by dramatizing it in brief. And in 2012 three disparate works of pop culture alluded to that signal conflict. On an episode of the Showtime drama series *Homeland,* the double-spy Brody took his family to the site and made a side trip to a tailor's shop for an explosive suicide vest. In the video for their top-of-the-pops single *Some Nights,* the band fun. donned blue and gray uniforms and mimed Civil War combat to a march tempo ("This is it, boys, this is war—what are we waiting for?"). And in the historico-horror action film *Abraham Lincoln: Vampire Hunter,* the fate of the Union rests on the President's mission to get a train through to Gettysburg while fighting off hundreds of the Confederate undead.

But for a century the movies have mostly been mute on the battle itself. One could almost say that Hollywood has dedicated not a single feature film to it.

The "almost" is *Gettysburg* (1993), Ronald F. Maxwell's four-and-a-half-hour war epic that was made for TV but, at the enthusiastic insistence of its sponsor, Ted Turner, released briefly in theaters. Turner backed the project after many executives at the major studios had rejected it—some more than once. The film's savior asked only that he appear fleetingly on camera. He plays a Confederate officer who shouts, "Let's go, men!" and is promptly killed. Noting that his scene needed to be shot only twice,

Turner told the director, "Just call me Two-Take Ted."

Though the film's source book, Michael Shaara's *The Killer Angels,* won the 1975 Pulitzer Prize for Fiction, Maxwell infused the story with suitable authenticity. Receiving permission to shoot on part of the battlefield, now a National Military Park, he recruited some 4,000 Civil War reenactors to serve as extras and amateur historians. Perhaps inevitably, this docudrama is stronger on docu than on drama. Some members of the professional cast, led by Tom Berenger as Union Lt. Gen. James Longstreet and Martin Sheen as Gen. Lee, seem as uncomfortable as the reenactors. The film's outstanding performance is by Jeff Daniels, as the college professor turned Union officer Joshua Chamberlain, who underlines the band-of-brothers theme by telling his men, "We're fighting for each other."

The battle scenes necessarily telescope the huge numbers of the warring troops—160,000, close to the population of Boston at the time—but adequately approximate the military strategies and, in the climactic and tragic Pickett's Charge, fitfully display a sad grandeur. A flop in movie theaters, *Gettysburg* found its true home on DVD and in schoolrooms, where it functions as a useful audiovisual aide to the observation by Civil War Gen. William Tecumseh Sherman that "War is Hell."

Glory: The War from a Black Perspective

Sherman's maxim is the conclusion reached by virtually all Civil War movies, whether or not they focus on the battlefield, and even if military service is the dream of the characters portrayed. The 1989 *Glory* describes the training of the 54th Massachusetts Volunteer Infantry, the first formal U.S. Army unit entirely composed of black soldiers, under the leadership of Col. Robert Gould Shaw (doe-eyed Matthew Broderick), the scion of wealthy white abolitionists. Written by Kevin Jarre from Shaw's letters, and directed by Edward Zwick, *Glory* nicely details the backgrounds of the volunteers: Thomas Searles (Andre Braugher), a free black; John Rawlins (Morgan Freeman), a gravedigger whom Shaw promotes to Sergeant Major; and Trip, an escaped slave (Denzel Washington in a subtle, powerful performance that earned him an Oscar for Best Supporting Actor).

The 54th distinguished itself in the second assault on Fort Wagner, S.C., two weeks and a day after the Battle of Gettysburg ended. It is hardy worth a spoiler alert to note that Fort Wagner was never taken, and that Shaw and most of his volunteers—who showed their bravery as

Racing against time
Actress Vivien Leigh, as Scarlett O'Hara, searches for acquaintances among the Confederate casualties during Sherman's campaign for Atlanta in David O. Selznick's classic 1939 film of Margaret Mitchell's 1936 bestseller, Gone with the Wind

much in the grace with which they endured the abuse of white Union soldiers as in their chimerical charge across the beach and toward the Fort—died in the attempt.

Gone with the Wind: Scarlett's Saga

Gone With the Wind is remembered as the love story of Scarlett O'Hara (Vivien Leigh) and Rhett Butler (Clark Gable)—misremembered, really, since the object of Scarlett's true and unrequited ardor is the prim aristocrat Ashley Wilkes (Leslie Howard). He is the idealized view of Southern gentility that so beguiles Scarlett, while moviegoers wait impatiently for her to get it on with Rhett. Her first husband, taken out of spite when Ashley rejects her affections, promptly dies in the War. Her second marriage, after the War, is simply a business decision, bringing her enough capital to rebuild her cherished homestead, Tara; her partner-husband also is quickly and conveniently killed. Still in love with Ashley, she marries Rhett—the "gentleman from Charleston, South Carolina" with, in Gable's performance, a crisp Yankee accent and a sulfurous erotic insolence—not for his sex appeal, which was evident to every female in the movie audience, but for his money, which will restore her social standing and maintain her estate.

Indeed, Scarlett's abiding beau—her constant lover and the spur to her ambition—is the land, Tara. Produc-

er David O. Selznick's film, no less than the Margaret Mitchell novel that spawned it, is really about real estate, the eternal obsession of warriors and homemakers alike. As the Confederacy sacrificed tens of thousands of lives to defend its notion of sacred property, so Scarlett O'Hara Hamilton Kennedy Butler will do anything, anything, to hold on to Tara. At the end, deserted by Rhett, she is bereft but unbowed, because the land is hers to fight for till death.

Less a war movie than a woman's picture, *GWTW* takes the traditional female view of military conflict; it is concerned not with battlefield heroism but with the loss of all those precious young lives. The movie's two largest scenes are of war's destruction (the burning of Atlanta) and its aftermath (the sight of hundreds of wounded warriors). Men will fight, and women will weep. Ashley spends the whole war leading his regiment, or as the prisoner of the Yankees. Even the cynical Rhett joins the Rebel army, though not until the late summer of 1864, because, he says, he believes in lost causes only "when they are truly lost." Yet the film skips the men's exploits and sticks with the women: Scarlett, Ashley's demure bride Melanie (Olivia de Havilland) and the Tara house servants Mammy (Hattie McDaniel) and Prissy (Butterfly McQueen).

While she fights to survive, Scarlett mourns her fallen

friends and relatives, the tragic deaths of her own two children and, finally, the end of her cherished way of life—the Confederacy. In portraying one of the strongest women in film history, this ultimate Hollywood movie also plays a requiem for a rich and tainted civilization that is "gone with the wind."

The General: Keaton's Triumph

"I think it's *the* Civil War movie," Orson Welles said of *The General* in 1971. "Nothing ever came near it, not only for beauty but for a curious feeling of authenticity ... Nobody except Keaton has brought us that close to the feel of the Civil War ... It's a hundred times more stunning visually than *Gone With the Wind*."

Unlike Selznick's epic, and Griffith's, *The General* was based on an actual war incident: the "Great Locomotive Chase." On April 12, 1862, James J. Andrews, a civilian spy for the Union, and a number of allies hijacked a Western & Atlantic Railroad train, the *General,* in Big Shanty, Ga.; they jettisoned most of the passenger cars and drove the locomotive north toward Chattanooga, Tenn., disrupting important Confederate supply lines. The train's conductor, William A. Fuller, pursued the *General,* first by foot, then on a handcar and then by commandeering another locomotive. When the locomotive ran out of fuel, Andrews abandoned it 18 miles from his destination. All the raiders were captured, and Andrews was hanged that June. Most of his abettors escaped, and were the first men ever to be awarded the Medal of Honor; Secretary of War Edwin Stanton did the honors. (In Spielberg's *Lincoln,* Stanton, played by Bruce McGill, is the one who complains to the chatty President that "I can't stand to hear another one of your stories!")

This true caper served as inspiration for a 1911 one-reel film, Sidney Olcott's *Railroad Raiders of '62,* and for the 1956 Disney feature *The Great Locomotive Chase,* starring Fess Parker (TV's Davy Crockett) as Andrews and Jeffrey Hunter as Fuller. The Disney version is told from the North's point of view, trumpeting the scheme's brazen ingenuity, as if it were a 19th-century *Argo. The General,* which Keaton co-wrote and co-directed with Clyde Bruckman, invests its sympathies in the Confederacy. Its "Captain Anderson" (Glen Cavender) is the hijacker and the Fuller character—Keaton's Johnnie Gray, here not the conductor but the engineer—pursues the kidnappers to reclaim the train he loves. Oh, he has a girl, with the Edgar Allan Poetic name of Annabelle Lee (Marion Mack), who is also in the Yankees' clutches. Yet when he

rescues her, she turns out to be a hapless heroine, 1920s-style. Exasperated by her "helpfulness" in trying to stoke the locomotive engine, Johnnie impulsively throttles her, then kisses her, then returns to the job at hand.

Beginning with Johnnie's rebuff at enlisting in the Confederate army (he's told his skills are needed instead as an engineer) and climaxing with a battle in which he almost inadvertently conquers the Northern foe, *The General* devotes nearly an hour of its 79-min. running time to the chase—a marvel of story construction and sight gags from the most inventive comedian in movie history. Watch Keaton's beautiful, compact body as it pirouettes or pretzels in tortured permutations or, even more elegantly, stands in repose as everything goes crazy around it. Watch his mind as it contemplates a hostile universe whose violent whims Buster understands, withstands and, miraculously, tames. And please, history buffs as well as movie lovers, make a date to watch *The General.* It's the one long-ago Civil War film that can be enjoyed with no apologies or footnotes, its thrills forever fresh, its moviemaking joy intact.

The Birth of a Nation: Griffith's Screed

Nearly a century after it was made, *The Birth of a Nation* stands as a monument to cinema's power both to use the medium to tell a complex story, in grand images the world could understand, and to shape and distort public opinion. The son of a former Colonel in the Confederate army, Griffith based his epic on Thomas Dixon's popular novel and play *The Clansman* (1905). That was the film's title at its world premiere in Los Angeles, before the opening a month later in New York City (at a top price of $2, when tickets to most movies cost a dime). Produced for $110,000, *Birth* was estimated to have earned $18 million in its first few years—the equivalent of more than $323 million today.

Griffith took this monumental risk without a real script, and using just one camera manned by his invaluable cinematographer, G.W. "Billy" Bitzer. At heart a Romeo-and-Juliet story extended to gargantuan proportions, the movie focuses on two families, the Northern Stonemans and the Southern Camerons, whose eldest sons fall in love with girls from the other clan. Though the Civil War places the young men on opposing sides, they retain respect for their old friends—Ben Cameron (Henry B. Walthall) stops mid-battle to comfort a wounded Stoneman—and love for their ladies. It is romantic chivalry, Griffith insists, that led to Southerners'

night rides against Negroes. In one scene, a rapacious black man stalks a young white woman until, to protect her virginity, she leaps off a cliff to her death. To avenge such indignities and defend the honor of white womanhood, Ben and his noble fellows give birth to the Ku Klux Klan. That, not the restored United States, is the nation of the film's title: the land of lynchings, voter suppression and second-class citizenship for Southern blacks.

Basing Austin Stoneman on Pennsylvania Congressman Thaddeus Stevens (Tommy Lee Jones in Spielberg's *Lincoln)*, Griffith turned the character, as played by Ralph Lewis, into a zealot who is dominated by his shifty biracial housekeeper-mistress, and who imposes humiliation on the white South in the name of Reconstruction. Black characters in the movie (usually white actors in corkface) are subhuman oafs or savages. So vile was the caricature of African Americans, so rousing the Klan's midnight ride to the Old South's idea of justice and so persuasive Griffith's storytelling through pictures that the NAACP demanded suppression of the film—and the modern Klan was born.

Yet *The Birth of a Nation* is nearly as antiwar as it is antiblack. The Civil War scenes, which consume only 30 minutes of the 3hr. 12 min. extravaganza, emphasize not the national glory but the human cost of combat. "On the battlefield," announces one of the film's intertitles, "War

claims its bitter, useless sacrifice." For all the spectacular panoramas of the battle footage, its explosions and ragged processions of soldiers, the most impressive and startling moments are the more intimate views of the battle's end. "War's peace," reads another intertitle, and we are shown a tableau of a half-dozen dead soldiers, as if taking a restorative rest after their fatal labor. These images have the impact of defiant art: Goya's *Disasters of War* or Picasso's *Guernica*. Griffith may have been a racist politically, but his refusal to find uplift in the South's war against the Union — and, implicitly, any war at all — reveals him to be a cinematic humanist.

War's price was evident to the Generals on the hill, every bit as much as to their cannon fodder below. In the 1993 *Gettysburg,* Robert E. Lee muses that "this war goes on and on, and the men die, and the price gets even higher. We are prepared to lose some of us, but we are never prepared to lose all of us ... We are adrift here in a sea of blood and I want it to end. I want this to be the final battle." Gettysburg was the bloodiest but not the final battle of the Civil War; hostilities would drag on, and casualties multiply, for another 21 months. No Audie Murphy emerged from it with hundreds of clean kills and a hero's luster. It was an exercise in organized slaughter. And that may explain why this crucial event has inspired so few movies. ■

Truth in advertising
The posters for three classic Hollywood films about the Civil War show their perspectives on the conflict: romance in Selznick's Gone with the Wind, *comedy in Keaton's* The General, *facial politics in Griffith's* Birth of a Nation

Abbreviations
GNMP: Gettysburg National Military Park
LC: Library of Congress, Prints and Photographs Division, *www.loc.gov/pictures*
MOC: The Museum of the Confederacy, Richmond, Va.
MOLLUS-MASS: Military Order of the Loyal Legion of the United States–Massachusetts
NARA: National Archives and Records Administration, *arcweb.archives.gov*
USAMHI: U.S. Army Military History Institute, Carlisle, Pa.

Online sites
Don Troiani paintings: *www.historicalartprints.com*
Military & Historical Image Bank: *www.historicalimagebank.com*

The Road to Gettysburg
i GNMP; iii Andria Patino/Corbis; iv-v Medford Historical Society Collection/Corbis; 1 Classic—Stock/Alamy; 3, 5 Liljenquist Family Collection/LC: LC-DIG-ppmsca-32050, LC-DIG-ppmsca-37551 (2); 6-7 Chris Hackett/Tetra Images/Corbis; 9 (from top) Fort Sumter National Monument/National Park Service, Culver Pictures/The Art Archive at Art Resource, NY; 10 North Wind Picture Archives/Alamy; 11 (from left) LC: LC-DIG-ppmsca-07636, A.C. McIntyre—Courtesy of the Boston Athenaeum; 12 North Wind Picture Archives/Alamy; 13 Andrew J. Russell/NARA: Neg. No. 111-B-514; 15 Michael Miley/Boule & Miley/MOC; 16 Andrew J. Russell/LC: LC-DIG-ppmsca-07322; 17 (from left) Gift of Robert E. Lee, III, Washington-Custis-Lee Collection, Washington and Lee University, Lexington, Va., Hulton-Deutsch Collection/Corbis, LC: LC-USZ62-20244; 18-19 LC: LC-DIG-ppmsca-33151; 20 Encyclopaedia Britannica/UIG via Getty Images; 21 *Brandy Station Review,* painting by Don Troiani; 22-23 LC: LC-DIG-ppmsca-33216; 24 LC: LC-DIG-cwpbh-03184; 25 Wadsworth Atheneum Museum of Art/Art Resource, NY; 28 Corbis; 29 MOC; 31 (from top) LC: LC-DIG-cwpb-07546, MOC

July 1, 1863
32-33 Chris Hackett/Tetra Images/Corbis; 34 (from top) Image courtesy of the Military & Historical Image Bank, Painting by Don Troiani; 36-37 Frederick Gutekunst/Courtesy of the Gilder Lehrman Institute of American History; 38 Painting by Don Troiani; 39 LC: LC-DIG-cwpbh-01218; 40-41 Painting(s) by Don Troiani; 42 James F. Gibson/LC: LC-USZC4-1827; 43 (from top) LC: LC-USZ6-285, Alfred R. Waud/LC: LC-DIG-ppmsca-21109; 44 Image courtesy of the Military & Historical Image Bank; 45 (from top) Adams County Historical Society, GNMP; 46 LC: LC-DIG-cwpbh-00764; 47 Mathew B. Brady/LC: LC-DIG-cwpb-01649; 48 *Lee Deliberates* © Bradley Schmehl, *www.bradleyschmehl.com;* 50 North Carolina Collection, University of North Carolina at Chapel Hill Library; 51 Painting by Don Troiani; 52 Bettmann/Corbis; 53 (from top) Timothy H. O'Sullivan/LC: LC-DIG-cwpb-01658, Tyson Brothers/Tipton Collection/Adams County Historical Society;

54-55 Mathew B. Brady/NARA: Neg. No. 111-B-192 & 111-B-17; 56 (from left) LC: LC-DIG-cwpbh-00463; LC-USZ61-504; LC-DIG-cwpb-07586;LC: LC-DIG-cwpb-07437; 57 (from left) LC: LC-DIG-cwpb-05951, Hulton Archive/Getty Images, LC: LC-DIG-cwpb-05828; 59 (from top) Mathew B. Brady/NARA: Neg. No. 111-B-16; Richard Cummins/Design Pics/Corbis; 61 Alexander Gardner/LC: LC-DIG-ppmsca-23719; 62 (from left) NARA: Neg. No. 111-B-2541, the Bridgeman Art Library, LC: LC-DIG-cwpb-06342; 63 (from left) LC: LC-DIG-ppmsca-08350, LC-DIG-cwpbh-00839, LC-DIG-cwpbh-01198; 65 LC: LC-DIG-cwpb-04407

July 2, 1863
66-67 Jon Arnold Images, Ltd./Alamy; 68 Painting by Don Troiani; 70-71 Timothy H. O'Sullivan/LC: LC-DIG-cwpb-04001; 72 Painting by Don Troiani; 73 Norm Shafer for the Washington *Post*/Getty Images; 74 Mathew B. Brady/LC: LC-DIG-cwpb-01793; 75 Alexander Gardner/LC: LC-DIG-cwpb-00887; 76 Timothy H. O'Sullivan/LC: LC-DIG-ppmsca-32841; 78 Edwin Forbes/LC: LC-DIG-ppmsca-22564; 79 (from top) the Dolph Briscoe Center for American History, the University of Texas at Austin, GNMP, New York State Military Museum; 80 Painting by Don Troiani; 81 James F. Gibson/LC: LC-DIG-cwpb-00072; 82-83 (from left) Mathew B. Brady/NARA: Neg. No. 111-B-98 & 111-B-127; 84 Painting by Don Troiani; 85 NARA: Neg. No. 111-B-258; 86-87 Edwin Forbes/LC: LC-DIG-ppmsca-22563; 88 LC: LC-USZ62-15176; 89 Timothy H. O'Sullivan/LC: LC-DIG-ppmsca-32844; 90 (from left) Mathew. B. Brady/Corbis, MOC, LC: LC-DIG-cwpb-07580; 91 (from left) LC: LC-USZ62-100480, LC-DIG-cwpb-04996, USAMHI; 93 (from top) Medford Historical Society Collection/Corbis, Pejepscot Historical Society; 95 SSPL/Getty Images; 96 Alexander Gardner/LC: LC-DIG-cwpb-03769; 97, LC: LC-DIG-cwpb-04095; 98-99 (from left) GNMP, Mathew B. Brady/NARA: Neg. No. 111-B-358

July 3, 1863
100-101 Pat & Chuck Blackley/Alamy; 102 Painting by Don Troiani; 104-105 Alexander Gardner/LC: LC-USZC4-1829; 106 Henry Augustus Duryea/LC: LC-USZ62-120894; 107 Edwin Forbes/LC: LC-DIG-ppmsca-22569; 108 Mathew B. Brady/LC: LC-DIG-cwpb-01643; 110 From the original painting *The Guns of Gettysburg* by Mort Künstler c. 1993 Mort Künstler, Inc., *www.mkunstler.com;* 111 James F. Gibson/LC: LC-DIG-cwpb-00159; 112 Mathew B. Brady/LC: LC-DIG-cwpb-01860; 113 LC: LC-USZ62-11089; 114-115 Edwin Forbes/LC: LC-DIG-ppmsca-22570; 116 LC: LC-B812-9105; 117 (from left) GNMP, MOLLUS-MASS/USAMHI, NARA: Neg. No. 111-BA-636; 118 LC: LC-B812-2914; 119 Timothy H. O'Sullivan/LC: LC-DIG-cwpb-00865; 120 Alfred R. Waud/NARA: Neg. No. BA-2030; 121 Bill Dowling; 122 LC: LC-DIG-cwpb-07540; 123 (from top) Painting by Don Troiani, LC: LC-DIG-ppmsca-33129, 124 (from left) LC: LC-USZ62-11613, LC-B812-2741, Courtesy North Carolina Museum of History; 125 (from left) LC: LC-DIG-cwpbh-00682, LC-DIG-

cwpb-06452, LC-DIG-cwpb-05876; 127 (from left) LC: LC-DIG-cwpb-06685, LC-DIG-ggbain-13584; 129 Alexander Gardner/LC: LC-DIG-cwpb-00907; 130-131 LC: LC-DIG-ppmsca-33752; 133 Timothy H. O'Sullivan/LC: LC-DIG-cwpb-00844; 134-135 Edwin Forbes/LC: LC-DIG-ppmsca-22572; 136 NARA: Neg. No. 111-B-5132; 137, LC: LC-USZC4-7948; 138 Timothy H. O'Sullivan/LC: LC-DIG-ppmsca-33357; 139 Edwin Forbes/LC: LC-DIG-ppmsca-20559

Gettysburg in Memory
140-141 Greg Dale/National Geographic Stock; 143 (from top, left to right) LC: LC-DIG-ppmsca-33171, LC-USZ62-39409, LC-DIG-ggbain-31646; 144-145 Negative by Timothy H. O'Sullivan, Positive by Alexander Gardner/LC: LC-B8184-7964-A; 146 Alexander Gardner/LC: LC-DIG-cwpb-00915; 147 Alexander Gardner/LC: LC-DIG-ppmsca-12562; 148 Brady-Handy Collection/LC: LC-DIG-cwpbh-03798; 149 George N. Barnard/LC: LC-B8184-10053; 150-151 Mathew B. Brady/LC: LC-DIG-ppmsca-33494; 152 Massachusetts Historical Society; 153 Alexander Gardner/LC: LC-DIG-cwpb-00673, LC-DIG-cwpb-00652; 154-155 Photographer unknown/LC: LC-DIG-ppmsca-32850; 157 (from top) Alexander Gardner/LC: LC-USZ62-12950, LC: LC-USZ62-3117; 158-159 LOC: LC-DIG-cwpb-02641; 160 Mathew B. Brady/LC: LC-DIG-cwpb-07136; 161 George N. Barnard/LC: LC-DIG-stereo-1s02515; 162-163 (from left) Tom Lovell/National Geographic Stock, LC: LC-DIG-cwpb-03908; 164 Abraham Lincoln Presidential Library and Museum; 165 LC: LC-DIG-ppmsca-23855; 166-167 Walter Bibikow/JAI/Corbis; 169 (from top) Todd Harrington, Alexander Gardner/LC: LC-DIG-ppmsca-12560; 170-171 (from left) Todd Harrington, Mathew B. Brady/LC: LC-DIG-ppmsca-32842; 172 Todd Harrington; 173 Alexander Gardner/LC: LC-B811-235; 174 (from top) Todd Harrington, Mathew B. Brady/LC: LC-DIG-ppmsca-32853; 175 Todd Harrington (4); 177 Everett Collection; 179 Silver Screen Collection/Getty Images; 181 Everett Collection (3)

Gatefold, Gettysburg Cyclorama: Henry Groskinsky

End Papers: Brian Cahn/ZumaPress/Alamy

Front Cover: Tony Savino/Corbis

Back Cover: LC-DIG-ppmsca-33151

Special Appreciation
Jeff Bridgers, Prints and Photographs Division, Library of Congress
Greg Goodell, John Heiser and Andrew Newman, Gettysburg National Military Park
Holly Reed, The National Archives
Benjamin K. Neely and Lauren Roedner, Adams County Historical Society, Gettysburg, Pa.